TOWARDS A NEW PRICE REVOLUTION

TOWARDS A NEW PRICE REVOLUTION

By

B. CSIKÓS-NAGY

AKADÉMIAI KIADÓ · BUDAPEST 1979

Translated from Hungarian by

L. HALÁPY

English text revised by

Professor ALEC NOVE

ISBN 963 05 1851 1

Printed in Hungary

CONTENTS

PREFACE

After *Socialist Economic Policy* and *Socialist Price Theory and Price Policy* this is my third work published in English and Hungarian at the same time. On this occasion Professor Alec Nove of Glasgow University undertook revising the English text. It is with his consent that I quote a passage from the comprehensive appraisal he wrote to the publishers. "Dr. Csikós-Nagy has a whole number of important and interesting things to say. Could I suggest that the form of presentation be reviewed, so that the arguments are more accessible and acceptable to the average Western economist. The barrier is essentially connected with the use of what I would call elementary Marxist phraseology. The reason why it is a barrier is that the words are unfamiliar to the Western non-Marxist reader, or have only reached him in the context of the abstractions of Marxist political economy."

On the basis of these critical remarks I have perused the manuscript again and again and have made changes. I have left out certain passages. And yet, I think that if Marxist phraseology constitutes a "barrier", I have not completely torn it down —because I have not been able to do so. This very fact makes me present to the reader, by way of an introduction, the episodes that caused me to write this work, episodes in the wake of which the problems to be dealt with in this book have taken shape.

In the course of the four decades I have spent in the study of economics I have always devoted the greatest attention to the price problem. For more than half of this period I have been engaged in performing the task confronting me as head of the Hungarian price office. But the *first episode* connected with the writing of this work fell to a time prior to this. As a relatively young economist I did important work in government planning.

The "theory of socialist accumulation" was the basis of planning. This theory considers the reduction of a specific input (the labour input of a product) an objective trend. Accordingly, the rate of economic growth is mainly determined by two factors: (1) The share of the national income allocated to accumulation; (2) the rate of cost reductions. According to this theory there is a reciprocal relationship between the increase of the productivity of labour and the decrease of production costs.

However, experience has shown me that in practice this reciprocity is accidental; there are cases when the costs rise, although productivity significantly improves. This can not be always explained by the deterioration of natural conditions. The "irregularity" can be observed in extractive and non-extractive sectors alike.

It does not need to be emphasized how significant a disequilibrium may ensue when the actual trend of specific inputs differs considerably from what has been planned. Already then it was my view that all the negative manifestations of what is called "repressed inflation" are strongly linked with the *a priori* theses of the theory of socialist accumulation. To put it more exactly: Marx formulated the law of decreasing commodity value under the conditions of classical capitalism. Thus his investigations were based on a free market system in which, though there already existed monopolies, nevertheless the competitive market was the predominant form. This model was the basis of the theory of socialist accumulation. I have always called into question the idea that an economic law can be severed from the socio-economic background against which it was formulated. But, independent of this, the question also puzzled me how the factors determining socio-economic development in our present times could be characterized.

The *second episode* is connected with the conditions under which a *rise of the price level* could be made acceptable in Hungary. When treating the price problem, Marxist economists set out from three hypotheses: (1) Value is the key to price; (2) planned pricing must be enforced by government control; (3) the decrease of commodity value must be expressed in a fall in the price level. All this taken as a whole presupposes two things. On the one hand, relying upon government planning, that the control of production according to needs will be consistently realized; that is to say, the equilibrium price always emerges on the basis of the value (input) price. On the other hand, again relying on government planning, that the economy will develop on the basis of overall equilibrium. In other words, that the value of the currency can be considered constant.

Today the older generation of Hungarians can recall a trend of price decreases only in the first half of the 1930s. That was, at the same time, the period of the Great Depression and, with it, of hopelessness. After the Second World War, in the three decades of socialist construction, a government policy of price reduction could be applied only in the short transitory period between 1952 and 1955. It should be added that, prior to that, the reform of consumer prices had raised the retail price level by about 40% at the end of 1951. In the past three decades only the way in which the rise of the price level has been managed has changed.

A regular rise of the price level in itself would not put the law of decreasing commodity (input) value into question. Though these trends appear to be contradictory, they could be harmonized if the price rose due to excess demand, i.e. to inflation, which means a decrease in the value of money. But manifold analyses of specific inputs convinced me that, in numerous cases, the factors that raise the value of inputs, and have accordingly a price raising effect, spring from the commodity side.

While writing the present work I started reading the book *Prices in a Planned Economy* by Yu. V. Yakovets,* Director of the Price Institute connected to the Board of Prices of the Soviet Union. It is a work most useful for those who wish to get acquainted with the history of price policy in the Soviet Union and with the criteria determining price policy there at present. For me the book had surprises in store. It was from this work that I learned that the policy of price reductions had been formulated in the second half of the 1920s and this decision was later repeatedly reaffirmed. At the same time this was the very period when prices rose extraordinarily rapidly. It was hard for me to understand why policy advocated price decreases, when curbing inflation seemed to be a more realistic task. The question also arose whether this inflation was a phenomenon of transition from capitalism to socialism or had greater significance. If we consider only price statistics then—as you will see—inflation in socialism is only a transitory phenomenon. From this angle inflation can be connected with the debates that took place in the Soviet Union in the 1920s about "primitive socialist accumulation". We may reach different conclusions if we direct attention to

* (Yakovets, Yu. V.) Яковец, Ю. В.: *Цены в плановом хозяйстве* (Prices in a planned economy), Moscow, 1974.

disturbances in commodity supply and the various manifestations of repressed inflation. But what are these conclusions?

The *third episode* is connected with the experiences gained during the oil price explosion brought about by OPEC in 1973. Hungary is one of the countries that has suffered heavy losses in consequence of the new prices on the world market. Certainly, I am not the only person asking the question what the power was that had enabled a group of oil exporting countries to take this step, totally unusual in the history of prices. This price policy could be contrasted with everything we knew about market prices and what had been laid down in economics as criteria of the equilibrium price. In fact, it was in this connexion that I made up my mind to contrast what is taking place at present on the scale of world economy with the price revolution of the sixteenth and the early seventeenth centuries.

Who was the first to use the expression "price revolution"? It may have been O. Wiebe, in his work *Zur Geschichte der Preisrevolution des 16. und 17. Jahrhunderts,* published in Leipzig in 1895. This is as difficult to ascertain as would be to clarify what is exactly meant by price revolution. Is it permanent inflation or something else?

And here I have reached the *fourth episode.* In 1975 the International Economic Association staged a conference in Salstjöbaden about "Inflation Theory and Anti-Inflation Policy". It was for the first time that the publication of the conference papers of the International Economic Association (MacMillan Press Ltd.) included not only the lectures but the debate as well. This may have been so thanks to Eric Lundberg, the eminent Swedish economist. Thus we have a publication that provides information not only about existing various inflation theories, but also presents in a manysided way the controversial elements of the individual theories. As a member of the Program Committee and an active participant of the conference I was deeply impressed by the debates, but—I must admit—I am unable to bring the new theories into harmony with the traditional theses of economics. All this has but strengthened my impression that the process taking place on a world scale can be characterized as a permanent structural crisis, which cannot be cured by traditional treatment.

Now the reader may perhaps understand how my thoughts on the "theory of socialist accumulation" induced me to write the present book and how the theme became of an increasingly "universal" character. Have I succeeded in adequately synthetizing the two aspects in this work? It follows from Alec Nove's remarks that I have only partly done so. Of course, I do not know what his opinion about the revised text is. But, when all is said and done, it will not do the Western economist any harm if he is tipped out of his everyday way of thinking. Anyhow, I hope to have made myself understood even where the terminology is unusual for a non-Marxist economist.

Budapest, January 1979

The Author

Chapter One

PRICE INTERDEPENDENCIES

1. Value and price

Price types and relative prices

The price of a commodity produced for exchange is regulated by its value, and its value by the quantity of work expended on its production. All investigations of price theory must be based on this. This is the point from which we have to start when we examine the causes of price movements: their nature, secular price trends and our opinion on price trends to be expected.

Today the quantification of the commodity value is feasible, though, of course, when interpreting secular price trends in *historic retrospect* we have to use hypotheses that cannot be unambiguously proved. And yet a static analysis of commodity value interdependencies offers knowledge useful in investigating price trends, both past and future.

Commodity value can be quantified by means of *price-type calculations*. These indicate the principle by which the financial system distributes net incomes among branches (products).

In a financial system consistently based upon *value price*, the budget derives the part of the revenue needed to cover public expenditure from the place where income is created in the process of production. Since live labour creates the new value, a tax proportionate to wage costs is appropriate to such a financial system. The system of value prices appears as a concomitant of such a financial system, in which—in principle—the ratio between net income (s) and wage costs (v) is equal in every branch of production (in every product) to the ratio between the total social net income (S) and the wage costs (V) of the whole economy.

In a financial system consistent with the *production price*, the budget derives the part of the revenue needed for covering public expenditure from the place where it is realized in the production process. The production price system appears as a concomitant of such a financial system, in which—in principle—the ratio between the net income (s) and the capital engaged (e) is equal in every branch of production (in every product) to the ratio between the total social net income (S) and the total capital engaged in production (E).

If the type of prices alters, costs change in their function. Costs presuppose set prices, indeed a whole price system. To determine the costs of any commodity one has to know, among other things, the prices of capital goods used in producing the commodity (buildings, machines, vehicles) as well as the prices of the materials contained in a unit of the commodity. Before one knows these prices one cannot calculate the costs of the end product. However, these prices differ, in price systems of the "value" type, from those of the "production" type. That is why with different types of prices the costs of commodities are different too.

In the value price system the costs of every product are calculated at their value price. In such a price system the cost of electrical energy, for instance, is calculated in terms of the value prices of the equipment of power plants, of coal, etc. In production price systems every product is expressed in costs at its production price. Thus costs are functions of the price system and, accordingly, costs are also of different types. The type of costs is determined by the type of prices. Regarding the matter from this aspect costs are "incomplete" prices for the products in question, but these products appear in their "complete" prices for every product in which they are used as inputs. The peculiar link between the type of prices and costs indicates clearly the mutual dependency of prices and the organic relationship of the prices of products within the price system; it also indicates that—other things equal—relative prices will change as a function of the type of prices.

We shall not undertake the manysided analysis of the interdependency of prices and, within it, the divergences of relative prices appearing as a function of the type of price in the Hungarian production structure and under the production conditions valid in Hungary. This, of course, limits the validity of the results obtained, since the institutional system of the social production organization, its sectoral composition, its macro- and micro-structure, the general level of the productivity of labour and of production standards—and within the latter the conditions of production—widely differ in different countries. Moreover, parallel with the development of productive forces these conditions will also systematically change within the same country too. But even so we may acquire knowledge that enables us to draw some conclusions which may even hold internationally. When calculating the type of prices, we have taken as a basis the input–output balance of the 1976 plan, comprising 19 sectors. In it gross output shows the following composition:

Table 1

The nomenclature of the input–output balance comprising 19 sectors

No.	Sector	No.	Sector
1.	Mining	11.	Agriculture
2.	Energy	12.	Forestry
3.	Metallurgy	13.	Economy of water supplies
4.	Engineering	14.	Transport and communication
5.	Building materials	15.	Domestic trade
6.	Chemicals	16.	Foreign trade
7.	Light industry	17.	Personal services
8.	Other industries	18.	Public health and social services
9.	Foodstuffs	19.	Administration and other services
10.	Construction		

When analysing the interdependency of prices, we have used—with a view to simplification—the terms "price of social product" and "sectoral price". In the calculations of the price index both appear as aggregated indices. The "price of the social product" is the price index which expresses the production structure of products and of services in all sectors of the economy. The "sectoral price" is the price index of the products produced and services rendered in the given sector.

To show the connexion between variants of the price type and the relative prices of a given sector, we have taken the value price, the production price as well as the type of prices valid in Hungary in 1976 as a basis. The net income pattern of the three price types is the following:

With respect to Hungarian economy, in 1976 prices of the value type could be obtained by a 100% supplement of the wage input, while prices of the production

Table 2

Variants of the price type

channels	Type of price		
	Value price	Production price	Hungarian 1976
In percentage of the wage input	100%	—	35%
In percentage of the capital input	—	25%	5%
Different channels altogether in percentage of the wage input	—	—	45%

type by supplementing 25% of the capital tied up in production. Thus the real type of prices in 1976 can be described as follows: taxes of 35% were levied on the wage input, and taxes of 5% on the capital tied up in production; besides, according to different branches (products), various kinds of taxes were levied, their total being 45% of the wage cost. The following differences can be observed in the relative sectoral prices.

Table 3

Divergences of the relative sectoral prices according to types of prices

Sector	Value price	Production price	Actual price
	actual price = 100	value price = 100	value price = 100
Mining	89.8	101.1	111.3
Energy	76.7	146.6	130.5
Metallurgy	77.4	113.7	129.1
Engineering	73.8	103.8	135.5
Building materials	79.0	119.4	126.5
Chemicals	74.4	115.6	134.4
Light industry	84.0	100.9	119.1
Foodstuffs	107.3	110.8	93.2
Construction	86.4	88.2	115.8
Agriculture	121.1	104.1	82.6
Transport	88.2	89.6	113.4
Personal services	99.1	78.6	100.9

Seven sectors of negligible significance in the present context have been omitted. In the connexion between the type of price and the sectoral ratio there are two questions, different in character, and therefore deserving separate investigation. One is the connexion between value price and production price and the other between value price and actual price.

In sectors (products) whose organic composition of capital is average, the production price coincides with the value price. That is to say the production price is a function of the sector's capital requirement, either below or above the level of value. At the same time value price and production price can be considered the two extreme poles from the point of view of all mixed price types which realize the *s* by two channels (proportionately to wages and capital), but differ from each other in the proportion of these two channels. Under the conditions of highly developed large-scale production based on a concentration of capital, the actual price will, evidently, tend to approximate to the production price.

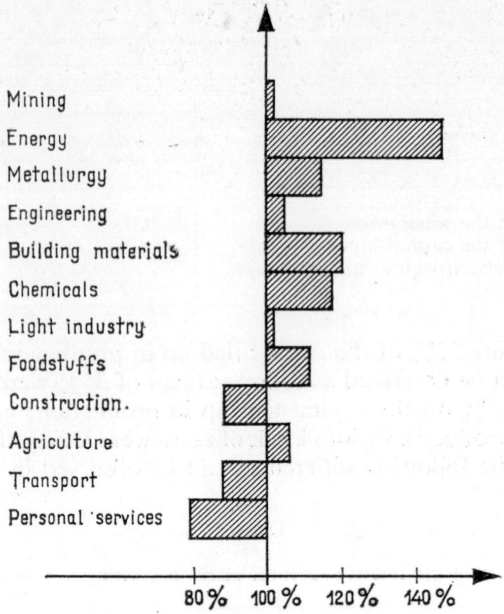

Chart 1. Divergence of the production price from value

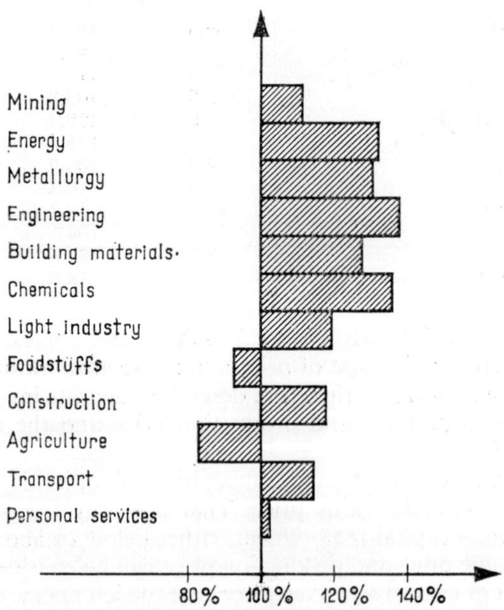

Chart 2. Divergence of the actual price from value

When judging the divergence between the actual price and the value price, it should be taken into consideration that *there are no fully neutral financial systems.* No pure value price or even production price system can be created in practice because in a diversified economy with even partially developed production forces the centralization of revenues inevitably takes place through several channels. And yet the examination of the divergences of relative prices in value price systems and in production price systems as well as the comparison of these relative prices with actual prices is useful. (1) Value and production prices are the two poles *within* which the actual relative price will emerge, depending on the price type applied. (2) To know the value and the production price is a condition of quantifying price deviations. This method may also play a part in designing an effective financial system.

Price characteristics based on the financial system

Only through the intermediary of a financial system can the price meet the requirements of the law of value. If a financial system could be completely neutral, price would diverge from value *only* as a function of demand and supply. The coincidence of the two would, in this case, indicate that the commodity has been produced in a quantity socially needed, namely in a quantity in which supply will be in equilibrium with demand at the very level of value. A divergence of the price from the value would, on the other hand, indicate that either more or less has been produced than is socially needed.

However, to repeat, a financial system cannot be wholly neutral, and that is why the price can never be a precise yardstick of social input. For the same reason one cannot draw a conclusion about the differences of labour input from the *national prices* of identical products made in different countries. Certain elements of the financial system may cause basic differences in national prices even if some countries decide to eliminate the major differences and bring their financial systems into line.

One might believe that the *exchange rate* will neutralize the differences of financial systems of different countries, since it determines the value relations of currencies in terms of national prices and not in national commodity values. This, however, would only be true if we considered the Social Product as "one" product. The peculiarities of financial systems appear in the very fact that they deflect relative prices from relative inputs. If we investigate various possible financial systems from the aspect of their effect on the price system, the following points deserve special attention.

1. *The participation of different sectors in a general and proportionate sharing of taxation.* If industry, agriculture and the tertiary sector pay proportionate taxes, it may be assumed that, within the same country, the sectoral price levels will be related symmetrically to their relative inputs. This, however, is not to be found in any country. The tax-bearing capacity of the various sectors assumes different forms. The tax-bearing capacity of industry—as a general rule—is higher than that of agriculture; the tax-bearing capacity of mass-production manufactures is higher than that of services. This differentiation is considerable even within the same sector. The fact that in certain countries taxes levied on agriculture are smaller than those levied on industry does not mean that certain branches of the foodstuff industry (tobacco, alcohol, etc.) are not subject to heavier taxation.

Every country will form its taxation system under the conditions prevailing in it and will change it according to its particular conditions of production or distribution. Consequently, a taxation system, uniform in all its elements and applicable to every country cannot be expected to exist.

2. *Participation of the spheres of production and of distribution in taxation.* If the government levies taxes mainly in the production sphere, the divergences of wholesale prices from retail prices are basically determined by handling costs. In such a taxation system we may speak of a *one-level price system;* i.e. the price levels of the means of production and of consumption goods are set on the same basis. This follows from the fact that the government does not make any difference—from the point of tax-bearing capacity—between means of production and consumption goods.

If the government levies taxes predominantly in the sphere of distribution, the divergences of wholesale prices from production prices and of retail prices from wholesale prices are decisively determined by the peculiarities of the taxation system. One of the peculiarities of such a taxation system can be to concentrate the process of central revenue-gathering on the final product. In such cases the means of production sold for further processing, may perhaps not be taxed at all. In such a taxation system we may speak of a *two-level price system,* in which the price level of the means of production is lower and that of consumption goods higher. This can vary depending on the circumstances under which the means of production are also subjected to taxation, though at a lower rate than when goods are sold by retail trade.

If a dual exchange rate is applied, the fact that a price system is two-levelled—with a different rate for foreign trade and for services—will not cause any problems in international transactions. This dual valuation of currency is indeed found in the relation between CMEA (Council for Mutual Economic Assistance) countries. But capitalist countries will—as a general rule—evaluate their currency at a uniform exchange rate.

3. *Taxation structure applied in the sphere of production.* This appears in different ways in capitalist and in socialist countries. In capitalism the process of production and the connexion between the labourer and the entrepreneur, the capitalist or landowner are shaped in and by the market. Thus it appears to be a matter of course not only that the workman sells his labour power, but also that the landowner claims his share of surplus value in respect of the land whose use he has transferred and the capitalist in respect of his invested capital. Under conditions of capitalism this participation (land rent and interest on capital) as well as the wages of labour are determined by market relations of the production factors. The market mechanism operating on such a large scale fosters the opinion according to which commodity value is nothing but the summary of values of these three factors of production summarized in the value of a commodity.

While accounting for the existence of the entrepreneur's profit, interest on capital and land rent, Marx showed that value could be created solely by labour. Thus the acceptance of the theory of the three production factors does not entail—in contrast to the view of numerous Marxist economists—a denial of the theory of labour value. Nevertheless, if land and capital are nationalized, the possibility exists for the state to put land and capital at the disposal of enterprises it owns free of charge. If this course is followed, the price calculation is of the so-called wage type: to the wage costs of the final production phase are added the wage costs of the previous production phases (material costs) and to these are added the enterprises' profits.

For a long time it was taken for granted that socialist countries should exclude from their calculation interest on capital and land rent. Later this point of view underwent a change. A socialist society operates the production forces at its disposal in the form of enterprises and not as a homogeneous mass. Enterprises are accounting units. Among enterprises the division of labour is organized in a system of commodity and money relations. Rational behaviour is demanded from every productive unit. To ensure rational behaviour, scarce resources at society's disposal must be used economically.

A socialist economy can be managed in different ways. The state, in its capacity of the owner of natural resources, can regulate the rate and manner in which these resources are to be exploited according to an exact plan. The utilization of the available land can take place according to central allocation, etc. These centralized control methods, outside the sphere of prices, are well known, and to some extent unavoidable. However, central prescriptions in physical terms cannot be a substitute for control based on the use of the prices and financial instruments.

Within the production process the factors of production can be substituted for one another—within a wider or narrower framework. The optimal combination of the production factors is one of the criteria of the enterprises' rational behaviour. From this it follows that nothing should be free of charge for the enterprise that is at the disposal of society only in limited quantities and is required for the expansion of production. But while in capitalism this is solved as a market price problem, in a socialist economy the relative evaluation of factor prices arises as an issue of the taxation system. That is why in a socialist economy the various forms of taxes in the sphere of production (taxes on wages and salaries, profit tax, turnover tax, etc.) must be complemented with a charge for the capital tied up in production and for the land used, as well as with various other forms of rent charges, levied on the use of exhaustible natural resources or on the agricultural use of land.

4. *The system of tax preferences.* The different extent of the participation of industry, agriculture and the tertiary sector in a general and proportionate burden of taxation does not necessarily mean that the state prefers one sector to another. If agriculture enjoys tax preferences as against industry but the industrial price level is higher than the agricultural price level, then agriculture does not occupy a financially privileged position compared to industry, since the difference in taxes is offset by a reverse deflection of price from value.

Of course, whether the differentiation of taxes according to sectors, branches, groups of commodities or products, implies a *policy of conscious discrimination* is open to debate. Accordingly, tax differentiation (or price subsidy as a negative turnover tax) could be interpreted as a government policy which is not to be explained by the differences in tax-bearing capacities, but rather by the conscious decision of the government to bring about an equilibrium of demand and supply at prices higher than the value of one product and lower than the value of another product. If one views taxes (subsidies) from this angle, they form a means by which the government carries out *income re-distribution* in society.

Naturally, price can perform an income re-distribution function through price differentiation by sectors (branches). Nevertheless, the more usual examples of this are provided by turnover taxes (subsidies) connected with specific products. This system of tax-discrimination differs basically in capitalist countries from that of socialist countries. The reasons will be dealt with when discussing the optimum concepts of the two socio-economic systems. But even within socialist countries preferences significantly differ. This springs from the fact that in a system of preferences ideological aspects interact with the level of economic development and with the conditions for economic growth, and, as far as the latter are concerned, there are significant differences between socialist countries.

Interpreting the taxation system as a system of preferences, the question also arises whether the government ensures identical conditions *for domestic sales and for exports.* Exemption from taxation (tax refunds) in export introduces a system of dual calculations, by which the national currency of a country, if reckoned at export prices, will be revalued as against the domestic value of the same currency. In view of all this the question is only to what extent the practices pursued in different countries correspond or differ.

These peculiarities of national taxation systems sufficiently explain why differences in labour input in different countries cannot be identified by comparing international prices. This, at the same time, explains the endeavours to unify taxation systems. An instance of this was the reform of indirect taxes realized within the framework of the European Economic Community: the discontinuation of taxes levied on gross turnover in certain countries, the introduction of value added tax (net turnover tax) and of a unified taxation system. The international alignment of taxation systems does not confront any special obstacles if the differences originate merely from traditions or from differing (subjective) judgments. However, such an approach is not realistic if the differences are rooted in the natural endowments of economies, or if they are due to differences in the conditions of economic growth (objective reasons).

5. *The normative regulation of enterprise profit for taxation.* Within the sphere of enterprise taxation, profit tax deserves special attention. This is again an area where similar features can be observed in capitalist and socialist cost calculations. Among production costs there are those which are measured as such, and there are also so-called normalized costs. The specific feature of normalized costs lies in the fact that they need not arise at the same time, in the same way and to the same extent as they are indicated in calculations. Among these latter, depreciation, costs of technical progress, etc. deserve major attention.

Although in capitalist countries there is no direct government regulation concerning normalized costs, there is—as a general rule—an indirect one. This is realized when the government determines how the profit that constitutes the basis of tax assessment is to be calculated. This is the indirect method of the regulation of normalized costs, based on tax liability. In socialist countries the government—in general—regulates in a direct manner the calculation of these normalized costs.

2. Micro- and macro-price structure

Real costs

In principle the value of a commodity can be calculated directly in terms of *work time* and in terms of *wage costs.* A direct calculation of the commodity value in terms of work time has never yet been achieved and, indeed, accounting methods under conditions of commodity production are not suitable for this purpose. Although we know production technologies and the time norms relating to the different units of a product, this is insufficient to calculate the work time needed per unit. First of all, the degrees of skill involved in producing a commodity differ. To summarize them one should work out the time norms of different operations in terms of *time norms for simple work.* Secondly, we know the time norms of operations only *in respect of the last phase of production.* The contribution of previous production phases to the commodity value is recorded in the form of material norms incorporated in one unit of the commodity. Thus, in order to quantify the commodity value directly in terms of work time, the material norms should be expressed in operational time norms, which requires switching back from one production phase to the earlier ones.

At the same time *commodity value can be approached by means of the aggregate wage costs used in producing the commodity.* The *c* appearing in the value of a commodity—which is the product of a previous phase of work—is also divided into

$c+v+s$. The c in this latter also consists of components of $c+v+s$, and so on. Thus the c (past labour) constituting a component of the value of the commodity can be traced back in the form of an endless convergent line to $v+s$, to past live work. Accordingly, the formula of the commodity value can be also put down as follows:

$$c+v+s = (V+S)+v+s.$$

This formula leads directly to live labour input. Thus the essence of the quantification of commodity value in money terms is a reduction of the input to aggregate wage costs attained by subtracting net income from value. By working our way back to all phases of production, along with the s we can also eliminate the c part of the value, and thus aggregate wages remain, that is to say, v. Calculations of the price type in an input–output balance are based on this method.

In the logic of Adam Smith, wage costs expressing real costs, offer a solution of the commodity value problem. According to this, (1) since the value of every commodity is determined by the quantity of labour included in it, and all labour needed for producing a commodity is decomposed into necessary labour (v) and surplus labour (s), the commodity value ($c+v+s$) can be expressed in these two component elements. In the final analysis commodity value cannot consist of anything else than $v+s$. (2) Since the surplus value is created in the production process by work, the commodity value ($c+v+s$) also expresses the supposition that the rate of surplus value $\left(\frac{s}{v}\right)$ is identical with respect to every commodity.* Under such conditions

– the relative real self-costs of different commodities compare with each other like their relative value,

– and the value of the commodity can be worked out if the constant $\frac{s}{v}$ is known.

Tracing back the value of a commodity ($c+v+s$) to a new value ($v+s$) finally enables us to quantify value by using the price category. To do this we must, however, adopt two assumptions: (1) that the wage included in the price corresponds to the value of labour and (2) that the commodity is fully divisible; input and profit are absolutely internal and there are no externalities. Needless to say, these assumptions are not fully justified. Wages may differ from the value of labour and even more can relative wages differ from the relative amount of work done. We also know that with the development of productive forces and the progress of the scientific-technical revolution and, in particular, with the increase of social expectations, the number of commodities characterized by partial indivisibility is increasing. We are going to revert to this problem later on, but will disregard it when examining price interdependencies.

Marx's criticism, known by the name of the "Smith Dogma", refers to the tracing back of $c+v+s$ to $v+s$.** Marx criticized the hypothesis according to which the value of commodities is "made up" from incomes and "is resolved" in incomes. He pointed out that, in addition to variable capital *(v)* and surplus value *(s)*, the reproduction of constant capital *(c)* must also occur. Equivalent exchange can only take place in pure form when commodities are exchanged as products of precapitalist small-scale production. When producers of commodities on a small scale establish

* Smith, A.: *Inquiry into the Nature and Causes of the Wealth of Nations*, Edinburgh, 1776. Marx's theory of surplus value is—as is well known—a further developed variant of A. Smith's theory of the labour value.

** Marx, K.: *Capital*, Vol. I, Moscow, 1967, pp. 598–602.

market relations with each other, the trend is for the producers of commodities to receive in exchange by way of commodity purchases as much labour from society as they did for society by the production of the commodities sold. On the other hand, *in capitalism commodities are the products of capital,* and thus surplus value assumes the form of profit.

In analysing the "Smith Dogma" Marx wanted to emphasize that A. Smith did not understand the social process of reproduction under conditions of capitalism. At the same time Marx considered A. Smith's explanations useful and important from the point of understanding the laws of the movements of *social* capital. Interpreting A. Smith's economic views, Marx admitted that the movement of *social capital*—that is to say the total of individual capitals—differs from the movement of capital belonging to each individual capitalist. For the individual capitalist the commodity value appears in its constant element, *(c),* as well as in the total of wages and surplus value. On the other hand, from a social point of view constant capital value vanishes.*

Marx came to agree with A. Smith about the latter's views on real costs. Marx demonstrated how the different components of the notion of commodity value can be expressed by the proportionate parts of the product itself. Marx's example about the components of the input of 20 lbs of cotton yarn is well known.**

Table 4

Components of the costs of 20 lbs of cotton yarn

Costs	Elements of value expressed in terms of cotton	Components of the value of the yarn	Quantity of work in material form
	lbs	shillings	work hours
Cotton used	13⅓	20	40
Auxiliary materials, implements, spindles etc. used and worn out	2⅔	4	8
The spinner's necessary labour	2	3	6
The spinner's surplus labour	2	3	6
Total	20	30	60

This formula wholly tallies with that of real costs. The real costs of 20 lbs are 15 shillings. Out of this the cotton workers' wages are 10 shillings, the spinners' wages 3 shillings and the wages paid for the production of the auxiliary materials, implements and spindles worn out in the process are 2 shillings. Thus, if we know the ratio between v and s, we can trace back the real costs from the product value as well as the product value from the real costs. Thus value can be obtained in two ways: either by determining values at the outset, or by establishing the real costs and raising them to a value level.

Why must Marx's formula be transformed? Because with Marx the calculations presented here only throw light upon the components of value, on the assumption of price being equal to the value. If, on the other hand, we have to find a method

* Marx, K.: *Capital,* Vol. II, Moscow, 1967, pp. 366–393.
** Marx, K.: *Capital,* Vol. I, Moscow, 1967, pp. 203–207.

by which the value can be identified, we must find a formula that eliminates the distortions caused by the price system. The transformation of the formula serves this end.

Value calculation

Value calculations are based on the supposition of a multi-directional flow of commodities. When modern mathematics and computer techniques are used in calculations, this is essentially matrix calculation performed in the price model or in the sectoral input–output balance. This matrix calculation will show the aggregate, quantitative connexions between different branches and thus provides a systematizing basis for the investigation of the interdependencies induced by price changes.

Cost indices of industrial branches (enterprises) provide data upon which matrix calculations can be based. In the course of the matrix calculation—adjusted to the accounting system of enterprises—the price structure undergoes a transformation, which simplifies the investigation of the connexions of prices and costs. We will demonstrate this kind of transformation of the price structure, using as an example *rolled aluminium,* taking the 1976 Hungarian data as a basis. Calculations were made in the Price Institute of the Hungarian National Board for Materials and Prices.

Table 5

Enterprise cost calculation of rolled aluminium (unalloyed, ton)

Price components	Price structure	
	Forint	per cent
Direct material costs	31,598	85.4
Direct wage costs	1,092	3.0
Technical development fund	71	0.2
Overhead costs	6,009	16.2
Enterprise profit	– 1,770	– 4.8
Price of product	37,000	100.0

This calculation schema is based on the so-called *cost phase* principle. Here we are not seeking to determine how much the commodity costs society, but how much it costs the enterprise. From the enterprise's point of view the value of the inputs it processes or uses up in producing the commodity it wants to sell does not matter. From the point of the enterprise the cost price is decisive, whether it is in fact lower or higher than value. In this very respect costs interpreted by political economy $(c+v)$ differ from those calculated in practice. This also explains why a business administrator well versed in cost calculations considers it an impossible task to establish the value of a commodity even if he knows its costs.

The organic connexion between accounting, the prescriptions of production technology and price calculations explains why costs can be only partly charged directly to a given product, and thus they are partly to be treated as overhead costs. In accountancy only such costs can be charged to the product directly of which it can be unambiguously stated by which product they were incurred at the time they arose. The prescriptions of production technology only record the (gross) quantities of material used for a product and the work time spent in its production. However, they do not determine the whole quantity of materials used in the enterprise and the whole work time expended there. The difference of the two is reflected by the proportions of overhead costs.

No problem arises in such a grouping of costs as long as it is only required that the price of a single product should be determined from its costs. The situation is entirely different when pricing several products closely connected with one another. If cost calculations do not clarify how much of the whole quantity is used specifically in the production of a given commodity, we cannot exactly determine the price and cost interrelations of this commodity. Thus it is easy to understand why calculation data must be transformed and turned into basic data that can be used in matrix calculations, by eliminating the separation of directly chargeable costs from overhead costs.

The separation of wage costs and material costs in production costs is due to the specific features of the social production structure and of the specialization of production, and it is adjusted to the form in which production is organized in different enterprises. As it has become evident from the above, material costs can be reduced to wage costs arising outside the enterprise. Can material costs really be considered in this way in enterprise calculation? No, they cannot. Calculations provide information only on the cost relations of the last process of production. Thus, calculation at an enterprise level will conceal the cost relations of the social productive organization in two ways: first when it divides a part of the input among several products by averaging, and, secondly, when it reveals cost relations limited to the last production phase only.

Thus, it is self-understood for an economist versed in real cost calculations that when, for example, the value of rolled aluminium products is to be determined, investigations cannot be restricted to the last phase of production only. On the level of a national economy the answer is to be given not to the question of how much and what kind of material is used by an aluminium foundry in producing one ton of rolled aluminium, but to the question of what and *how many products are to be produced in all branches of the social production organization for producing one ton of rolled aluminium.* The difference between the two can be summarized as follows:

In the former case only such materials are taken into consideration as are used in the product directly, whereas in the latter case all materials directly or indirectly used are considered. In the first case costs are counted on enterprise level, whereas in the second, the calculation is on the level of the national economy, with all means of production taken into consideration in principle, since there is no kind of means of production that would not be in some relationship with all the others.

In cost calculations on the level of a national economy *technical co-efficients are cumulated,* in contrast to enterprise cost calculations, where account is taken only of the direct use of materials. When among material costs the costs of one ton of rolled aluminium are calculated in aluminium metallurgy, only the quantity of specific electric energy is counted that arose in the metallurgy phase. Electrical energy used in previous phases of production is taken into account in the price of alumina, etc. On the other hand, if we want to determine the cost of one ton of rolled aluminium on the level of the national economy, we must know how much electrical energy was needed for its manufacture in all branches of production.

In calculations for the whole of the national economy the accumulated technical co-efficient used by every product is, as a general rule, more than one. It must be at least one, because, as a matter of course, the commodity in itself had to be produced. As a general rule it is more than one because, while it was produced, or in the production of some other means of production, a part of it has been consumed.

Matrix calculations are prepared by disaggregating—by means of estimates—general costs into material and wage costs, and by transforming material costs (value indicators) into indicators in kind (technical co-efficients). According to the rules of matrix algebra, if the matrix of technical co-efficients is subtracted from the unit matrix and the square matrix inverse obtained is calculated, the result is a matrix which contains the co-efficients comprising the cumulated material inputs of the product.

Table 6

Technical co-efficients of rolled aluminium (unalloyed, ton)

Material	Quantity unit	Enterprise	Cumulated
		technical co-efficients	
Fuel	t	2.08	13.62
Electrical energy	1,000 kWh/t	0.49	12.99
Bauxite	t		5.73
Alumina	t		1.91
Aluminium ingots	t	1.00	1.11
Rolled aluminium goods	t	—	1.00

If cost calculations are built on cumulated technical co-efficients and not on enterprise ones, the justification of a division of costs into material costs and wage costs lapses. Here all costs assume the form of wage costs and, accordingly, in the price structure of the national economy costs can be related only with the elements of net social income. This is a direct consequence of the circumstance that, in price calculations on an enterprise level, wage costs and net income are expressed in terms in which they appeared in previous work processes. Thus, in the structure of the national economy the price is constituted from the items of wage costs and net incomes which are connected with cumulated technical co-efficients. (See Table 6.)

Table 7

Price components of products connected with rolled aluminium goods (unalloyed, ton)

Name of product	Quantity unit	Share of the product's price falling to		
		the last phase of production	the other phases of production	all phases of production
Fuel	Ft/t	510	363	873
Electrical energy	Ft/1,000 kWh	374	447	821
Bauxite	Ft/t	326	160	486
Alumina	Ft/t	1,318	3,997	5,315
Aluminium ingots	Ft/t	2,033	27,015	29,048
Rolled aluminium goods	Ft/t	5,402	31,598	37,000

Thus, to learn the price structure of rolled aluminium on the level of the national economy, we must know the part of the prices of all other goods connected with the production of rolled aluminium goods, which falls to the share of the wage costs of the last phase of production and to the elements of net income realized there.

The price structure of rolled aluminium can be indicated based on the cumulated technical co-efficients and the amount of the prices of materials used in the last phase of production. (See Tables 7 and 8.)

Table 8

Price structure of rolled aluminium goods in the national economy (unalloyed, ton)

Name of product	Unit of quantity	Cumulated technical co-efficients	Part of price falling to the share of last production phase	Price structure of rolled aluminium goods
Fuel	t	13.62	510	6,946
Electrical energy	1,000 kWh/t	12.99	374	4,858
Bauxite	t	5.73	326	1,868
Alumina	t	1.91	1,318	2,517
Aluminium ingots	t	1.11	2,033	2,258
Other products	t	.	.	13,151
Rolled aluminium goods	t	1.00	5,402	5,402
Altogether				37,000

Here we can see again the Ft 37,000 price of one ton of rolled aluminium. This, however, was not reached on the basis of the calculation of the enterprise, but by price elements of the national economy. If we know the price structure of a product in the national economy, the real costs of the product can also be calculated, by eliminating net incomes. Let us examine this on the example we have chosen:

Table 9

Structure of the price and of real costs of rolled aluminium (unalloyed, ton)

Branch of industry	Real costs ($V+v$)	Net incomes ($S+s$)	Price
	Forints		
Fuel	2,556	4,390	6,946
Electrical energy	1,214	3,644	4,858
Bauxite	687	1,181	1,868
Alumina	697	1,820	2,517
Aluminium smelting	1,880	5,780	7,660
Others	1,069	12,082	13,151
Altogether	8,103	28,897	37,000

Thus the price of the commodity can be calculated *within two structures:* In the first case the quantity of products used by the enterprise in manufacturing a unit of the commodity (that is to say in the last phase of production) is to be multiplied by their price. The wage costs arising at the enterprise and the net incomes realized there are added to the material costs calculated in this way. In the second case we consider the means of production in the system as a whole, in the way they had to be produced and cumulated to manufacture the commodity in question, and then we multiply the quantities so derived by the price applicable to the final phase of production. However, to achieve such a transformation of the price structure, the system in which the material connexions are considered requires to be essentially changed and so does the price structure itself. Based on linear algebra, the transformation of technical co-efficients and price structures can be performed by electronic computers or by inverse operations.

Value movements and price movements

If one knows the real costs, one can also establish the *quantity of work time* spent on the product. If one divides the product's wage costs by the average hourly wage of the branches in which the majority of the work was applied to the product, one gets the number of working hours needed for producing a unit of the product. Calculated in this way 3,500 hours were needed in Hungary to manufacture 1 ton of rolled aluminium in 1976. This, of course, is only an approximate magnitude, but it serves our purposes.

Value calculations have been conducted in Hungary since 1957, and this enables us to prepare comparative analyses of value and price movements in two decades' survey. In 1957, 4,200 hours were needed to produce 1 ton of rolled aluminium. Thus, within two decades the value of the product diminished by 16.7%. It is expedient to complete such calculations with an examination of manufacturing technologies, and the results achieved in money terms are absolutely justifiable in the case of rolled aluminium. The established technology is the so-called two-phase Bayer–Hall–Heroult process:

- the processing of the ore (Bayer), and
- the smelting of alumina in fusion electrolysis (the Hall–Heroult process).

In spite of the fact that the technology is almost a hundred years old, by the perfecting of the technology and by other means the specific labour input could be considerably reduced. Of particular significance in this respect were the followings: (1) In the *bauxite* phase the opening of tropical bauxite mines, the increase in open-cast mining and the reduction of transport and loading costs. (2) In the *alumina* phase the specific energy and the consumption of caustic natron could be significantly reduced; the ten–twentyfold enlargement of works of alumina factories diminished the consumption of specific energy. (3) In the *aluminium* phase: when new aluminium smelters are constructed, smelting works of 500 thousand tons are built and used, instead of the former tenthousand ones; so are silicium-diode rectifiers instead of the formerly used mercuryarc ones. Owing to this, the current-transforming degree of efficiency is increased by 6–8%; the strength of current is increased (10–15 times) in the cells where alumina are electrolyzed; modern technical plants are constructed by which energy and auxiliary materials can be saved—e.g. by the introduction of various types of aluminium electrolyzing cells.

Not only has the value of aluminium decreased, but so has its *relative value*. Due to the difficulties of its production, aluminium used to be a metal dearer than silver. Only when, at the end of the nineteenth century, the electrolytic method of its production was elaborated did the production costs of aluminium decrease sufficiently to render its industrial use possible.* In the 1890s the aluminium production

* Geleji, S. (ed.): *Alumínium kézikönyv* (Handbook of aluminium), Budapest, 1949.

of the world was only 1,000 tons annually, but by 1904 it rose above 10,000 tons and by 1916 above 100,000 tons. In 1941 production reached 1 million tons, and 14 million tons in 1976. Prognostications indicate that by 1980 production will reach 20–25 million tons and by 2000 50–70 millions. By establishing the technology of mass production and by its continual modernization, aluminium—as against other non-ferrous metals—has become gradually cheaper.

Table 10

Informative world market prices of non-ferrous metals* and their relative prices compared to aluminium ($/ton)

Year	Aluminium	per cent	Copper	per cent	Lead	per cent	Zinc	per cent
1935	482	100	172	35	69	14	68	14
1950	370	100	472	127	300	81	210	57
1955	500	100	500	100	332	66	273	55
1958	551	100	572	104	269	49	229	42
1960	577	100	712	123	265	46	287	49
1965	545	100	780	143	260	48	320	59
1970	614	100	1160	189	304	49	296	48
1972	610	100	1100	180	320	58	375	61
1972 as per cent of 1935	127		640		463		543	

* With the average of the 1935–1970 prices.

Table 10 also shows that the relative cheapening of aluminium took place parallel with the rise of the world market price of aluminium. For reasons to be discussed later, the divergent movements were even stronger in Hungary: in the period 1957–1976 the price of 1 ton of rolled aluminium rose by 11%, although its value diminished by 40%.

When making price forecasts, it should be borne in mind what place within general price trends a certain concrete product may occupy due to the major role played by foreseeable changes in manufacturing technology. In the case of aluminium, price planners in Hungary set out from the fact that the possibilities offered by the Bayer–Hall–Heroult process are on the point of being exhausted. Indeed this method has some considerable shortcomings: the high requirement of energy, high investment costs and environment pollution. In addition to bauxite there are other raw materials containing aluminium, but among them only the laterites can be processed by the Bayer technology. But, in addition to them, cyanites, nefelines, clay-shale, clays and organic shale offer potential possibilities. No wonder that numerous papers and patents on the production of aluminium have appeared. The grouping of the most frequent methods of producing aluminium is the following:

- metallothermic processes,
- carbothermic (electrothermic) processes,
- plasma-chemical methods,
- other methods.

In their essence the new processes of production differ from the traditional method in so far as the former attempt to manufacture aluminium either from the basic material (bauxite, clay, etc.) directly, or else they are aimed at producing metal-aluminium from pure subcompounds ($AlCl_3Al_2S_3$).* A general shortcoming of various methods for producing aluminium is that the purity of the metal obtained is not satisfactory and that it can be rendered suitable for use only by means of expensive purifying processes. On an industrial scale only the traditional method is used to produce aluminium for the time being. At present price forecast cannot take into account new methods.

3. Spill-over effects of price changes

A survey of the interdependency of price changes

The micro-price structure relates to economic life with a focus on enterprises, whereas the macro-price structure views it from the aspect of the national economy. On the basis of our value calculations it is clear that price interdependencies can be appropriately studied only in their macro-structure, which is rendered possible by a survey of the spill-over effects of price changes. This method also enables us to calculate ideal price systems. When we wish to transform an actual price system into an ideal one we correct the net income *(s)* included in sectoral prices by the method of causing spill-over price changes so that:

– in case of a value price system the $\frac{s}{v}$ included in the sectoral prices should be equal;

– in case of a production price system the $\frac{s}{e}$ included in the sectoral prices should be equal;

– in case of a mixed type price system the net income included in the sectoral prices should be consistent with the chosen price type.

The *consistency* of the price system is an important condition of the investigation of the spill-over effects of price changes. In the calculation of ideal systems this goes without saying, since in that case the net incomes included in the prices must conform to some mathematical formula. But even independently of this, the consistency of a price system involves consistent treatment of spill-over effects on prices. Accordingly, if the price of product "A" changes and, on account of this, production costs of product "B" also change, the price of product "B" must also change, and to such an extent that the price structure of "B" *should not* change. In other words, if a survey of reciprocal effects of price changes is in the focus of our investigations, we may leave out of consideration whether prices elaborated in this way can be enforced in practice.

In view of the above-mentioned limiting factor, it must be emphasized that the consistency implied by the spill-over method of price changes, evidently cannot result in a price system consistent with the relationship between supply and demand. The new relative prices attained by the method of spill-over effects must, inevitably, differ to a greater or lesser extent from the changes of relative prices brought about by price movements of the market. Nevertheless, the analysis of price interdepen-

* Miskei, M.–Lakatos, T.: A hagyományostól eltérő alumínium-előállító módszerek és eljárások (Methods and processes different from the traditional one for producing aluminium), Budapest, 1972. (Manuscript.)

dencies is not to be considered a useless pastime. After all, it is only in this way that every effect exerted by the price movement of a given product (products) can be examined in its connexions of the production structure of society in a static state. And these effects are vitally important in the mechanism of decision-making that shapes the supply structure.

The *iteration method* applied in value calculations indicates the peculiarity of the social production structure according to which the change of the price of product "A" changes that of the others, among them the price of product "B", in such a manner that the feed-back effect of the latter *also* changes the price of product "A". The to-and-fro movement of the effect of price changes is general and asserts itself for all products. (1) Price changes of *export products* will change the value of the national currency in relation to all other currencies and—in a consistent price system—they affect, through the change of the exchange rate, the price system. (2) The changes of prices of *consumption goods* will change the real value of wages and—in a consistent price system—they react on the price system through changes in nominal wages. (3) The change of the prices of *capital goods* will change the real value of investments, including also depreciation, and will—in a consistent price system—react in this way upon the price system as a whole.

We have deliberately picked out export products, consumer goods and capital goods, since, when the interdependencies of price changes are examined in an input–output balance, these products are—as a general rule—treated as if their price changes did not have a feed-back effect. When the methodology is applied, this gives rise to the differentiation in the range of products, depending on whether the effect of their price changes proceeds only outwards, moves to and fro, only passes through them or, finally, moves only inwards.

(1) The price changes of *products that exert an effect only outwards* do react upon all other products, but the changed prices of these latter do not affect the prices of the former. Import goods, for instance, belong to this group of products. (2) Some means of productions produced domestically (such as coal, electrical energy, bauxite, cement, iron mouldings, cotton yarn, sawn goods, etc.) belong to the group of products having *to-and-fro effects,* the price changes of which act sensitively upon the prices of other products, and, as a reaction the price changes of these latter change the prices of the means of production too. (3) The products *through which the effects of price changes only pass* react to the price changes of commodities belonging to the first two groups. Their prices when they change affect the prices of products belonging to group 4, but price changes do not react upon goods belonging to the first two groups. A fairly high number of the means of production belongs to this group, whose price changes, as shown by specific analyses, do not significantly affect prices of goods produced in previous phases of production. (4) Industrial finished goods, and among them consumption goods, belong to the group of products whose price changes have *only an inward effect.* These goods are subject to the effects of price changes but do not participate in conveying effects (to and fro, or passing through them).

We shall investigate the interdependencies of price changes

– in the system of sectoral price changes,
– in the effect of price changes of some basic materials, as well as
– in the relations of prices and wages.

Real processes taking place in the production structure of society and the essential laws of their movements are comprehensively reflected in the interdependencies of sectoral prices. The knowledge we may gain in this way is extraordinarily useful even if we know that within the sector real price movements take place with a marked differentiation.

Sectoral price changes and their effects

The investigations of the mutual effects of price changes must start with the examination of sectoral price changes. In this instance, too, we have used the Hungarian input–output balance of 1976. The calculations were made in the Price Institute of the Hungarian National Board for Materials and Prices. The question to which we are seeking an answer is: what effect does a 10% rise in the sectoral price exert in the prices of all the other sectors, and what repercussions these effects will have on the sectoral price that set off the price movement? As there is a feed-back effect of price changes, the price in the given sector must rise by more than the 10% increase of the sectoral price, so as to cause the relative price of the sector increase by 10%.

Table 11

Co-efficient of price level cumulation
in case of a 10% sectoral price level increase

Sector	Cumulated co-efficient
Mining	11.7
Energy	10.9
Metallurgy	12.6
Engineering	11.0
Building materials	10.8
Chemicals	12.2
Light industry	12.5
Foodstuffs	11.7
Construction industry	10.4
Agriculture	14.2
Transport	10.4
Personal services	10.3
Gross output	18.5

As shown by this table, if every sector wants to raise its own price level by 10%, this—if the consistency of the price system is to be preserved—can be achieved only by raising the Social Product price by 18.5%. At the same time the table shows a considerable dispersion of the cumulated co-efficient according to sectors. The cumulated co-efficient is particularly large in agriculture (1.42), in metallurgy (1.26) and in the light industry (1.25). The extent of *verticality* differentiates these three sectors from all the others. In these three sectors the cumulated co-efficient is high not only because, in contrast to the other sectors, the feed-back effect is in this instance considerable, but because vertical cumulation within each of them is considerable. In *metallurgy* verticalities appear in crude iron, steel and rolled goods; in *light industry,* in yarns, in grey and finished fabrics as well as in ready-made garments and in *agriculture* in fodder and livestock. Price cumulation is a peculiar manifestation of the gross output.

As in the comparative analysis of price types, here too we have picked out 12 sectors of the 19 of the input–output balance, and based on these 12 we present the connexions of sectoral price changes.

Table 12

Spill-over effects of a relative 10% rise

Sector	Mining	Energy	Metallurgy	Engineer-ing	Building materials
Mining	11.7	2.4	0.4	0.4	1.3
Energy	0.3	10.9	0.3	0.2	0.5
Metallurgy	0.2	0.2	12.6	1.5	0.8
Engineering	0.5	0.6	0.6	11.0	0.5
Building materials	0.1	0.1	0.2	0.1	10.8
Chemicals	0.7	1.4	0.3	1.0	0.6
Light industry	0.4	0.3	0.3	0.5	0.4
Foodstuffs	0.1	0.1	0.1	0.1	.
Construction	0.1	0.1	0.1	0.1	0.1
Agriculture	0.4	0.4	0.2	0.1	0.1
Transport	0.7	0.4	0.4	0.4	0.8
Personal services	0.1	0.2	0.2	0.1	0.1
Gross output	16.1	17.8	16.7	16.6	16.9

The effect of sectoral price changes upon *the Social Product price* varies substantially between sectors. In case of most sectors the effect of a 10% rise of the relative price on the Social Product price remains within 1%, or is about 1%. However, in case of agriculture it is 3.4%, for the engineering industry it is 2.1%, for the chemical industry 1.7% and for light industry 1.6%. In the effect the sectoral price exerts upon the Social Product price it is, first and foremost, the production structure that plays a decisive role. The particularly large effect of agriculture in the quantified model is only due to the fact that the input–output balance reflects the production structure of an industrially intermediately-developed country and the conditions of production given under such circumstances.

Interdependencies of sectoral prices reflect the internal technological connexions of the organization of social production. Price rises in *mining* will touch most markedly the price of electrical energy (the effect is 2.4%), since in the production costs of electrical energy the expenditure on fuel plays an important part. *Metallurgy* affects the input of the engineering industry most strongly (the effect is 1.5%), since rolled goods are the most important basic material of the engineering industry, but the effect on the construction industry is also significant (0.7%), and is even enhanced by the expansion of up-to-date construction methods (e.g. light weight constructions). The price rises of the *building material industry* influence, above all, the prices of the construction industry (0.7%). The effects of price rises in the *chemical industry* are particularly far-reaching, because chemical products play significant and ever more important roles in the production of electrical energy—as fuels; in transport—also as fuels; and as synthetic materials in practically all sectors. The effect of price rises in *light industry* on prices of the construction industry (0.9%) originates, first of all, from the wood industry. The link between prices in the *food industry* and in agriculture is especially close. An increase in prices in *agriculture* by 10% will raise prices of the *food industry* by 8.4%, while a 10% increase of prices in the food industry will affect agricultural prices only to the extent of an increase of 1.1%. The rise of transport charges affects, clearly first of all the sectors particularly dependent on transport (construction industry, building material industry, mining, etc.).

of sectoral prices* (in per cent of the price)

Chemicals	Light industry	Foodstuffs	Con-struction	Agri-culture	Transport	Personal services	Gross National Product
1.0	0.3	0.3	0.3	0.2	0.2	0.4	0.7
0.4	0.3	0.2	0.2	0.2	0.2	0.2	0.5
0.2	0.2	0.4	0.7	0.4	0.4	0.3	1.1
0.3	0.3	0.7	1.3	0.9	1.1	0.6	2.1
0.1	0.1	0.2	0.7	0.2	0.2	0.4	0.4
12.2	0.6	1.0	0.9	1.0	0.7	0.4	1.7
0.8	12.5	0.4	0.9	0.3	0.5	0.5	1.6
0.2	0.2	11.7	0.1	1.1	0.1	0.1	1.7
0.1	0.9	0.1	10.4	0.2	0.2	1.8	1.1
0.4	0.6	8.4	0.3	14.2	0.4	0.1	3.4
0.5	0.5	0.5	1.0	0.3	10.4	0.6	1.1
0.1	0.1	0.1	0.2	0.1	0.1	10.3	0.4
17.1	18.2	25.2	18.2	19.9	15.1	16.3	18.5

* Calculation made in the Price Institute of the National Board for Materials and Prices.

When one knows the interdependencies of sectoral prices, it is easy to judge the effect of different price movements on prices of a given sector. If, for example, the price level of agriculture rises by 15% and that of the chemical industry decreases by 30%, prices in the food industry must rise—in a consistent price system—by 9.6%. The effect within the food industry is: $1.5 \times 8.4 - 3.0 \times 1.0 = 12.6 - 3.0 = 9.6\%$. Calculations of a similar kind can be performed for any sector, or any interrelationship, if this is required, by the examination of the effects of price movements of the world market or else of effects of changes in production conditions in different sectors.

Spill-over effects of price changes of materials

The sectoral price is a price level measured in a given production sructure, and it changes in the function of the price movements of the product. The more detailed the breakdown in the input–output balance in which the mutual flow of products is investigated, the more accurate the information we can get about these movements. This refers, first of all, to so-called homogeneous branches of industry, where the branch may cover one product (e.g. in coal mining) or a narrow range of related goods (e.g. in some branches of the building material industry). Calculations performed in the input–output balance with 10–16, 30–40 or 60–80 sectors are a characteristic example. The degree of aggregation is determined by the nature of the question to be examined.

However, in many sectors there is an extremely diversified product mix. In these sectors some of the goods produced are closely related, while others differ greatly both in the technology of their manufacture, and the use for which they are destined. If we want to examine spill-over effects of related price changes, we can do so only in a *product type price model.* Product type price models are set up with a view to *representing* the price system, the endeavour being that they should adequately characterize the production structure, taking also into consideration the verticals within the individual sectors. In the few countries where price models of the product type are made, they embrace positions from some hundred to some thousand.*

The construction of price models is particularly useful in an examination of the spill-over effect of price changes of raw materials. In this case we are interested, first of all, in the intensity and the range of spill-over effects and not so much in their effect on the Soctal Product price level, though this too may be significant.

Table 13

The effect of a 100% price rise of some products on the Social Product price level

Name of product	Social Product price level = 100
Crude oil	105.5
Copper	100.7
Sugar	100.5
Fertilizers	100.5
Ox-hide	100.2

Spill-over effects may be considered of a high intensity if the 100% price rise of one product brings about a price change of at least 40% in the price of another. See some cases of spill-over effects of great intensity in Table 14.

Table 14

Some cases of spill-over effects of great intensity (in per cent)

Changing price of product		Spill-over effect of price changes	
Electrical energy	100	Ferro silicon	48
		Caustic soda	45
		Hydrochloric acid	43
Pig iron for steel	100	Steel ingots	71
		Bar steel and profile steel	59
		Steel springs	45
Aluminium ingots	100	Rolled aluminium goods	85
		Aluminium foil	66
Cellulose	100	Wrapping paper	56
Cotton fabrics	100	Cotton goods (coat)	44

Spill-over effects may be considered of medium intensity if a 100% price change of one product causes a 10–40% price change in another product.

* Csikós-Nagy, B.–Ganczer, S.–Rácz, L.: Az első termékrendszerű ármodell (The first price model of the product type), *Közgazdasági Szemle,* 1964, No. 1.

Table 15

Spill-over effects resulting from a 100% price increase in fuel (in per cent)

Product	Price change	Product	Price change
China insulators	37	Aluminium ingots	28
Alumina	36	Machine implements	27
Bar and profile steel	36	Steel ingots	26
Ferro-silicon	31	Black steel sheets	26
Hydrochloric acid	30	Caustic soda	25
Screws	29	Bricks	24
Steel springs	29	Rail transport	19

Spill-over effects of prices may be considered of a low intensity if a 100% price change in one product causes a price change of 2–10% in another one.

Calculations have shown that in a product model of adequate size and of reasonable accuracy, the number of indirect co-efficients may amount to fifteenfold of that of direct co-efficients. However, 85% of the indirect co-efficients are of insignificant intensity. Interdependencies of an intensity of 1–7% covered about 10–12% of the total co-efficients, and only 3% of the co-efficients were of a higher intensity.

The grouping of products according to the extent of the spill-over effect of price changes is based on the features of products which are expressed in different spill-over-effect curves. From this angle, three basic types of products can be distinguished. There are, firstly, product prices whose spill-over effect is general, secondly those whose spill-over effect covers a wide sphere and finally others affecting a narrow one. Fuel, for instance, has a general spill-over effect, pig iron for steel effects a wide sphere, whereas price changes of aluminium ingots spill over a narrow range only.

The spill-over effects of wage changes

When examining the spill-over effect of wage changes, we are again interested in the interdependencies of price and not in the factors that trigger off the price movements. We include the price–wage interrelations within our investigations only because, without doing so, we cannot obtain a full picture of the price interdependencies.

It is to be borne in mind, however, that the examination of price–wage movements is traditionally connected with the question whether price rises set off wage rises or the other way round, whether the rises in wages, by causing increased production costs, render price rises inevitable. The question can also be put in general terms: Can the analysis of price interdependencies be severed from the investigation of the causes of price movements? Causes lying behind price movements are highly intricate. The price movement of product "B" is, from the point of product "A" a cause, but from the point of product "C" it is a result.

When we analyse price movements, we shall differentiate between external and internal factors, between original and derivative ones. We shall consider *internal* and *derivative* such price movements as take place in consequence of the interdependencies of prices. This should be regarded as a formal–theoretical distinction, since we should be confronted with unsurmountable difficulties if given the task of determining, in accordance with this classification, the factors governing the price trends of a certain given period.

Let us remember what has been said above with regard to value calculations and, within this framework, to the category of real costs. Real costs are wage costs, and, in the last analysis, value is composed of wages and net income. If we examine the price relations applicable to a given country in terms of the extent to which they are adjusted to value relations, or to which they differ from them, we can determine this by examining the proportion of wages and net incomes expressed in the price of the sector (or product). Primary inputs, in the form of a unit of net national production, may also be expressed as follows, using the figures for Hungary for 1974:

Table 16

The structure of sectoral price traced back to $v+s$

Sector	v	s	Price
Mining	58.3	41.7	100.0
Energy	38.3	61.7	100.0
Metallurgy	36.1	63.9	100.0
Engineering	37.5	62.5	100.0
Building materials	41.3	58.7	100.0
Chemicals	44.7	55.3	100.0
Light industry	44.5	55.5	100.0
Foodstuffs	63.2	36.8	100.0
Construction	45.0	55.0	100.0
Agriculture	68.0	32.0	100.0
Transport	51.6	48.4	100.0
Personal services	49.2	50.8	100.0
Social Product	46.0	54.0	100.0

Here labour, as a commodity, appears representing all products and services. This springs from the fact that value is produced by human labour and the value of a product is measured by the labour input. If we suppose that wages paid in Table 16 are related to the quantity of work, the deviation of sectoral prices from the value proportions are measured exactly by the different proportions of $\frac{v}{s}$ in the price structure of the national product and of the sectoral price. If—furthermore—wages rise proportionately in every sector, only the total price level will rise in a value-price system, but the relative sectoral prices will remain unchanged. This follows from the preceding argument. Product value is labour value, and, in the last analysis, so are relative inputs. In a value-price system $\frac{s}{v}$ is identical in all sectors (products). Consequently, a uniform increase of wages cannot affect relative price proportions.

True, prices are increased by enterprises. The organization of social production operates in a determined institutional framework, in which economic calculations are based on the summarized forms of the factor prices, viz. land, capital and labour. Obviously in the price structure of particular sectors or products, wage costs will appear to be widely differentiated by sectors if we consider production costs as they show themselves directly ($c+v+s$), and again in different forms if we trace the price structure back to value-added ($v+s$). In Hungary's input–output balance of 1976 the proportion of wages calculated in this way appears as follows:

Table 17

The $c+v+s$ structure of the sectoral price

Sector	v	$c+s$	Price
Mining	21.4	78.6	100.0
Energy	6.0	94.0	100.0
Metallurgy	6.9	93.1	100.0
Engineering	11.5	88.5	100.0
Building materials	14.2	85.8	100.0
Chemicals	4.4	95.6	100.0
Light industry	11.8	88.2	100.0
Foodstuffs	5.3	94.7	100.0
Construction	17.4	82.6	100.0
Agriculture	14.5	85.5	100.0
Transport	21.6	78.4	100.0
Personal services	26.1	73.9	100.0
Social Product	12.9	87.1	100.0

Let us have a look again at Table 12 which offers a picture of the spill-over effect of a relative 10% increase of the sectoral price. And let us take the case when wages rise by 100%. In the Gross National Product price, wages represent 12.9%. By sectors this ranges between 4.4 (chemical industry) and 26.1 (personal services). The question is: what are the spill-over effects that follow a 100% increase of wages. It is still being assumed that wage increases are proportionate per sector (per product).

At first sight the price movement triggered off by the sectoral differentiation of the wage ratio (capital structure) will both raise the price level and change relative prices. But, in fact, even under such conditions the higher price level will be accompanied by unchanged relative sectoral (product) prices. This is the consequence of feed-back effects. If we bring about a spill-over effect while preserving the consistency of the price system and of the original price structure, the effect—irrespective of the type of price—will be the same as in the value-price system.

This thesis, which can be proved mathematically, can be explained logically too. When analysing the connexions between the price type and the relative price, we found that every possible type of mixed prices would cause relative prices to be between the value price and the production price. The extent to which relative prices diverge from relative values reflects the extent to which the net income element in the prices is not proportionate to wages. Consequently, by merely raising the wages new relative prices do not emerge, due to the spill-over effect of prices, which preserves the consistency of the price system.

This is a specific feature of price movements induced by proportionate wage rises. In case of a 100% increase of wages, the Gross National Product price will, naturally, not rise by 12.9% (see Table 17), but to a much greater extent. This is logical because in most individual sectors the greater part of costs consists of the value-part c, and this c comprises in an indirect way significant wage elements of previous phases. Accordingly, the final relative sectoral (product) prices are shaped by feed-back effects. The 10% rise of sectoral prices in Table 12 led to a cumulated co-efficient of 18.5%. Accordingly, a 100% proportionate wage rise brings about in an indirect way almost the same indirect wage increase, and the price level at which the original relative sectoral (product) prices can be re-established comes into force not by a 12.9% but almost by its double, by a 23.9% (12.9×1.85) increase of the price level.

In practice the extent of wage increases is not 100%, but, say, 10%. In this case its effect on the price level will only be 2.4%. Moreover, through any time-period, price rises can only be viewed in the context of the productivity of labour. When wages only alter with changes in productivity of labour, this cannot, under a consistent price system bring about price movements. Under such conditions price movements could be interpreted only to mean that, in case of price reductions, wages are above the value of labour, whereas in case of price increases, they are below the value of labour.

Let us suppose that the productivity of labour increases by 5% on an annual average. In this case there is considerable scope for wage rises which can take place under unchanged price relations. On the other hand, if possibilities of improving the productivity of labour vary widely by sectors (products), then a proportionate wage increase in line with average productivity would cause price rises in some sectors and price decreases in others, but without changing the overall price level.

Chapter Two

SECULAR MARKET PRICE TRENDS

1. The law of general price rises

Possibilities and limits of the analysis of prices

In what follows we are presenting a historic survey of price trends. The more we know of the past, the better can we understand the present. Indeed a historic survey may provide a basis for price prognostication.

The types of price movements can be divided into two groups.

1. The movements which adapt themselves to the decrease of commodity value owing to increases in productivity of labour. These movements only distribute the additional commodities created by the growth of the productive force of labour in harmony with the state of equilibrium of the production structure. Reflecting the actual conditions of production, these changes of relative prices take place consistently with either decreases or increases in the general price level. In the former case the prices of goods benefiting from higher productivity will decrease, whereas in the latter case the prices of goods whose productivity rises little or not at all will increase.

2. The price movements which lead to a re-distribution of value produced on a scale of society among classes of society or within the same class among several groups (e.g. among capitalists). If we consider such processes on a world scale, this re-distribution can—and does—take place among countries too. Behind such re-distributions there are always social forces, and the struggle among them and the real context determine the extent of re-distribution and its social effects. These movements are not connected with value in production, but with the re-distribution of the total value. Their effect on the price level may be very considerable depending on the economic–social forces in the area or areas affected.

In reality it is rather difficult to distinguish the various factors causing price movements, since they often merge and interact. And yet it is important to distinguish them theoretically, because the interpretation of general price movements in a given period depends on this.

We wish to focus our attention in Chapters Two and Three of the present work on the examination of the trend of the *general price level.* As it were, we suppose that the trend of commodity value was hyperbolic in the past centuries: consequently, if the price level did not decrease, or if it rose, this can be interpreted as an inflation. In Chapter Four we shall inquire whether the law of the decrease of the commodity value has prevailed in the twentieth century or will do so in coming decades. The intricate questions of the trend of relative prices will be discussed, in connexion with the so-called North–South problem, in Chapter Five.

Now we should like to draw attention to the statistics that determine the trend of the general price level. We will then examine price formation separately in capitalism and in socialism. Differentiation according to socio-economic systems is justified, because in a capitalist economy price movements are—in general—regulated by the market mechanism, whereas in a socialist economy this is done by government decision. Of course, the law of value asserts itself in both socio-economic systems, but its manifestation is basically different if prices are regulated by the market rather than by the government.

Economic historians, statisticians and economists have devoted surprisingly great efforts to the history of price trends. In this research—particularly in Europe—specialists of nearly every country have taken part.* Not only the monographs on price history in general, but also general histories of economy are of considerable significance. The present work, however, *does not aim to analyse the complete historic background of price trends.* If this had been our purpose we should have studied thoroughly the French literature of the subject, since French scholars may have contributed most to the history of prices.** But we only wish to characterize secular price trends. Accordingly, it seems to be desirable to concentrate on England, setting out from the historic role of the Pound Sterling.

As a preliminary, let us point out that *a precise system of price statistics* has existed for hardly a hundred years; indeed the construction of such a system has not yet been completed. Even today there are "blank spots" in price statistics, although in some industrially developed capitalist countries calculations of the *implicit price deflator**** have been introduced. There are economists who call into question the reality content of the aggregated price index. According to them, price formation cannot be characterized by a comprehensive index.° Such an index, however, seems to be indispensable. Besides, there is another practical use of the implicit price deflator. It is still a shortcoming of price statistics that data represented in different qualities and types, etc. differ. Owing to this, one cannot draw unambiguous conclusions from price data as to the effect that import prices, domestic prices, costs and consumer prices, etc. exert upon one another. The calculation of an implicit price deflator presupposes a system of price statistics in which the different kinds of prices (costs, wholesale prices, retail prices, export–import prices, etc.) and the prices appearing in various sectors interrelate.

In March 1973 experts discussed the questions of the statistical *integration of the price index and the volume index* at a conference organized by the Economic Com-

* A survey of literature of price history can be gained from the following works:
Mass, W.: Zur Geschichte der Preise in Polen, Österreich und Oberdeutschland. VSWG. 1938, pp. 357–371.
Lerner, F.: Neue Beiträge zur Geschichte der Preise und Löhne in Deutschland, Holland und Italien. VSWG. 1952, 3, pp. 251–265.
Hoszowski, St.: L'Europe Centrale devant la révolution des prix. XVIe et XVIIe siècles. Annales 1961, pp. 441–456.
Zimányi, V.: Bibliográfiai áttekintés a külföldi ár- és bértörténeti kutatásokról (Bibliographical survey of foreign research of price and wage history), Világtörténet, Tájékoztató a külföldi történeti irodalomról, Budapest 1964, No. 4.

** Cf. particularly:
Fourastié, J.: *L'évolution des prix à long terme,* Paris, 1969.
Baulant, M.: Prix et salaires à Paris au XVIe siècle, Annales (Économies, Sociétés, Civilisations) 1976/5.
Labrousse: *La crise de l'économie française à la fin de l'Ancien Régime et au début de la Révolution,* Paris, 1944.
D'Avenel, G.: *Histoire économique de la propriété des salaires des denrées et de tous les prix en général depuis l'an 1200 jusqu'à l'an 1800,* Paris, 1894–1926. (6 Vols.)
Vilár, P.: Remarques sur l'histoire des prix, Annales (É.S.C.) 1961/1.
Simiand: *Le salaire, l'évolution sociale et la monnaie,* Paris, 1932.

*** Brunner, K.: Fiscal and Monetary Policies in Moderate Inflation, *Journal of Money, Credit and Banking,* February 1973, pp. 313–353. (Co-authors: Fratiani, M., Jordan, J. L., Meltzer, A. H., Neumann, N. J. N.) The paper contains calculations of the implicit price deflator, of price relations in the USA in the period 1948–1950.

° Erdős, P.: *Contributions to the Theory of Capitalist Money, Business Fluctuations and Crises,* Akadémiai Kiadó, Budapest, 1971.

mission for Europe. At this conference the opinion was expressed that, in a consistent set of value, price and volume indices, consumption cannot be satisfactorily measured. According to this view the increase in the volume of consumption is partly based on an increase in the quantity of commodities available to consumers and partly on the change in the quality composition of consumption, mainly by an increase of the proportion of dearer articles of a better quality. The former can be considered a quantitative component of increased consumption and the latter a qualitative one. Thus, if one were to characterize the course of the volume of consumption, the quantitative factor should be separated from the qualitative one.

Price statistics based on a comparative analysis becomes considerably more difficult if we want to calculate the price index for *several centuries of the past*. The problem is not due to the lack of appropriate price data. If one undertakes the effort of exploring the *records of prices* to be found in national archives, in libraries of statistical offices and in other centres of documentation, one will see how rich the source-material is and how important the information on prices was considered in every era. The real problem is how to quantify numerically and more or less unequivocally the *changes of the price level*. From this point the investigations conducted by Gayer, Rostow and Schwartz deserve particular attention.* They compared the price indices they had made for the period 1790–1850, or for a part of it, with the five available English wholesale price indices, prepared by Jevons, Sauerbeck, Silberling, Kondratieff and Rousseaux.** The comparison revealed significant differences, which can be traced back to different causes. By way of an example we refer only to the following: The Silberling index included 35 commodities which can be interpreted better as a business barometer than as a measure of changes in the general price level. Oriental products are represented with a relatively important weight in Jevons's index, consequently the specific price movements of these products cause this index to diverge from the others.

The foundation in 1930 of the International Scientific Committee on Price History was well justified. It has elaborated the rules to observe when a price index is being prepared; rules that often used to be left out of consideration.*** It is hardly possible to devise historic price statistics which can satisfy all requirements. Nevertheless, the chief directions of secular price trends can be summarized with a fair probability.

Alternative basic hypotheses

The Economist published noteworthy data on the formation of market prices in Britain.° By presenting them we are beginning the investigation of secular market price trends.

* Gayer, A. D.–Rostow, W. W.–Schwartz, A. J.: *The Growth and Fluctuation of the British Economy, 1790–1850*, Vol. I, Oxford, 1953.

** Jevons, W. S.: The Variations of Prices and the Value of the Currency since 1782, *Journal of the Statistical Society*, XXVIII, 1865. Sauerbeck, A.: Prices of Commodities and the Precious Metals, *Journal of the Statistical Society*, 1886. Silberling, N. J.: British Prices and Business Cycles, 1779 to 1850, *Review of Economic Statistics*, 1923. Kondratieff, N. D.: Die langen Wellen der Konjunktur, *Archiv für Sozialwissenschaft und Sozialpolitik*, Dec. 1926. Rousseaux, P.: Mouvements de Fond de l'économie Anglaise, 1800–1913.

*** Ramsey, P. H. (ed.): *The Price Revolution in Sixteenth-Century England*, London, 1971. Hammarström, I.: The Price Revolution of the Sixteenth Century: Some Swedish Evidence, *Scandinavian Economic History Review*, 1957, No. 5.

° *The Economist*, July 13, 1974. "Back to an Age of Falling Prices?"

Table 18

Price formation in Britain since 1661 (1661 = 100)*

	0	1	2	3	4	5	6	7	8	9
166–		100	103	101	96	96	92	88	88	84
167–	85	84	81	80	86	92	88	81	82	87
168–	85	82	82	80	81	83	84	74	74	73
169–	75	76	75	78	87	87	89	90	95	98
170–	85	74	73	70	73	66	75	65	68	79
171–	90	100	75	72	76	77	73	70	69	72
172–	75	74	68	66	70	72	75	71	73	77
173–	70	65	66	63	65	66	64	69	67	66
174–	74	80	73	70	62	63	69	67	70	71
175–	70	67	69	67	67	68	68	81	78	74
176–	73	70	70	74	75	78	79	81	80	73
177–	74	79	87	88	86	84	84	80	87	82
178–	81	85	86	95	93	89	88	87	90	87
179–	92	90	90	95	101	109	114	110	110	118
180–	157	169	129	115	119	138	136	138	151	157
181–	153	152	175	180	155	141	127	140	144	128
182–	115	105	101	104	106	115	102	102	97	95
183–	95	97	95	93	97	97	107	102	103	113
184–	111	105	96	91	94	95	95	100	87	82
185–	82	79	82	97	108	108	108	110	96	100
186–	104	100	104	105	103	102	104	102	100	93
187–	95	100	111	110	105	102	100	95	88	85
188–	89	86	88	88	82	76	72	70	73	73
189–	76	75	71	71	64	62	63	64	68	73
190–	79	75	75	75	72	75	81	84	76	80
191–	84	86	91	91	91	116	146	193	207	222
192–	270	167	141	139	150	146	136	131	129	124
193–	104	89	86	85	103	103	106	110	113	113
194–	152	205	195	177	195	191	191	205	219	227
195–	234	251	269	273	276	287	301	312	319	319
196–	322	333	347	354	365	379	396	404	425	446
197–	474	513	545	595						

Figures for each decade are along a horizontal line; e.g. that for 1667 = 88, for 1944 = 195.
* Linked index. Main sources: Mitchell and Deane. Abstract of British Historical Statistics, and Department of Employment, British Labour Statistics Historical Abstract 1886–1968.
Basic series: Schumpeter-Gilboy price index 1661–1697 (1697 = 100) and 1696–1823 (1701 = = 100); Rousseaux price indexes 1800–1923 (1865 to 1885 = 100); Sauerbeck-Statist price indexes 1846–1938 (1867 to 1877 = 100); DE index of the internal purchasing power of the pound 1914–1968 (1963 = 100).
Series rebased on 1661 = 100 using the multipliers: 1697 = 100, 0.9174; 1701 = 100, 0.7399; 1865–1885 = 100, 0.8679; 1867–1877 = 100, 1.0761; 1963 = 100, 3.5417.

Apart from a short period during the Second World War, prices have risen in Great Britain without a break since 1933. By means of price regulations and budget subsidies, the Government stabilized the cost of living index during the war. This index radically differs from the secular price trends of the preceding centuries. According to the data published in *The Economist,* inflationary cycles unfolded generally only in the wake of war, in periods before 1933. In most cases they lasted three years. Only after the First World War did the run of inflation take six years.

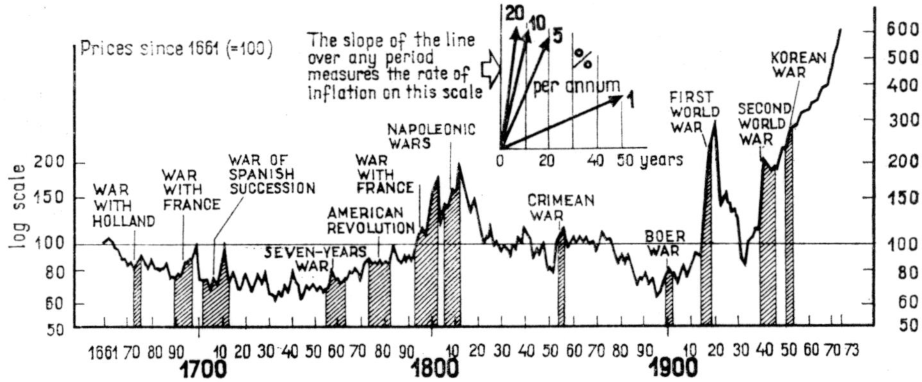

Chart 3. The trend of inflation in Britain since Cromwell (1661 = 100)
The chart plots prices on a logarithmic scale

In the years that followed, prices decreased considerably. We can read in *The Economist* that more could be bought in 1911 for one pound sterling than at the time of the 1665 plague, and more than twice as much as in 1813 during the Napoleonic wars.

The hypotheses formulated in *The Economist* summarize a widely held view. And yet, it is a surprise for those who have closely explored secular price trends. Let us compare the previous chart with the one that R. G. Lipsey published in 1960.* This latter is based on the price statistics of Ph. Brown and Sh. Hopkins and presents a survey of price formation in Southern England back to 1264.**

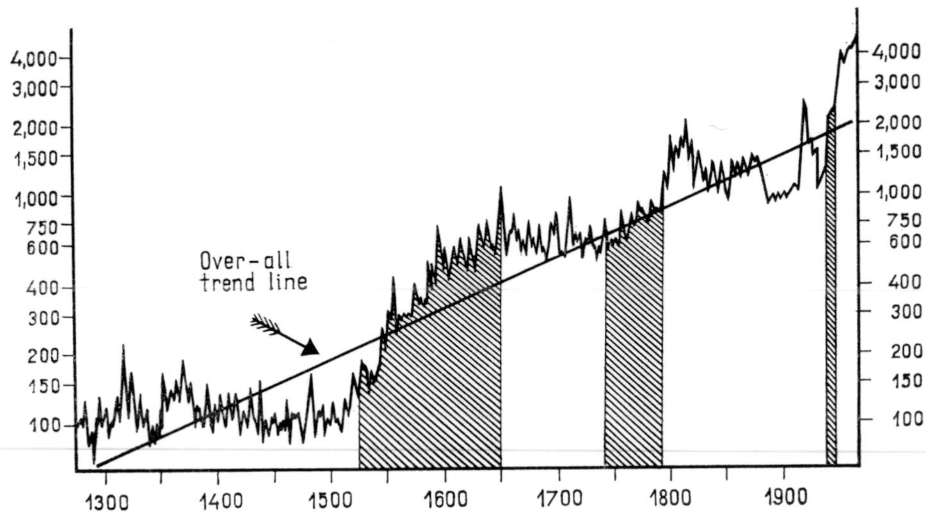

Chart 4. Price index of consumables in Southern England 1275–1959
(1451–75 = 100; shaded areas indicate periods of unreversed inflation)
The chart plots prices on a logarithmic scale

* Lipsey, R. G.: Does Money always Depreciate? *Lloyds Bank Review*, Oct. 1960, pp. 1–13.

** Brown, Ph. and Hopkins, Sh.: Seven Centuries of the Prices of Consumables, Compared with Builders' Wage Rates, *Economica*, Vol. XXIII, No. 92, 1956.

The chief components of the basket are cereals, meat and fish, butter and cheese, beverages, fuel and lighting, garments. The line of prices from 1264–1954 was continued by Lipsey with data of the consumer price index till 1959.

The difference between the two charts is striking. The Lipsey chart confirms *the law of general price increases*. The difference may be partly explained by the fact that *The Economist* started the price line only following the death of Oliver Cromwell (1658), with the justification that annual data are available only from 1661 on. Thus no account was taken of the critical period of 125 years—to be examined separately later on—in which, according to Lipsey's graph, the price level rose by 550%. The deviation in the data of price trends in the years following 1661 may also be conspicuous. In Lipsey's graph cyclical price movements show an upward direction; the value of the Pound Sterling was less in 1911 than in 1665.

The history of English wheat prices

Uncertainties about price index calculations reaching back several centuries make us lay the foundations of our study of secular price trends by the price history of a commodity which, in a certain meaning, may indicate general price trends too. Grain, or more exactly wheat, seems to be suited to this purpose. We have fairly accurate price information about wheat. Besides, wheat is not "one" commodity "in a vast forest", but a commodity which has an outstanding importance from the point of politics, social and economic affairs in price history. Man in our times can realize this only if he is able to put himself amidst the conditions prevailing before the industrial revolution. Periods in which the supply of the population with grain was a question pushing all others into the background, recurred again and again. We need not even point to the distant past. At its birth and quite a long time after it, economics could not free itself from the effect of Physiocrats. What Quesnay formulated in his essay "Grains" in the *Encyclopedia* indicated for many people and for a long time the way of economic thinking.

We are greatly indebted to the work of Th. Tooke, J. E. Th. Rogers and others for revealing the history of grain price.* The work of Th. Tooke and J. E. Th. Rogers in the history of economics was a source for many others studying the formation of grain prices. Now we shall investigate *wheat prices prevailing in the 14th–19th centuries in Britain.* We may safely disregard Antiquity as well as the beginning of the Middle Ages, since at those times grain was subject to trade by barter. But even in the 12th century, when urban life was growing and landowners sold their produce on fairs, grain was not a considerable commodity, owing to the primitive means of transport. We have deliberately concentrated our attention on Britain. The emergence of the modern world economy, being determined by the industrial revolution—at least up to the First World War—was closely connected with the leading role of Britain.

In a separate publication the Ministry of Agriculture, Fisheries and Food published

* D'Avenel, G.: *Histoire économique de la propriété des salaires, des denrées, et de tous les prix en général depuis l'an 1200 jusqu'à l'an 1800,* Paris, 1894–1926.

Pagnini, G.: Saggio sopra il giusto pregio della cose, la giusta valuta della moneta et sopra il commercio dei romani. 1751. Scrittori classici italiani di economia politica. Parte moderna. Vol. 2. Ed. Custodi Milan, 1809.

Rogers, J. and Edwin, Th.: A History of Agriculture and Prices in England from the Year after the Oxford Parliament (1259) to the Commencement of the Continental War. 1793. Four volumes, London, 1866–82.

Tooke, Th. and Newmarch, W.: A History of Prices and of the State of the Circulation from 1793 to 1856. Six volumes, London, 1838–57.

price statistics in respect of one cwt of wheat, barley and oats from 1771–1966.* The same publication contains the price for 25-year periods from 1316 to 1820, also calculated for a unit of one cwt. Prices for 25-year periods can be calculated on the basis of annual prices up to 1966.

Table 19

Wheat prices at Exeter (per cwt)

Year	s	d	Year	s	d
1316–24	1	11	1650–74	10	0.75
25–49	1	3	75–99	8	7.5
50–74	1	10.50			
75–99	1	3.25			
			1700–24	8	3
			25–49	7	6.25
1400–24	1	6	50–74	7	4.25
25–49	1	6	75–99	12	5.25
50–74	1	6.25			
75–99	1	6.6			
			1800–24	18	9
			25–49	13	5
1500–24	1	9	50–74	11	10
25–49	2	3	75–99	7	10
50–74	4	6.75			
75–99	6	9.25			
			1900–24	9	8
			25–49	10	9
1600–24	7	9.25	50–66	23	10
25–49	9	9.5			

In terms of arithmetical averages, and extending the data up to 1975, the following average prices for a century can be obtained:

Table 20

Formation of the average wheat price in Great Britain[1]

	Price of one cwt		Index	
	s	d	14th century = 100	Previous century = 100
1316–1399	1	6	100	—
1400–1499	1	6	100	100
1500–1599	3	10	253	253
1600–1699	9	1	607	240
1700–1799	8	11	593	98
1800–1899	12	6	800	140
1900–1975	16	0	1,067	128

[1] Up to 1922 in British price statistics the wheat price referred to a measure of capacity: 1 quarter. Only after 1922 has the measure of weight, the 1 cwt been used for wheat. The figures of equivalence are the following:
1 quarter measure of capacity = 480 lbs = 217.7 kg
1 cwt measure of weight = 112 lbs = 50.8 kg.

* *A Century of Agricultural Statistics, Great Britain, 1866–1966,* London, Her Majesty's Stationery Office, 1968.

On examining the data, it cannot escape our attention that the average price of wheat was lower in the last quarter of the 19th century and in the first quarter of the 20th, than in the third quarter of the 17th century. Viewed from this aspect, the trend indicated by *The Economist* can be confirmed by the data on wheat prices. At the same time the table clearly indicates that wheat prices rose quite steeply in the third quarter of the 17th century. Thus it does not seem particularly fortunate that *The Economist* chose 1661 as its base, when characterizing secular price trends. As soon as we analyse price formation in a wider time horizon, the two kinds of basic hypotheses cease to exist. *The law of general price rises seems to assert itself in economic development*. This, however, did not come into being in consequence of a process of continual price rises, but rather in the wake of periodical price explosions, price rises by leaps and bounds. Price stability and even price decreases occurred between such price explosions. So, if we *a priori* suppose a decreasing trend of commodity value, the law of general price rises should be interpreted as a constant decrease of the value of money. And, indeed, studies analysing secular price trends are based on the hypothesis of periodically recurring inflations.

The six great inflations

Anna J. Schwartz attempted to summarize the price history of 2,500 years and to explain the background of essential price movements.* Almost 2,000 of the years examined introduce the reader to various forms of money inflation and to its reasons. In the survey of the 14th–20th centuries, on the other hand, we can gain a picture of fluctuations in the price level. The following summary picture can be obtained from the tables published by A. J. Schwartz.

Table 21

Changes of the price level in the 14th–20th centuries

Period	England	USA	Germany	France
	average annual extent of price level changes			
1320–1350 – 1351–1375	1.2	—	—	1.9
1376–1400 – 1476–1500	0	—	—	0
1501–1510 – 1593–1602	1.7	—	—	2.1[1]
1593–1602 – 1643–1652	0.6	—	—	1.6[2]
1643–1652 – 1693–1702	0	—	—	0[3]
1693–1702 – 1731–1740	−0.5	—	—	—
1731–1740 – 1781–1790	0.8	—	—	—
1790 – 1815	2.8	3.3	3.2	.
1815 – 1850	−2.2	−2.3	−1.9	−1.0
1850 – 1873	0.9	5.3	1.9	1.2
1873 – 1896	−1.7	−1.8	−0.8	−2.5
1896 – 1920	4.7	4.2	11.0	8.2
1920 – 1934	−4.1	−3.9	−1.2	−8.4

[1] 1501–1525 – 1576–1600
[2] 1601–1625 – 1626–1650
[3] 1626–1650 – 1676–1700

* Schwartz, A. J.: Secular Price Change in Historical Perspective, *Journal of Money, Credit and Banking*, February 1973, pp. 243–269.

As can be seen, six great waves of inflation left their mark upon the price trends of the past seven centuries:

– from the second decade of the 14th century a silver coin inflation that lasted over six decades,
– the so-called great price revolutions of the 16th and of the early 17th centuries,
– the inflation preceding the Napoleonic wars by half a century,
– the inflation of the Napoleonic wars,
– the inflation of the First World War,
– the inflation of the Second World War (this period is not covered by the table).

Schwartz's historical investigations also cover wages, capital interest and money supply. Thus the conclusions she has drawn from the historical evidence well deserve attention.

1. Periods of rising prices have alternated with periods of declining prices, apparently for as long as money has been used as a medium of exchange.

2. Until the 18th century, the sources of monetary expansion and contraction were the output of precious metals and the debasement or restoration of the coinage. These sources have since been supplemented or substituted by paper money issues of banknotes or deposit currency. All forms of money issue have been subject to government control.

3. Before the era of 20th-century central banking, governments tended to be passive in relation to long-term changes in the precious metal output of the world and the changing rate of accrual to their national stocks. In earlier centuries, debasements and restorations of coinage seem to have been determined mainly by fiscal needs.

4. Long-run price changed consistently parallel the monetary changes, with one exception for England in the 16th century.

5. With the exception of war and immediate postwar periods and in earlier centuries of plagues, as well as of the economic disaster of 1929–32, output has apparently grown both during periods of secular price rise and fall.

6. Discrepancies between movements of the ratio of the money stock to real output and price movements reflect long-run changes in the public's demand for money balances.

7. In recent centuries, price fluctuations occurred at approximately the same date in numerous countries. The mechanism for the diffusion of price changes was the mutual adjustment of price levels between countries by international trade and the re-distribution of the world stock of monetary reserves. This was the case both under the gold standard before 1914, when the quantity of money in each country was a dependent variable, which had to adjust to produce a level of prices relative to prices abroad consistent with balance of payments equilibrium, and in the period after the war, when the monetary authorities had more leeway with respect of controlling the quantity of money.

8. Over the centuries it has been alleged that factors other than the ratio of money stock to output have caused secular price movements. These factors have ranged from changing population growth to changes in costs of production and to the presence or absence of speculation. If each price-period were a response to a constellation of factors other than money, it would then be necessary to show that constellations produced either a change in money stock or in velocity associated with a particular period. No one has done so.

9. Costs of production are affected by the same monetary influences as are prices

of final goods. Prices of factors that did not change in line with commodity prices would indicate a defect in the market for labour or capital.

The evaluation of seven centuries' price movements performed by Schwartz, who belongs to the Chicago monetary school, grasps the essential elements of reality, but not its entirety. In what follows we shall concentrate on three price episodes. These are:

– the price revolution of the 16th and of the early 17th centuries;
– the trend of price reductions accompanying the industrial revolution of the 19th century, and finally
– 20th century inflation, which has become continuous.

2. The price revolution

The evolution of world economy

Let us have another look at Chart 4. We can see three hatched areas. It is the common feature of the first two that inflation was not followed by deflation; the inflationary price level became the starting point of secular price trends in later periods. The first figures in the history of prices as the price revolution.* It embraces the time between 1525 and 1650. During those 125 years the price level rose by 550%.

The coincidence of the periods allows a reference to the fact that *both world economy and capitalism emerged in a price revolution.* It was the world economy still based on the colonial system, and its principal beneficiaries were some West European countries. Adam Smith's well-known exaggeration has been often quoted: the discoveries of America and of the way to India around the Cape of Good Hope were the greatest and most important events in the history of mankind. Furthermore, that was still the capitalism of which the *different phases of primitive accumulation* were characteristic. Karl Marx wrote the following: "The discovery of gold and silver in America, the extirpation, enslavement and entombment in mines of the aboriginal population, the beginning of the conquest and looting of the East Indies, the turning of Africa into a warren for the commercial hunting of black-skins, signalised the rosy dawn of the era of capitalist production. These proceedings were the chief momenta of primitive accumulation. On their heels there trod the commercial war of the European nations, with the globe for a theatre. It began with the revolt of the Netherlands from Spain, assumed giant dimensions in England's Anti-Jacobin War, and is still going on in the opium wars against China, etc.**

* It was with this that Hamilton began his significant paper on the price revolution. Hamilton, E. J.: American Treasure and the Rise of Capitalism, *Economica,* XXVII, 1929, pp. 338–357. I. Helferich was among the first to use the denomination "price revolution" in characterizing the price movements of the sixteenth and the early seventeenth centuries. (Helferich, I.: *Von den periodischen Schwankungen im Wert der edlen Metalle von der Entdeckung Amerikas bis zum Jahre 1830,* Nürnberg, 1843.) The concept itself, however, became generally accepted on grounds of George Wiebe's work. (Wiebe, G.: Zur Geschichte der Preisrevolution des XVI. und XVII. Jahrhunderts. Staats- und Socialwissenschaftliche Beiträge, ed. A. von Miaskowski, Leipzig, 1895. II. 2. (By price revolution Wiebe meant the general rise of the prices of products taking place in West Europe in the sixteenth century and brought about, in his opinion, first of all by the silver flowing to Europe from the American territories the Spanish had conquered. Historians of economy deem the price rise to have been revolutionary, though rather in its effect than in its rate.)

** Marx, K.: *Capital,* Vol. I, Moscow, 1967, p. 775.

Adam Smith, too, supposed that capitalist accumulation was preceded by a previous accumulation, which was thus the starting point and not the result of the capitalist mode of production.*

This process was analysed by Marx particularly fully. We shall revert to those of its elements which are connected with the revolution. First we should like to call attention to the intricate, manifold and sometimes even inconsistent character of this process. This too may play a part in the debates about the character of the price revolution and the assessment of causes triggering off inflation.** The available information suggests that it was as a result of numerous factors, both on the monetary and on the commodity side that the price revolution became permanent. In various periods different factors played the principal role.

With the evolution of the world economy, the most important elements of the price revolution appeared on the monetary side, with an increase of the stock of precious metals and with the acceleration of the velocity of money circulation. Within a couple of decades the European stock of gold got doubled, the stock of silver rose 3–4-fold. This was decisively due to the gold and later silver flowing in from the areas of the Spanish conquest in the New World. The extension of markets and, based on it, the development of industry, as well as commercial expansion played a part in the acceleration of the circulation rate of money.

Processes occurring *in Europe* also contributed to the price revolution, but owing to national ambitions, these too were in one way or another connected with the evolving world economy. We refer only to one factor, perhaps the most important one, that of growing state debts. Governments (monarchs) time and again resorted to debasing the coinage, in order to finance wars or the growing power of the state. The money scandal that took place in England between 1542 and 1551 was perhaps only the greatest among the recurring events. At that time the gold content of coins was reduced by a quarter and the silver content by three quarters.

The price revolution can be interpreted as an organic concomitant of capitalism, which, based on the colonial system, evolved on a world scale.

Profit inflation

Analysing the price revolution, Hamilton found that the prices of commodities rose faster than land rent and wages. He mentioned the following example to illustrate the process. Let us suppose that in the beginning of the 16th century out of 100,000 Pounds Sterling of commodity value 60,000 fell to the share of wages, 20,000 to rent and 20,000 to profit in Britain. The same commodity could be sold by the end of the century at 250,000 Pounds Sterling, but the wages of this commodity did not surpass 75,000. On the unrealistic assumption that rent rose proportionately with profit, this amounted to 50,000. Thus profit reached 125,000 Pounds Sterling, that is

* Smith, A.: *The Wealth of Nations.*

** Out of the extraordinarily rich literature see:

Brenner, J. S.: The Inflation of Prices in Early Sixteenth-Century England, *Economic History Review,* 2nd series, XIV, (1961–62), pp. 225–239. The Inflation of Prices in England, 1551–1650, *ibid.,* XV, (1962–63), pp. 266–284.

Hamilton, E. J.: American Treasure and the Rise of Capitalism (1500–1700), *Economica,* XXVII, 1929, pp. 338–357.

Hammarström, I.: The "Price Revolution" of the Sixteenth Century: Some Swedish Evidence, *Scandinavian Economic History Review,* V, 1957, pp. 118–154.

Gould, J. D.: The Price Revolution Reconsidered, *Economic History Review,* 2nd Series, Dec. 1964, pp. 249–266.

to say 100% of the original production value. Profit had risen fourfold.* That is why Hamilton treated the price revolution as a profit inflation. He plotted the changes in the proportion of price and wages as follows:

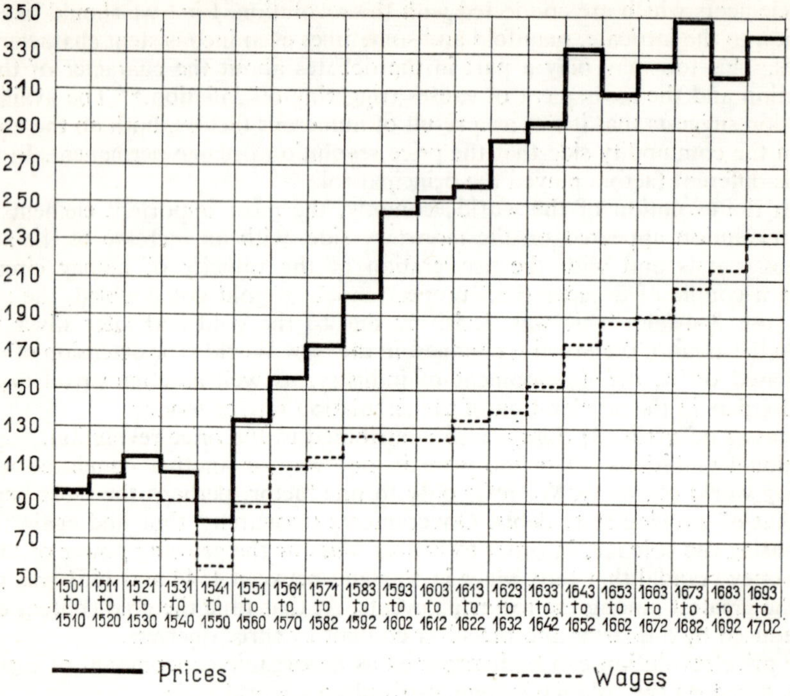

Chart 5. Index numbers of prices and wages in England, 1500–1702
(Index for 1451–1500 = 100)

Several economists protested against his interpreting the price revolution as a profit inflation. In fact, this encouraged Gould to write a paper on the re-evaluation of the price revolution.** J. N. Nef referred to the fact, among others, that side by side with wages and rents other costs had also arisen, e.g. timber, whose price had considerably increased.***

Evidence of a price rise in the means of production does not, of course, refute the hypothesis of a profit inflation. Let us recall what we have stated about the interdependencies of prices. If inflation really assumes the form of profit inflation, this can take place only in the following way: the capitalist increases output prices to a greater extent than would be justified by the rise of the input prices (means of production, wages, rent). That is to say, profit inflation must be accompanied by a redistribution of profit within the capitalist class (between branches of production and companies) and, in connexion with this, by the differentiation of increasing profit rates. Hamilton was right to leave out of consideration the rise of the prices of means

* Hamilton, E. J.: *Op. cit.* pp. 355–356.

** Gould, J. D.: *Op. cit.*

*** Nef, J. N.: Prices and Industrial Capitalism in France and England, 1540–1640, *Economic History Review*, VII, (1937), pp. 155–185.

of production, since he wanted to characterize the inflationary process in one product, and in this case c disappears from commodity value, everything being summarized in $v+s$. Such an approach has the advantage, in respect of class relations under capitalism that it renders possible an analysis of income distribution and changes therein.

E. Kerridge considered the statements about the land rent debatable.* Quite a few papers refer to rapid increases in land rent.** Gould might be right in asserting that no re-distribution of incomes between the capitalist class and the landowner class could take place in the way Hamilton supposed it had. It is even probable that the owners of agricultural land may have been greater beneficiaries of the price revolution than the owners in the industrial sector.*** But all this does not change the character of the inflation.

Nef called in question even Hamilton's data on wages, pointing out that the money wages of the periods examined could not be wholly compared. Nevertheless there seems to be a general agreement on the point that wages lagged considerably behind the increase of profit and land rent.

Returns of industrial and loan capital

But let us stay with the hypothesis of a profit inflation. Those who agreed with Hamilton that the increase of wages lagged behind the increase of profit continued the debate about the causes behind the increase of the profit rate. According to G. L. Bach the effect of price rises upon industrial profit did not originate from the fact that wages lagged behind prices, but rather from capital costs lagging behind price increases.°

In a period of continuous price rises the price of machines also increases, but as soon as their "historical cost" has been fixed, and the cost of depreciation is based on historical costs, it means a decreasing proportion in the gross income originating from price income. Or, more exactly: if all the other costs (including wage costs) increase in proportion to the price of the end product, the net profit originating from the operation of the machine tied up in production will rise more than the rise of the price level.

All this is only true if the writing off of fixed capital is based on historical costs and not if the cost of replacement is used in calculations, which is quite possible in practice. Seen from this angle, a part of the actual profit is a consequence of inappropriate depreciation and this is offset when the machine has to be replaced. On the other hand, if the machine is not discarded when it has been already written off—which might have been characteristic of the Tudor and Stuart periods—this too could be a source of the high profit rate.

But let us proceed: the profit from the operation of a machine installed in the inflationary period may rise not only because the conventions of accountancy adjust the depreciation to historical costs (and not to replacement costs), but it may also rise because *the interest on loans obtained to be invested in the machine decreases compared to the price income.* In the view of C. N. Cipolia the real economic revolution of the

* Kerridge, E.: The Movement of Rent, 1540–1640, *Economic History Review*, 2nd series, VI, (1953–1954), pp. 16–34.

** Simson, E. A.: *The Wealth of the Gentry*, Cambridge, 1961, Chapter V. Tawney and Power: Tudor Economic Documents, 1953, Vol. III, pp. 305–310.

*** Gould, J. D.: *op. cit.*, p. 263.

° Bach, G. L.: *Inflation*, Providence, R. I., 1958, pp. 33 ff, and 79 ff.

16th and early 17th centuries was not so much the rise of the price level but rather the decrease of the interest on capital.*

Now we should like to draw attention to S. Homer's work, who examined the interest rates of long-term credits by fifty-year periods (see Table 22).**

Table 22

Review of medieval and modern Western European and American long-term interest rates

Date	England	France	Dutch Republic—Holland	Spanish Netherlands—Belgium	Germany	Sweden	Spain	Switzerland	Italy	United States
	Minimum rates on best credits by half centuries[1]									
13th century										
1st Half				8.00						
2nd Half		14.00		8.00					$6\frac{5}{8}$	
14th century										
1st Half				8.00					$4\frac{7}{8}$	
2nd Half				8.00					$5\frac{1}{4}$	
15th century										
1st Half		10.00		8.00			4.00		6.00	
2nd Half		10.00		8.00	5.00		4.00		5.00	
16th century										
1st Half	10.00	$8\frac{1}{3}$	$8\frac{1}{3}$	4.00	4.00				4.00	
2nd Half	10.00	$8\frac{1}{3}$[1]	$6\frac{1}{6}$	4.00	4.00				4.00	
17th century										
1st Half	8.00	$8\frac{1}{3}$	5.00							
2nd Half	4.00	5.00	3.00							
18th century										
1st Half	3.05	5.00	3.00?		4.00			5.00	4.00	
2nd Half	3.13	5.00	2.50		4.00			4.00	4.00	
19th century										
1st Half	3.26	4.06	4.53	4.43	3.84					4.55
2nd Half	2.47	3.03	2.93	2.71	3.53	3.68				3.23
20th century									Canada	
1st Half	2.79	3.06	3.20	2.94	3.64	3.04		3.31	2.93	2.31

[1] Lowest decennial average where available; otherwise lowest reported rate. Lowest yield or yields are given in italics for each time period.

* Cipolia, C. M.: Note sulla storia del saggio d'interesse, *Economia Internazionale*, V, (1952), pp. 255–274.

** Homer, S.: *A History of Interest Rates*, Rutgers University Press, New Brunswick – New Jersey, 1963.

	Decennial Averages								
	England	France	Holland	Belgium	Germany	Sweden	Switzerland	Canada	United States
18th century									
1st decade	7.00?								
2nd decade	6.00								
3rd decade	3.40								
4th decade	3.05								
5th decade	3.22								
6th decade	3.13								
7th decade	3.59								
8th decade	3.75								7.49
9th decade	4.64								
10th decade	4.54	14.00	6.42						6.23
19th century									6.39
1st decade	4.80	8.66							
2nd decade	4.57	7.29	5.95		5.45				
3rd decade	3.72	4.21	4.79		4.91				4.55
4th decade	3.40	4.06	5.11	5.05	4.05				4.95
5th decade	3.26	4.14	4.53	4.43	3.84				5.41
6th decade	3.16	4.45	4.02	4.25	4.08	4.64			4.33
7th decade	3.27	4.37	4.21	3.62	4.03	5.41			5.34
8th decade	3.19	4.71	4.17	3.72	4.29	4.91			4.98
9th decade	2.97	3.67	3.55	3.38	3.82	3.73			3.60
10th decade	2.47	3.03	2.93	2.71	3.53	3.68			3.23
20th century									
1st decade	2.79	3.06	3.20	2.94	3.64	3.74	3.68	3.80	3.17
2nd decade	3.81	4.06	4.00		4.72	5.10	4.52	4.76	3.93
3rd decade	4.63	5.22	4.50	5.25	7.25	4.72	5.20	5.07	4.26
4th decade	3.54	3.98	3.50	4.04	6.26	3.48	3.94	3.88	3.34
5th decade	3.06	3.60	3.24	4.27	4.70	3.04	3.31	2.93	2.31
6th decade	4.31	5.68	3.52	4.41	6.01	3.65	2.96	3.67	2.99
7th decade[2]	6.96	5.80	5.69	6.05	6.78	5.50	4.11	5.96	4.77

[2] Completed by the author.

Key to table.

England: 13th–17th centuries: lowest reported private mortgage rates. 18th–20th centuries: decennial average of annuity and consol yields at market.
France: 13th–18th centuries: lowest reported rates on census annuities and *rentes*. 19th–20th centuries: decennial average of *rentes* at market.
Holland: 13th–18th centuries: lowest reported rates on government annuities. 19th–20th centuries: decennial average of perpetual annuities at market.
Spanish Netherlands and Belgium: 13th–16th centuries: rate for Spanish Netherlands; lowest reported rates on census annuities. 19th–20th centuries: decennial average of Belgian *rentes* at market.
Germany: 15th–16th centuries and 18th century: lowest reported rates on census annuities. 19th–20th centuries: decennial average of long-term government bonds, including mortgage bonds at market.

Sweden: 1850–1920: decennial average of offering yields of new issues of long-term government bonds. 1920–1960: decennial average of government bond yield at market.
Switzerland: 18th century: lowest reported rates for census annuities. 1900–1960: decennial average of government bond yields at market, 5-year maturity or over.
Italy: 13th and 14th centuries: lowest market yield of Venetian *prestiti*. 15th and 16th centuries: lowest reported rates for census annuities.
Canada: 1900–1920: decennial average of market yields on province of Ontario bonds. 1920–1960: decennial average long-term Dominion bonds.
United States: Decennial average of market yields of long government bonds 1798–1829, of prime municipals 1830–1839, of long government bonds 1840–1869, of prime municipals 1870–1889, thereafter to 1939 of prime long corporate bonds adjusted to theoretical taxable government bond yields by subtraction of 30 basis points throughout. After 1940, average of long taxable governments.

A few of the "decennial averages" in this table cover less than 10 years because of the lack of data.

Homer has also plotted a chart, based on fifty-year periods for nine countries using the lowest rate in the chosen nine countries. He set out from the following point: interest on capital at any given time varies. In fact there is only one specific limit: the lowest rate of interest. Under the influence of various factors this lowest interest increases or decreases. In his opinion this is the only rational basis on which the trend of interest rates can be determined. In the chart the lowest averages per decades are indicated from 1700 on.

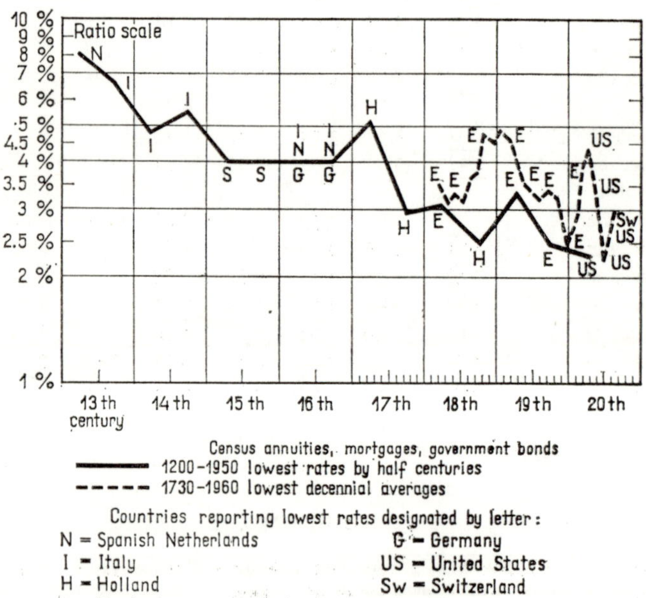

Chart 6. Long-term interest rates in Western Europe and North America

The chart shows a *tendency of long-term interest on capital to decrease,* which can be followed through the centuries. Though the decreasing trend slowed down, it did not turn upwards over any long period. Temporary turns can be observed in the 16th century and in the second half of the 18th. Apart from that, the trends either show a downward line or a horizontal one. The largest decrease in the lowest interest rate occurred in the early 13th and in the 17th centuries. Its level was the lowest in the mid-twentieth century.

The secular trend of a general rise of the price level of commodities and of a general decrease of the level of interest on capital can be qualified as a re-distribution of profit by capital in favour of industrial capital. This, at the same time, explains why self-financing has gained ground in the process of industrialization and why the interest received by the creditor can be negative in inflationary periods. This is always the case when the interest rate is less than the inflation rate. But, in spite of this, the profit rate of banking organizations may reach and even surpass the profit rate of industrial capital. Banking organizations supply services. The interest margin is the price of the credit service. Banks re-distribute the savings accumulated by them and distribute the accessory outflow of money.

Thus the depositor is the real loser of the negative interest. In this way a re-distribution of the profit of industrial capital in favour of interest on loan capital also takes place, however, because of intertwined links between different kinds of capital it does not seem to be justified to make a sharp differentiation between industrial capital and loan capital.

Wage scissors

The problems of the price revolution can be approached from different angles. But there is a question that we cannot evade. How could wages lag behind price rises, and, moreover, lag far behind them? Marx examined this question in particularly great detail. He referred to the *laws aimed at the forcing down of wages,* on account of which the conditions of workers strongly deteriorated in the 16th century. "The money wage rose, but not in proportion to the depreciation of money and the corresponding rise in the prices of commodities. Wages, therefore, in reality fell," he wrote.*

Wage scissors, so characteristic of the price revolution, could not have come into being if the governments had not set severe limits to the labour market. At the historical emergence of capitalist production the rising capitalist class needed the power of the state and used it to get *wages "regulated"*, which *was considered by Marx an essential feature of primitive accumulation.*

As early as in the 14th century the Statute of Labourers of Edward III set the wages for country and town, for piece-work and day-work in England. It was forbidden, under pain of imprisonment, to pay higher wages than those fixed by statute, but the taking of higher wages was more severaly punished than the giving of them. The labour statutes of 1349 and after were characterized by the fact that they set maximum wages, but left the lowest ones to the market. At the period of the manufactures (handicraft industry), the capitalist mode of production had grown strong enough to render a statutory regulation of wages impracticable and, at the same time, superfluous, but it did not want to abstain from using the weapons of the old armoury, in case they again became useful.

In general the 16th–17th century *labour market* did not operate on the same principles as the capital and land markets. The view that employer and employee could act on the labour market under similar conditions would be particularly ill founded. Profit inflation and wage scissors are natural manifestations of primitive accumulation.

* Marx, K.: *Capital,* Vol. I, Moscow, 1967, p. 763.

The basis of this process—and here Marx's explications should be followed*—was the expropriation of the agricultural population from the land.

The capitalist system pre-supposes the complete separation of the labourers from all property in the means of production by which they can realize their labour. The process, therefore, that clears the way for the capitalist system, can be none other than the process which takes away from the labourer the possession of his means of production, a process that transforms, on the one hand, the social means of subsistence and of production into capital, on the other, the immediate producers into wage labourers. The so-called primitive accumulation, therefore, is nothing else than the historical process of divorcing the producer from the means of production. It appears as "primitive" because it forms the pre-historic stage of capital and of the mode of production corresponding to it.

The transformation of money and commodities into capital can only take place under certain circumstances, involving two very different kinds of commodity-possessors who must come face to face and into contact; on the one hand, the owners of money, means of production, means of subsistence, who are eager to increase the sum of values they possess, by buying other people's labour power; on the other hand, free labourers, the sellers of their own labour power, and therefore sellers of labour. Free labourers, in the double sense that neither they themselves form part and parcel of the means of production, as in the case of slaves, bondsmen etc. nor do the means of production belong to them, as in the case of peasant-proprietors.

The prelude of the revolution that laid the foundation of the capitalist mode of production, occurred in the last third of the 15th and the first decade of the 16th centuries. A mass of free proletarians was hurled on the labour-market by the breaking up of bands of feudal retainers and by the forcible driving of the peasantry from the land. But this "free" proletariat could not possibly be absorbed by the nascent manufactures as fast as it was thrown upon the world. On the other hand, these men, suddenly dragged from their accustomed mode of life, could not adapt themselves overnight to the discipline of their new condition. They were turned *en masse* into beggars, robbers, vagabonds. Hence at the end of the 15th and during the whole of the 16th century, throughout Western Europe there were adopted drastic laws against vagabondage.

Hence, the historical movement which changed the producers into wage-workers, appeared, on the one hand, as their emancipation from serfdom and from the fetters of the guilds, on the other hand, these new freedmen became sellers of themselves only after they had been robbed of all their own means of production and of all the guarantees of existence afforded by the old feudal arrangement. And the history of this, their expropriation, is written in the annals of mankind in letters of blood and fire.

3. Falling price level

The evolution of modern world economy

Now we are going to investigate the period after the Napoleonic wars, or to be more exact, the 80 years between 1813 and 1893. In Lipsey's diagram this period is characterized by a substantial, 51%, decrease in the price level. If one is inclined to interpret economic history, and within it the history of prices, as an alternation of inflation and deflation, one will obviously think that price relations became "normalized" in the

* Marx, K.: *Capital,* Vol. I, Moscow, 1967, pp. 740–757.

nineteenth century and prices approximated the level prevailing prior to the Napoleonic wars. In fact this price trend expresses the decreasing tendency of commodity value which, in the nineteenth century, asserted itself through the industrial revolution with the modernization process of world economy.

Parallel with the development of capitalist production, the comprehensive network of the capitalist world system, *incorporating every country into capitalist development*, came into being. It was a world economy in which conditions of subordination were striking in the connexions between industrially developed countries and the colonies, semi-colonies and, in general, the economically less developed countries. At the same time the forms of sharp competition emerged, reflecting the contradictions between capitalist big powers for a territorial division and re-division of the world.

The colonial expansion policy of a few countries and the international spread of their monopolists created the capitalist world system. Colonization and the economic dependency of vast territories brought about a tendency towards unification and, at the same time, set the small group of oppressor countries against the immense majority of colonial and dependent countries. Even at the end of the Second World War, 43% of territories belonging to the capitalist world system were colonies, where 57% of the population of the capitalist world lived. Only in our own time has the colonial system been done away with.

This makes it evident that the whole development of the capitalist world was greatly affected by colonial exploitation and by the state of dependency between the ruling countries and the territories serving them—a situation that made this unequal economic position permanent. Relying on its political rule the mother country realized an absolute and exclusive monopolistic control in the colony. It levied taxes, controlled finances and transport. It expropriated land and natural resources. It freely pursued prospecting and mineral development. Indeed, the mother country could compel its colony to sell its products cheap, and to buy those of the mother country at a high price. It kept wages low in the colony, etc.

In stark contrast to the manysided production structure (polyculture) of the mother country, the *colonial economic policy* developed the colonial economy into a specialized mining and plant cultivation (oligocultural) direction, since by this it could create "optimal" economic conditions for exploitation. The one-sided economic development of colonial territories was carried out by the monopolies of the mother country since, in most cases, they were able to organize production in colonial territories in their capacity as owners. Essentially this was the basis of the international expansion of the monopoly organizations of colonial powers. The expropriation of the resources of the colonies enabled them not only to supply cheap raw materials to the mother country, but also enabled the latter to organize capitalist trade in world economic dimensions thus ensuring for itself the monopolistic extra profit based on colonial trade.

In the capitalist world market too the centralization and concentration of capital led to the domination of monopolies. The monopolies established international organizations. Dividing the market among themselves they strove to realize a uniform production policy and price policy. The leading (sometimes exclusive) role in international monopoly organizations was held by the capitalist powers. The alliance of some capitalist great powers' monopolists had control over the world market even when such products were produced by other capitalist countries of the world.

The doctrine of comparative costs was born in the first half of the nineteenth century in Britain, and acquired adherents there. At that time Britain was the greatest colonial power. She transacted the overwhelming part of world trade and organized or controlled the exchange of goods between other countries as well. If a capitalist country can gain such a privileged position, it is a matter of course that she stands for free trade, which ensures the greatest advantages for her. In such a capitalist country capitalists do not need any special government protection, because this is secured by the power position of the country (colonies, merchant navy, etc.) better than by anything else. Under such conditions the greatest freedom of capitalist activity attracted effective government support, which can take ruthless forms in the colonies, while also ensuring privileges in the internal markets of politically independent countries.

In the period of classical capitalism the role of the state in economic life was practically limited to ensuring the conditions for the competitive struggle and for a free formation of prices, relying on the automatic regulation of the market within the country and in the international exchange of goods, which accorded with the national interests of the capitalist class. It was in the 1860–1870s that classical capitalism reached the summit of its development. In the last third of the nineteenth century the transition from pre-monopoly capitalism into monopoly capitalism took place.* While monopolies were gaining ground, the institutions of state capitalism also evolved.

Monopolies used state capitalism more and more in their own interests. And yet, it would be wrong to explain government interference with economic life merely by the desire of monopolies. The whole process of state protectionism came into being and grew stronger, first and foremost as a result of the tremendous pressure of the forces of production in the leading capitalist countries and of the re-organization of the national economies in the economically developing capitalist countries.

For this reason there is nothing unusual in the United States and the European capitalist countries pursuing in the last century a policy of government protective tariffs to defend themselves against British economic hegemony. Ever since, protection against foreign competition has been the most important form of aid provided by the government to capitalist enterprise in industrially developed countries. In capitalist countries the capitalists take it for granted that by means of tariffs and other trade prescriptions the state should curb imports, thus creating favourable conditions for capitalist enterprises on the home market. They also consider it justified—or even indispensable for industrial development—that the government should contribute to the maintenance and expansion of export markets.

Protectionist industrial policy gave rise to keen debates among non-Marxist economists already in the last century. Many of them considered protectionism as impeding the development of productive forces. And yet, in capitalist countries following this course, the development of productive forces accelerated in the wake of the adoption of a policy of protective tariffs. The United States took over the leading role from Britain in the capitalist world, while some West European capitalist countries were catching up with the latter. Britain, having been the chief trustee of the idea of free trade, has adopted within this century not only the mechanism of government protection of industry, but has, in a certain respect, developed it even further. Thus, already after the First World War, state protectionism was generally acknowledged; a fact which has not been essentially changed in the capitalist world by integration tendencies asserting themselves after the Second World War.

* Lenin, V. I.: *Imperialism, the Highest Stage of Capitalism,* See: Fundamentals of Marxism-Leninism, edited by O. Kuusinen, London, 1961.

We know the story of British wheat prices. But let us confine ourselves now to the course of wheat prices in the nineteenth century.* In the nineteenth century the average price of a quarter of wheat was 56 shillings. The 83.9 shilling price of the first decade fell to 28.3 shillings by the last decade. The high price prevailing in the early nineteenth century can be explained by wars, poor crops and the chaotic financial situation. Suffice it to point to one instance. The continental blockade ordered by Napoleon occurred at that time. To offset it, land uncultivated up to then was sown with grain in Britain.

Conditions at the end of the nineteenth century were radically different. There were no wars. Thanks to the development of rail transport, of steamships, of telephone and telegraph communication, international grain trade, which had been undeveloped in the early nineteenth century, grew very rapidly. In the seventies and eighties of the nineteenth century freights, both rail and shipping, were considerably reduced. This was due to the development of transport techniques and of the establishment of long-distance transport of mass products. The freight charge for wheat from New York to Liverpool, which was 14.30 cents in 1868, became only 5.34 by 1888.

The history of grain prices in the nineteenth century confirms the conclusions of Marx about the effect of the industrial revolution in its capitalist form upon commodity value. The marked reduction of grain prices in Britain in the last decades of the nineteenth century rightly attracted widespread interest and set off a lively discussion among economists. In these debates the same elements were emphasized on which Marx based his theory of decreasing commodity value: the competitive battle and technical progress, based on the ruin of others.

Competition within the same branch of production is aimed at a more advantageous sale of commodities and at a surplus profit. Production conditions of different enterprises are different, while the price of commodities is determined by the socially required input of labour (their social value). Accordingly, enterprises, in which production techniques are more developed and the productivity of labour is higher than the average level in that branch of production, gain advantages and draw an extra profit. That is why it is in the capitalists' interest to reduce the *individual* value of commodities produced in relation to their *social* value. Competition compels owners of backward factories to introduce the technologies applied in the more advanced ones. By this, again, the average conditions of production undergo a change, that is to say the *social value of commodities decreases;* the extra profit comes to an end, and, on a higher technical level than before, a further differentiation will come into being.

The organic composition of capital rises with the development of capitalism. When the entrepreneur replaces workers with machines, he endeavours to make production cheaper, to sell more commodities and to acquire extra profit. The degree of productivity of labour in a given society—as Marx stated—is expressed in the relative magnitude of the means of production that one labourer, during a given time, with the same work effort turns into products. The mass of the means of production which he thus transforms increases with the productivity of his labour. But these means of production play a double part. The increase of some is a consequence, that of the others a condition of the increasing productivity of labour.

With the division of labour in manufacture and with the use of machinery, more

* Földes, B.: *Statisztikai vizsgálódások a XIX. század gabonaárainak alakulásáról* (Statistical examination of the formation of wheat prices in the nineteenth century), Budapest, 1905.

raw material is worked up during the same time, and, therefore, a greater mass of raw material and auxiliary substances enter into the labour process. That is the consequence of the increasing productivity of labour. On the other hand, the mass of machinery, etc. is a condition of the increasing productivity of labour. But whether condition or consequence, the growing extent of the means of production compared with the labour power incorporated in them, is an expression of the growing productivity of labour. The increase of the latter appears, therefore, in the diminution of the mass of labour in proportion to the mass of means of production moved by it, or in the diminution of the subjective factor of the labour process as compared with the objective factor.*

In Marx's logical system the cheapness of goods, *ceteris paribus,* depends on the productivity of labour, and this again on the scale of production. Therefore, the larger capitals beat the smaller. Among the economic factors springing from the constant improvement of machines he mentioned the following: (1) the improving of the material of machines: e.g. iron instead of wood; (2) the cheapening of machines owing to general progress in machine production so that the value of the constant part of constant capital will continue increasing due to the development of large-scale organization; nevertheless it will not increase proportionately with it; (3) special improvements enabling the existing machines to work more cheaply and effectively, e.g. the perfecting of steam boilers, etc.; (4) a decrease of waste due to the use of better machines.

A comparative analysis of the price of handicraft products or goods produced on a small scale and those of machine products will reveal that with machine products the component of value that can be put down to the account of capital equipment shows a relative increase but an absolute diminution. Marx's famous example: "The first steelpens were supplied by the handicraft system in the year 1820, at £ 4 7s the gross; in 1830 they were supplied by manufacture at 8s, and today the factory system supplies them to the trade at from 2s to 6d the gross."**

"The battle of competition is fought by cheapening commodities", Marx wrote.*** But he also stated: "...a fall in the value of labour-power is also brought about by an increase in the productivity of labour and by a corresponding cheapening of commodities in those industries, which supply the instruments of labour and the raw material that form the material elements of the constant capital required for producing the necessaries of life."°

Let us follow Marx's analysis: "But if... the value of a day's labour-power (is) ... reduced from five shillings to three, the surplus value increases from one shilling to three. Ten hours were necessary for the reproduction of the value of the labour-power; now only six are required. Four hours have been set free and can be annexed to the domain of surplus-labour. Hence there is imminent in capital an inclination and constant tendency, to heighten the productiveness of labour, in order to cheapen commodities, and by such cheapening to cheapen the labourer himself".°°

As we can see Marx bounded the theory of diminishing commodity value on the battle of competition and set forth his theory in an organic connexion with the diminishing value of labour (diminishing wages). Two further important corner stones of the theory are the limits to mechanization and the Industrial Reserve Army.

From a social point of view the use of machines is advantageous either if the work

* Marx, K.: *Capital,* Vol. I, Moscow, 1967, pp. 635–637.
** Marx, K.: *Capital,* Vol. I, Moscow, 1967, pp. 463–464.
*** Marx, K.: *Capital,* Vol, I, Moscow, 1967, pp. 635–642.
° Marx, K.: *Capital,* Vol. I, Moscow, 1967, pp. 300–311.
°° *Ibid.*

involved in producing the machine is less than the work saved in using it, or if the machine facilitates work. However, from the capitalist point of view it is the saving of wages that matters and not the saving of social work or facilitating the labourers' work. *Therefore, from the capitalist point of view the use of machines has narrower limits.* These limits are determined by the difference between the price of the machine and the saving in wages paid to labourers due to the operation of the machine. Thus it is evident that the lower the wages of labourers the less does the capitalist endeavour to introduce machines.*

Under the conditions of a capitalist society the demand for labour relatively decreases with the increase of the organic components of capital in the course of capital accumulation, although parallel with the development of capitalism, the proletariate will increase numerically. In consequence of this a significant mass of workers will not find jobs for their labour. *A part of the labouring population will prove "superfluous"*, and a so-called relative overpopulation will come into being. This overpopulation is relative because a part of the labour force will prove superfluous only compared to the requirements of capital accumulation. The aim of capitalist production—the striving to acquire surplus value—sets certain barriers to the expansion of capitalist production. In a capitalist society, while a part of the working class in condemned to harder and excessive work, another part is forced into unemployment.**

Price–wage parity

In the Marxian definition of the general laws of capital accumulation the creation of an Industrial Reserve Army is the decisive factor. First of all, it should be borne in mind that in the period of the unfolding of classical capitalism the population proliferated more quickly than before and afterwards. Even on a world scale there was a closer connexion at that time between the development of the forces of production and the population increase; moreover, a major increase in the population seemed to be an indispensable condition of the quick growth of the *per capita* national product. The demographic "explosion" in the developing world is a novel phenomenon. This is extensively discussed in Simon Kuznets's collection of essays,*** from which we have taken the table set out by Durand. In it the population increase in ten years' averages is shown in three consecutive periods, in the economically developed European countries and the rest of the world. (See Table 23.)

In the period of classical capitalism the natural growth of the population—and within it that of the working class—was powerful and the increasing employment

Table 23

Population increase in ten years' averages

	1750–1850	1850–1930	1930–1960
Area of European Settlement	6.0	9.6	4.7
Rest of the world	4.3	4.8	14.3

* Marx, K.: *Capital*, Vol. I, Moscow, 1967, pp. 382–391.
** Marx, K.: *Capital*, Vol. I, Moscow, 1967, pp. 642–655.
*** Kuznets, S.: *Population, Capital and Growth*, New York, 1973.

of women and children also played a role. The relative but accelerated diminishing of variable capital within the total capital also resulted in the increase of the number of workers being slower than that of the absolute number of the proletariat. *Unemployment* was at the same time an inevitable consequence of cyclical development fraught with recurring economic crises.

In that period the Industrial Reserve Army was the chief means of keeping labour in check, and keep wages within the value of labour-power. The expropriated agricultural population were driven from their land, becoming vagabonds, and were then whipped, branded, forced by harsh laws into accepting the discipline of the wage system.

The advance of capitalist production developed a working class, which by education, tradition, habit, came to regard the conditions of that mode of production as natural. The organization of the capitalist process of production, once fully developed, breaks down all resistance. The constant generation of a relative surplus-population keeps the law of supply and demand of labour, and therefore keeps wages in a rut that corresponds to the needs of capital.*

Anna J. Schwartz's paper provides some information on prices and wages within the period under examination.**

Table 24

Development of prices and wages between 1815–1896 (annual average, in per cent)

	1815–50	1850–73	1873–96
	Annual average rate of change, per cent		
Great Britain:			
prices	−2.2	−0.9	−1.7
money wages	−0.6	1.9	−0.1
US			
prices	−2.3	5.3	−1.8
money wages	.	.	−0.3
Germany			
prices	−1.9	1.9	−0.8
money wages	.	.	−0.2
France			
prices	−1.0	1.2	−2.5
money wages	−0.1	0.07	−0.1

The assertion of price–wages parity presupposes that in the phase of price increases nominal wages rise correspondingly and fall when prices decrease. This, however, did not occur, or, if it did, in most cases it was not proportionate to the changes in price levels. Lowe searched for a solution in indexing.*** He thought that agreements which linked wages to prices would cause capitalists, on the one hand,

* Marx, K.: *Capital,* Vol. I, Moscow, 1967, p. 761.

** Schwartz, A. J.: Secular Price Change in Historical Perspective, *Journal of Money, Credit and Banking,* February 1973, pp. 243–269.

*** Lowe, J.: *The Present State of England in regard to Agriculture, Trade and Finance,* 1822. Schumpeter referred to G. Sh. Evelyn's pioneering work *Philosophical Transactions,* in which he, as early as in 1798, used a price index to measure the decrease of the value of money. According to Schumpeter, Lowe, taking Evelyn's ideas as a basis, suggested the price index to be used merely to provide money and money incomes with equal values and to reduce the adverse effects of fluctuation. See Schumpeter, J. A.: *History of Economic Analysis,* Oxford University Press, New York, 1966, p. 526.

to be more inclined to raise wages during inflation and, on the other, workers would tend to accept wage-reduction during times of deflation. It was under the effect of the class antagonisms of nineteenth century British industrialization that Lowe propagated indexing, in the wake of the stoppages of work and strikes by which workers reacted to refusals of their wage claims during periods of inflation. Marshall also took up a stand for indexing. In his opinion the workers' misgivings that if nominal wages were once reduced, they would not be easily raised again had some foundation.*

The indexing of prices did not strike root in the nineteenth century. Accordingly, the adjustment of nominal wages to changing price levels was difficult to realize. Since in the nineteenth century the price level fell, real wages rose considerably. This gave rise to Marx's criticism of the thesis of wages adjusted to the value of labour. Economists criticizing Marx left out of consideration the social element of the value of labour. Only the physical elements of the value of labour are included and not the many other elements indispensable for the mere subsistence of the working class, whereas the *social* element of the value of labour comprises the requirements springing from the social conditions of the life and education of people of different countries. Thus the social element is the value of those commodities of consumption, the changing quantity of which is determined by the socially customary way of life.

This also explains that the value of labour is different in different countries. In countries where capitalism unfolded under favourable conditions (e.g. in Britain and the US) the value of labour, due to the higher level of the productivity of labour, is smaller and the mass of goods embodying value is relatively bigger than in developing countries.

The formation of the value of labour is, in classical capitalism, basically determined by the movement of the productivity of labour. Along with the development of capitalist production, the productivity of labour increases. The increase of productivity has the effect of decreasing the value of labour in general. At the same time certain factors work against the decrease of the value of labour. Such a factor is the rise of the level of the working class's requirements and the growth of the social element in the value of labour. Therefore *the value of labour decreases more slowly than productivity in prime necessities increases.* In the mid-nineteenth century real wages indeed considerably surpassed the level prevailing at the beginning of the century. In the same way, however, the requirements of man in the mid-nineteenth century left far behind those of the early century or those of eighteenth century man.

4. The present inflation

Secular changes in world economy

The third price episode is connected with the economic history of our present time. On analysing the price history of seven centuries one is struck both by the extent of the present inflation and by its having become permanent. In the past seven centuries the annual average rise in price levels was about 1.5% and even in the 125 years of the so-called price revolution it did not exceed 5%. All this is normal price development compared to the present inflation of the capitalist world. Moreover, all previous periods of inflation took place by way of short-run cyclic price movements and had

* Marshall, A.: Remedies for Fluctuations of General Prices. In: Pigou, A. C. (ed.): *Memorials of Alfred Marshall,* London, 1925, p. 191.

to be terminated by a currency reform. The present one, on the other hand, is a steady inflation in which, as a general rule, exchange rate policy is used for influencing the inflationary process.

It seems to be expedient to lay the foundations of the examination of this price episode by analysing its background in world economy. Attention is to be called to the secular changes that have taken place in world economy. The birth of the Soviet Union and later the evolution of the socialist world economic system, the liquidation of the colonial system and the formation of independent countries, indicate basic changes in world economy.

The 1917 October revolution overthrew capitalism in Russia, and the socialist Soviet Union came into being. In one sixth of the earth capital has been deprived of its rule. *By this capitalism ceased to be the comprehensive and sole economic system covering the whole globe.* The world was divided into capitalist and socialist systems. During the Second World War and following it several countries became separated from the capitalist system. By this, socialism exceeded the boundaries of a single country and became a world system. Side by side with the old capitalist world market, a new, socialist one came into being. The weight of the two economic systems in world economy is shown in the following indices.

Table 25

Comparative indices (per cent) of the two systems of world economy

Index	1917		1962		1976	
	capitalist	socialist	capitalist	socialist	capitalist	socialist
	system of world economy					
Area	84.0	16.0	74.1	25.9	73.9	26.1
Population	91.8	8.2	64.7	35.3	67.4	32.6
Industrial output	97.0	3.0	65.0	35.0	60.0	40.0

Központi Statisztikai Hivatal (Central Statistical Office): *A szocializmus győzelmes előrehaladása* (The victorious advance of socialism), Budapest, 1977.

The two socio-economic systems are opposed. Capitalism wants to reconquer its lost position. The ascending new class, the working class fights all over the world to keep the positions it has obtained and to render socialism the comprehensive and only economic system of the globe; this contrast is antagonistic. However, the fight is pursued under peaceful conditions. In the period of nuclear weapons the only possible and reasonable policy is a peaceful co-existence and economic competition.

The opposition of the two socio-economic systems and the struggle in the spirit of economic competition have inevitably given rise to attempts at *integration.* Socialist countries have rallied around the Soviet Union and have created the Council for Mutual Economic Aid (CMEA) to ensure institutionally the foundations of planned economic co-operation. Though capitalism is predominant in the world, in socialist countries the rate of growth of industrial production is faster. (See Table 26.)

The socialist camp has set as its chief economic aim to catch up with and surpass the capitalist world system, or rather the leading capitalist countries in the absolute extent of industrial and agricultural production, in terms of *per capita* production and consumption and in the productivity of labour. This is a historical consequence of the fact that so far socialist revolutions were victorious chiefly in economically less developed countries.

Table 26

Some indices of economic growth according to groups of countries

Groups of countries	National income	Industrial production	Agricultural production
	1976 in per cent of 1950		
Socialist countries	613	11.5-fold	227
Developed industrial countries	293	332	172
Developing countries	337	673	210
World total	365	528	201
	Annual average growth in 1951–1976		
Socialist countries	7.2	9.8	3.2
Developed industrial countries	4.1	4.8	2.2
Developing countries	4.8	7.6	3.0
World total	5.1	6.6	2.7

Központi Statisztikai Hivatal (Central Statistical Office): *A szocializmus győzelmes előrehaladása* (The victorious advance of socialism) 1917–1977, Budapest, 1977.

In colonial territories the liberation movements pursued after the Second World War have led to the establishment of independent states, and this *put an end to colonial economic policy*. These newly emerging countries have naturally focussed their attention on the national aspects of economic development. They judge their integration with world economy first of all from the point of improving their own economic conditions. From this aspect secular changes can be formulated as a shift from an *oligo*-centric world economy to a *poly*-centric one. When peoples take into their own hands the direction of their destiny, they will, as a matter of course, turn against the market spontaneity which governs them as an elementary law. This is the cause of the trend emerging in the poly-centric world economy, according to which the framework and chief conditions of the international division of labour should basically not be organized on the level of micro-economy but on that of macro-economy. This relates to a centrally controlled intertwinement of the production of independent national economies and as such it belongs to the domain of economic policy.

Steady economic growth

Up to the crisis of world economy, classic economic trends represented the capitalist market economy as a harmonious system in which there are always investment possibilities ensuring an appropriate profit for capital goods, and thus development takes place with a satisfactory level of employment.* They deemed regularly recurring crises as natural phenomena compatible with the theory of harmony. *Crises,* they said, *were an objective necessity, the natural price so to speak to be paid*

* Say, J. B.: *Cours complet d'économie politique pratique*, Paris, 1828–1829.

for economic growth, since, in the general course of growth, the economy needed a self-corrective process.

But after the Great Depression between the two world wars the classical theory of crises became untenable. In that crisis, the superiority of the socialist system became particularly striking, a superiority based, among other things on steady economic growth and full employment. Nor could it escape attention that at that time only the Soviet Union was able to avoid the crisis. This shook to its foundation the faith that market laws acted like forces of nature. Thus it became more or less evident already in the thirties that capitalism would not be able to survive another crisis of the extent of 1929–1933.

Owing to the existence of the Soviet Union, economic growth became a central problem of the capitalist world as well. Here too the end pursued by economic policy was first of all economic growth. All this would have been unthinkable before. On the other hand, ever since the thirties, the capitalist countries have considered the utilization of every means by which the explosion of the crisis could be stayed, means which capitalism would never have used if it existed as the only socio-economic system.

Finally the view which regarded every kind of state intervention into economic life as *a priori* harmful reached an impasse. Four decades ago non-Marxist economics became dominated by Keynes.* The objective necessity of an *anti-cyclical economic policy* met with general approval and today it is admitted that some anti-cyclical economic measures are justified, even by those who generally oppose government intervention. At the same time the neo-classics have regarded the only function of the state as being to ensure economic growth without crises by regulating the amount of money in circulation.** In their opinion this task is not solved satisfactorily by the state (by the bank of issue). That is how the old crisis debate became an inflation debate. The same kind of economic thinking that four decades ago considered crises a natural price of economic growth, considers inflation today a natural price of economic growth without crises. Inflation—Röpke wrote—is inevitably present if full employment and economic growth enjoy priority as against equilibrium.***

With the evolution of the poly-centric world economy the theory of growth—as illuminated by practical experience—had also to be laid on new foundations. It could no longer be divorced, as it had been before, from the justified endeavours of national societies to have their integration into world economy assessed, primarily from the point of the growth of national economies. By now the growth theories differ from one another, some of them considering the structural transformation concomitant with economic growth in a proportionate adjustment to the *demand structure,* while others consider the point of proportion in the *production structure* as essential.

C. Clark deems growth in the consumption structure to be a typical course of economic development.° In the relationship of the three main branches of production (primary production, manufacturing and services) this means that in the course of economic progress the share of manufacturing increases first, chiefly at the cost of agriculture, whereas, at a later phase of development, services increase fastest, whilst the weight of agriculture decreases considerably and that of manufacturing also to some extent. This development is confirmed by the transformation of the consumption structure, the rise of living standards, demand for industrial products increases first, and that for services later, to a more than average extent.

* Keynes, J. M.: *General Theory of Employment, Interest and Money,* London, 1947.

** Friedman, M.: The Role of Monetary Policy, *The American Economic Review,* 1968, No. 3.

*** Röpke, W.: Der Kampf gegen die Inflation unserer Zeit (Inflation und Weltwährungsordnung), Erlenbach, Zurich and Stuttgart, 1963.

° Clark, C.: *The Conditions of Economic Progress,* London – New York, 1957.

What is expounded in this theory is really a generalization of experiences gained in countries in the vanguard of economic development. Adjusting themselves to this, R. Nurkse and others endeavoured to formulate the theory of balanced growth in a way suitable for solving the structural problems of developing national economies, arising at the transition period from an under-developed into a developed state.* Essentially, balanced development is development taking place in many directions proportionately, orientated by the demand of the market. This is a course of industrialization in which branches of industry organically complement one another, ensuring a market and reciprocal aid to one another. Development and structural formation orientated to demand (the national market), raise questions as to the relationship of development problems to economic policies, which were formulated by the classical laws of the market for the conditions of capitalist production. According to this, if an increase of production is distributed among various products in the way dictated by private interest, it will bring about or rather create its own demand.

The theory of economic growth of a *production structure* has been formulated by Hirschmann and others.** Setting out from the advantages of mass production and from the restricted amount of available investment resources, this theory considers the direction of development to be basically a problem of investment variants. Several economists have contrasted economic growth judged by the efficiency of the production structure—as a *theory of unbalanced growth*—with the theory of market orientation. This theory emphasizes the criteria under which the production structure in a state of transformation will best ensure the efficient operation of productive forces.

Unbalanced growth—particularly in market economies, where the state is a neutral observer of price formation—will, as a matter of course, bring about inflation and render it permanent.

Creeping, accelerated and galloping inflation

As early as in the fifties, a special committee of the American Bankers' Association dealing with questions of inflation commissioned J. M. Clark to investigate the related questions of price and wage increases. This sets out the view prevalent in capitalist countries—at least at that time—which based inflation on the *theory of the price—wage spiral.* According to this theory the inflation following the Second World War was of a novel kind, basically different from previous ones and thus it could not be explained by the classical theory.

In his work published in 1960, J. M. Clark*** differentiated between demand inflation and cost inflation. In his opinion in certain periods it is accessory demand and in other periods rising production costs (above all wage costs) that bring pressure to bear upon prices. In the theory of cost inflation the supposition is in Clark's terms that inflation originates from the increase of prices, the reason for which is the increase of production costs. According to the "classical" theory, inflation is always accompanied, rendered possible and caused by an increase in the supply of money. However, according to the modern price theory, price rises may precede the increase of the quantity of money, and in such cases the increase of the quantity of money and of the volume of credits is the result of price rises and not its cause.

In Clark's view inflation is brought about in the United States, on the one hand, by

* Nurkse, R.: *Problems of Capital Formation in Under-developed Countries,* Oxford, 1953.

** Hirschmann, A. O.: *The Strategy of Economic Development,* New Haven, 1958.

*** Clark, J. M.: *The Wage-Price Problem,* The American Bankers' Association, 1960.

the trade unions and, on the other, by the monopolistic enterprises ruling the market and making use of their power in the direction of inflation. They increase wage irrespective of the extent in which productivity is rising and then raise prices. If wages are raised in one branch of industry, the country's wage structure alters. But wage-relationships can be modified only to a certain degree. The market tolerates divergences in wage rates only up to a certain limit. As soon as differences exceed this limit, wage increases will occur far surpassing the extent of the increase of productivity. In such a case the rise of costs forces an increase of prices. On the other hand, there are goods whose producers even if costs fall, do not decrease prices unless they are compelled by competition to do so. High profits will then encourage trade unions to demand wage increases.

According to the "modern" non-Marxist theory, inflation is created by the trade unions' wage policy. Capitalists will respond to wage increases and higher costs by raising prices. This will become the starting point of further wage increase demands. Price is adjusted to the changing costs of the product, and wages to the changing costs of living. This so-called wage–price spiral is essentially an infinite chain which legitimizes the inflationary element of the economy by rendering wage and price increases continual. In non-Marxist economic thinking all this appears as a conscious or tacit agreement of capitalists and trade unions, realized at the cost of consumers.

On grounds of this theory the historical process should be characterized as

– the *primitive* accumulation of the 16th–17th centuries, the *capitalist* accumulation of the 19th–20th centuries and the *re-distribution of surplus* of the 20th century being links in a chain following each other, which

– appeared in the 16th–17th centuries in the form of *wage scissors,* in the 18th–19th in the form of a *price–wage parity* and finally in the 20th as a *price–wage spiral.*

In fact the improvement of the position of the working class in the 20th century differs only in its appearance from what could be observed already in the 19th, and it indicates the changes in the social elements of the value of labour. In the 19th century real wages rose only because nominal wages decreased to a lesser extent than the price level, the decrease in the value of labour was lagging behind the rise in the productivity of labour. In a situation of inflation, on the other hand, real wages can only be increased by means of nominal wages. The price–wage spiral can be said to express this process, but it is hardly an explanation of inflation itself.

Depending on the *rate* of price rises, J. M. Clark differentiates between creeping, accelerated and galloping inflation. The inflation is creeping if prices rise by 2–2.5% per year. In the case of accelerated inflation the annual rate of price rises is twice as great as this. But if prices rise even faster, inflation is considered to have entered its galloping phase. The view was still prevailing in the fifties that in industrially developed countries price levels could only rise slowly and moderately, and that galloping inflation was a specific feature of the developing world. At that time price statistics mirrored this view as shown in Table 27.

However, contrary to what was expected, inflation has accelerated. In the period 1965–1970 the annual inflation rate came up to 4.1% and in the period 1969–1974 to 6.9% in the ten industrially developed capitalist countries.* It was in 1974 that the rise in price levels reached a two-digit level for the first time.** (See Table 28.)

Inflation accelerated conspicuously in the developing world too, particularly in Latin America. (See Table 29.)

* The ten countries are the following: Belgium, Canada, France, German Federal Republic, Italy, Japan, the Netherlands, Switzerland, the United Kingdom and the United States.

** For further details see: Genberg, H. and Swoboda, A. K.: *Causes and Origins of the Current Worldwide Inflation, Inflation Theory and Anti-Inflation Policy,* London, 1977, pp. 72–108.

Table 27

The inflationary process in capitalist world economy in the 1950s

Country	Average annual growth of the cost of living index in the years, based on the 1950 basic indices per cent: 1950–1954	1954–1958	1958–1960
	1	2	3
Countries in the phase of creeping inflation			
Switzerland	1.7	1.6	0.4
United Kingdom	6.0	4.0	0.7
Belgium	2.7	1.8	0.8
Italy	4.6	2.4	0.8
Canada	3.1	1.9	0.8
Austria	8.8	2.1	1.3
German Federal Republic	2.0	2.5	1.6
Norway	7.8	2.9	1.6
Denmark	3.9	3.8	1.8
United States	2.0	2.2	2.0
Finland	5.0	6.2	2.2
Holland	3.6	3.8	2.2
New Zealand	7.0	3.1	2.3
Japan	8.6	0.4	2.5
Countries in the phase of accelerated inflation			
Sweden	6.4	4.0	2.6
Australia	9.9	2.9	3.0
India	3.6	2.3	3.1
Lebanon	1.0	4.7	3.4
Venezuela	1.7	0.9	4.0
Spain	2.4	8.5	4.2
Mexico	7.4	9.2	4.2
France	6.5	5.1	4.9
Countries in the phase of galloping inflation			
Greece	10.3	3.3	5.4
Colombia	4.8	9.4	5.8
Iran	9.0	3.8	9.0
Paraguay	58.7	16.5	10.5
Peru	7.8	6.4	10.8
Turkey	4.2	11.8	15.3
Bolivia	65.4	82.5	15.7
Indonesia	18.7	25.5	22.0
Chile	33.9	44.7	23.7
Brazil	17.5	18.7	36.0
Uruguay	11.5	16.8	39.0
Argentina	19.3	20.3	65.0

Source: BRD Statistisches Jahrbuch, 1960.

Table 28

The inflation rate of industrially developed capitalist countries[1]

Year	Consumer price[2]	GNP deflator[3]	Real[3] GNP	Nominal[3] GNP	Money[4]
1949	−0.2	2.0	3.3	5.3	
1950	1.7	1.6	8.9	10.7	5.4
1951	8.9	8.4	7.3	16.2	7.4
1952	3.7	4.0	3.5	7.6	7.5
1953	1.0	1.2	4.7	6.0	4.8
1954	1.3	1.6	0.8	2.4	4.3
1955	0.5	1.8	7.3	9.2	5.4
1956	2.2	3.9	3.2	7.2	4.4
1957	2.8	3.7	2.7	6.5	3.3
1958	3.4	3.2	0.4	3.6	4.5
1959	1.3	1.9	5.9	7.9	6.5
1960	2.0	2.0	4.3	6.4	5.3
1961	2.0	2.3	3.8	6.2	6.4
1962	2.7	2.4	5.7	8.3	6.7
1963	2.8	2.6	4.6	7.3	7.5
1964	2.5	2.7	6.2	9.0	7.9
1965	3.0	3.0	5.4	8.6	7.2
1966	3.4	3.4	5.8	9.4	6.1
1967	3.0	3.2	3.6	6.9	7.2
1968	3.9	3.7	5.7	9.6	9.1
1969	4.9	4.8	4.7	9.6	7.5
1970	5.6	5.9	2.6	8.7	7.7
1971	5.1	5.4	3.7	9.4	10.7
1972	4.5	4.8	5.7	10.7	12.2
1973	7.6	7.0	6.2	13.9	10.2
1974	12.5	11.7	−0.2	11.4	7.9

1 The USA, Great Britain, Austria, Belgium, Denmark, France, the German Federal Republic, Holland, Norway, Sweden, Switzerland, Canada and Japan.

2 In the annual average change of the price index some countries are weighted with the 1970 GDP.

3 Some countries are weighted with the GNP of the previous year.

4 Some countries are weighted with the GDP of 1970. There are changes between the money stocks in the beginning and at the end of the year. Money means banknotes and demand deposits.

Source: International Monetary Fund, Research Department; calculation based on IFS data. See: Fleming, J. M.: *International Acpects of Inflation, Inflation Theory and Anti-Inflation Policy,* London, 1977, pp. 153–182.

Table 29

The consumer price index in the most important countries of Latin America
(Increase in per cent)

Country	Annual average of 1970–1972	1973	1974	1975	1976
Argentina	34.5	43.9	39.9	338.8	401.0
Brazil	19.6	13.6	34.1	30.8	44.1
Chile	41.2	507.7	373.9	340.7	180.0
Colombia	10.0	25.0	27.0	18.0	26.0
Mexico	5.3	20.2	20.9	18.3	22.4
Peru	6.3	13.7	19.1	24.0	40.2

Source: El Comercio, 29 Jan., 1977.

The anti-inflationary policy of capitalist countries

In the capitalist world—and in particular in industrially developed countries—attempts have repeatedly been made to curb inflation, basically by means of financial policy—that is to say by monetary and budget instruments. Only temporarily and in cases of emergency are price and wage regulations put into force. Even today debates are pursued whether a capitalist state may transgress the "taboo" set up by market-conform economic policy.

The introduction of a price and incomes policy poses a graver dilemma than that of introducing an *anti-cyclical economic policy*. When introducing anti-cyclical policy measures, the co-ordination of the market mechanism with state intervention was based on the principle of *market-conform economic policy*. This policy did not change the approach that the market-clearing function of price asserted itself as an effect of the factors of demand and supply, although, in the new situation the market could provide only the technical framework for the regulating process in which the financial policy of the state was a determining factor.

However, after the introduction of *a price and wage policy,* capitalist production *can no longer* be organized on a market orientated basis, since direct regulators are an integral part of the market mechanism. In agriculture this restriction has been used for long by capitalist countries. However, economics, of which agriculture was a significant sphere of exploration, has grown for several decades now into a science centred on consumption and industry. Prices and incomes policy is opposed to the classic theses of economics interpreted in this way, and these theses have intermingled with the ideology of bourgeois democracy. This dilemma is in the background of debates pursued in the capitalist world about the scientific investigation of accelerated inflation and about anti-inflationary policy.

Among western economists, attention is directed, first and foremost, to what happens in the Anglo-Saxon world; in Great Britain, where the classical theory was born, and in the United States of America, the leading power of the capitalist world. In these two countries the *so-called three-phase variant of* the anti-inflationary program has been tested. In the first, short-run phase prices and wages are frozen, in the second short-run phase sectoral guidelines are set up for price and wage movements, whereas in the third—permanent—phase social responsibility (contracts) brings about a stabilizing behaviour. This program, however, did not come up to expectations.

If in monetary policy impulse and restraint are the chief principles of regulation, the inclination will be strong to introduce into price and incomes policy an economy of alternates "stop" and "go". But impulse and restraint have raised problems that are growing ever graver. This is because today the market no longer reacts so sensitively to changing market conditions as is supposed by monetary policy. The nature of society is undergoing a transformation. Mobility is changing into immobility and flexibility into rigidity. But, what is more: if enterprises assume that the "stop" policy must at a certain stage change into a "go" policy, decisions will not tally with the suppositions of monetary policy. Social reality will tend to be neglected by the makers of monetary policy.

What is true in the case of monetary policy holds good even more for prices and incomes policy. *Price is a delicate phenomenon.* Enterprise behaviour will become particularly irrational if, in an inflationary period, enterprises assume that prices and incomes policy will take the form of "stop" and "go". Even in intermediately developed national economies, which are not too big, the number of kinds of goods whose prices can be differentiated from one another runs into several millions. Change in product type is exceedingly rapid, on account of technical development, of changes in fashions and of other factors. Various kinds of goods can be exchanged and substituted for one another. Under such conditions price and incomes regulation *demands a high degree of organization and expertise.* It should also be borne in mind that the feasibility of prices and incomes regulation depends not only on the success of the anti-inflationary policy but also on whether it endangers rationality. This latter fact is more decisive if we consider the problem not of a temporary price-stop, but as a long-term state activity, which is an organic part of economic policy. The principles of a selective prices and incomes policy are easy to formulate legally, but to put these principles into practice is much more difficult. The high degree of organization and of expertise needed for this can hardly be expected from an institution created only for a short, transitory time.

It should be added that the problem with which the government is confronted cannot be evaded by an appeal to social responsibility in the hope that the *self-discipline of the participants of the market* will render anti-inflationary behaviour permanent. Even in socialist societies it can be observed that enterprises are able to interpret social interest only when legally enforceable measures limit their freedom of decision-making. Even more characteristic is this of market economies. It is impossible to utilize the motive power of the free market and to hope, at the same time, that the participants of the markets will be guided by ethics and not by market laws.

Numerous arguments against stabilization policy can be raised. However, no unambiguous conclusion can be drawn without consideration of all the other possibilities. Analyses are rendered difficult by the fact that in countries with market systems more and more instruments which do not conform with the market system are used in overt or hidden forms. Thus two questions ought to be answered: (1) Why have the programs aimed at stabilization not been successful so far? (2) What situation would emerge if economic policy gave really free rein to market forces? Here we have only raised these questions: in the final chapter of the present book we shall revert to them.

Chapter Three

PRICE TRENDS IN SOCIALIST ECONOMY

1. The concept of planned price

Socialist commodity production

In the pages that follow we will examine price trends in socialism. Of course there are fewer experiences in this field than those we could rely on when investigating secular price trends. The horizon of time extends over six decades, out of which the period during which the Soviet Union was the only socialist state within the system of capitalist economy covers nearly three decades. When examining price trends in the Soviet Union, it should also be taken into account that the socialist revolution took place in the course of war inflation, that in the hyperinflation following the First World War an attempt at experimenting with direct barter also played a part, and that the Second World War was also fraught with inflationary manifestations.

Thus the problem we have to face when investigating price trends in socialism is connected not only with the short horizon of time but also with the fact that the conditions under which socialism emerged and grew strong introduced elements into price trends "alien" to the socio-economic system. This partly explains the deviations between the political expectations professed by communist parties in socialist countries on the one hand, and actual practice on the other. We will investigate price trends in socialism, emphasizing what actually happened, without trying to explain why practice differed from what had been formulated theoretically. This latter question is to be dealt with when the problems of foreseeable price trends are discussed.

In principle a socialist society can organize its economy in two ways: on the basis of a barter (money-less) economy and on a commodity economy.

In a barter economy the needs of society are calculated exactly and production is regulated accordingly. The goods produced are distributed among the members of society according to their needs. In a barter economy the categories of a commodity economy, such as money, price, trade etc. are not used. *Direct barter* (money-less economy) renders the application of these categories superfluous. Productive units organize their activity according to social instructions. Working people are given vouchers to meet their needs and thus society regulates the distribution of products. In short: consumer goods reach the consumer in the system of direct barter. Production and the satisfaction of needs are here economic processes mutually and directly determining each other.

In a *commodity economy* products are produced as commodities and their distribution is realized by the *exchange of goods*. Production appears in the form of supply and needs in the form of demand. The exchange of goods takes place on the market and the movement of commodities is accompanied by a movement of money. Productive units receive the price of the products they have sold, whereas workers receive a money income for their work. For their money they can buy products according to their choice. In such an economic system

– there must be a universal equivalent (money), which serves as an intermediary in the exchange of goods;

– there must be prices, which is the expression of value in terms of money;

– and there must be a market where the exchange of goods takes place.

The question arises again and again whether *the application of categories of a commodity economy is compatible with the endeavours of a socialist society.* At first sight a direct exchange of products, that is to say a barter (money-less) economy, could be considered a natural regulator of connexions between people, since the communist principle of distribution according to needs pre-supposes direct barter. Marx imagined the economic structure of a socialist society as one where production is organized by the state directly according to needs. In this concept both the market exchange of goods and commodity economy would vanish. Marx supposed such a development of productive forces which would render the unrestricted satisfaction of human needs possible, if production were not curbed by the capitalist's profit motive. It was for this reason, among others, that he considered an economy organized on a socialist basis superior to an economy organized in a capitalist manner.* Engels had the same in mind when he wrote that when society has taken possession of the means of production, commodity production will come to an end and so will the rule of products over producers.**

It should be, however, added to this that Marx and Engels thought that socialist revolutions would first and at the same time be victorious in industrially developed countries and that developed socialist societies would overthrow market economies too when defeating private ownership.

Lenin first revised Marx's thesis on the historic process of socialist transformation and then that of the economic order of socialist society. As early as before the First World War Lenin reached the conclusion that the victory of socialism was possible in some capitalist countries—or even in only one—at first, and that a socialist revolution had the greatest chances of success in a place where the links of the capitalists' chains girding the whole world economy were weakest. The victory of the 1917 socialist revolution in Russia, and the foundation of the Soviet Union bore out Lenin's ideas.

But then the Communist party, led by Lenin did follow Marx's guidance in setting up the economic order of socialist society. It introduced a barter (money-less) economy for the short historical period called *war communism.* However, it soon turned out that the ousting of trade and of the function of money caused many disadvantages, and that the disruption of the economy caused by the world war could not be put right in this way. Therefore money, price, commodity exchange, that is to say the categories of market economy, were again set into operation in the Soviet Union. Lenin professed and introduced the New Economic Policy (the NEP) in the Soviet Union according to the guiding lines he had elaborated. Since then literature sufficient to fill a whole library has been written to reveal why, at a given phase of the development of productive forces, the preservation of commodity and money relations makes a more efficient economy possible, than would be the case if socialist societies shift over to a system of direct barter.

The starting point of socialist political economy is the fact that *commodity production and capitalist production are different things.* There can be no capitalist production without a prevalence of commodity production. However, commodity production can exist under non-capitalistic conditions too. Stalin formulated this idea

* Marx, K.: *Critique of the Gotha Programme,* New York, 1938.

** Engels, F.: *Herr Eugen Dühring's Revolution in Science,* New York, 1939.

as follows: "Commodity production must not be identified with capitalist production ... Capitalist production commences where the means of production are centralized in private ownership and labourers, deprived of the means of production, are compelled to sell their working power as a commodity. No capitalist production can exist without this.* Socialist society regulates the methods of producing and distributing commodities by means which depend on the conditions of production relations. In the first phase of the building of communism, income distribution according to work done and commodity distribution based on the market-clearing function were used, because of the relative scarcity of products. Only under the conditions of an abundance of goods is it possible to put into practice the principle of distribution according to needs. Under these latter conditions the abundance of goods and the extraordinarily developed state of the productive forces eliminates the need for restricting channels of distribution, in other words, when the objective circumstances eliminating commodity economy have come into being. Thus, from the point of a socialist society *price is a transitional category,* which, however, exists for a relatively long historical period.

The specific features of price in socialism appear, first of all, in the circumstance that *the state considers the price category an organic part of its function in organizing the economy.* Commodity production subsists, but the automatism of the market disappears. The state plans the processes of an extended re-production and distribution and regulates, in harmony with them, prices and wages. This is commodity production in which freedom to restrict the market mechanism operates in a relatively wide sphere. A system of regulating economic processes may emerge, which, in the historical development of capitalism, is used in war time only, that is to say in emergency situations. Socialist society has come into being and is developing *under the conditions of antagonism with and a struggle against capitalism.* For this reason, difficulties associated with a restrictive economy can be socially explained for a shorter or longer time.

The theory of socialist accumulation

We are going to base the investigation of price trends in socialism by setting forth the *concept of the planned price.* As an element of socialist planned economy the concept of the *planned price* was formulated in the Soviet Union.** Essentially it belongs to the same type as the market price in capitalism: serving for the expression of commodity value in terms of money; consequently, the measurement of the quantity of labour needed socially and embodied in the commodity can be performed by means of the price. Accordingly, the planned price—similarly to the market price—does not measure directly the social input; the law of value is manifested indirectly in price trends. When all is said and done, the concept of the planned price is meant to emphasize that the basic theses of the Marxist theory of labour value about the law of value, about the content of prices and the factors determining the trend of prices, remain valid in socialism too. The changes of the price level and of price ratios of commodities follow the changes of their values.

Thus the basic starting point of the concept of planned price is the general tendency of the movements of value, that is to say that, as a result of the development of productive forces and of the productivity of labour, *live and embodied labour, necessary for producing one unit of the commodity, decreases and so does the magnitude of value.*

* Stalin, J.: *Economic Problems of Socialism in the U.S.S.R.,* Moscow, 1952.

** (Yakovets, Yu. V.) Яковец, Ю. В.: *Цены в плановом хозяйстве* (Prices in a planned economy), Moscow, 1974.

This is an expression of the general economic law of labour-saving, a law that has gained primary significance in socialism. The decrease of the socially necessary labour input for producing commodities and realizing services is a precondition and, at the same time, a result of technical progress, moreover an indispensable condition for satisfying the rapidly rising needs of society, the number of whose members is constantly increasing.

According to the concept of planned prices, favourable circumstances are created in a developed socialist society, in which this law can assert itself. Scientific–technical progress is accelerated and so is the trend to specialization and co-operation in production as well as in labour productivity. The technical reconstruction of agriculture, of the construction industry and of services and the introduction of industrial methods to these fields, new technologies in industry, in transport and communication, the raising of the educational and vocational level of workers, the improvement of methods of controlling the economy will lead to the cheapening of products and to decreasing socially necessary labour input.

The *theory of socialist accumulation* is in the background of the plan-price concept. In this connexion attention should be drawn, first of all, to the debate under the slogan "Industrial Dictatorship" taking place in the Soviet Union in the 'twenties, after the introduction of the New Economic Policy (NEP). As a theoretical generalization of the experiences of Soviet economy Yu. Preobrazhensky formulated the concept of the critical stage of transitional economy*, according to which in the period of transition from capitalism into socialism the socialist system was not in a position to realize all its organic internal advantages, though, at the same time, it nullified all the internal economic advantages of a well developed capitalist system. That is why for a socialist government it was a question of life and death to get over that period as quickly as possible. In that transitional period the extent of accumulation was the crucial question. A high rate accumulation had to be ensured, for which industrial accumulation was not sufficient. As an analogy with Marx, Preobrazhensky interpreted the phase of transition into socialism as the phase of primitive socialist accumulation. In this phase the financial resources of the small-scale units including peasant farming were to be skimmed off to the greatest possible extent. However, no reference to primitive accumulation was made by Soviet economists when they first formulated the political economies of socialism.** According to this formulation, socialist industry is in an advantageous position as against capitalist industry in ensuring the increase of accumulation. With regard to large-scale production and the centralization of production socialist industry stands first: it is centralized on a nationwide scale and, what is more, in socialist industry the laws of competition and of anarchy of production cannot assert themselves. The socialist ownership of the means of production, planned industrial development, a rational utilization of industrial resources, the industry and devoted work of the working class and the swift development of technology—all this creates the conditions under which the productivity of labour continually rises.***

The improvements in technology and the increase in productivity must, according

* (Preobrazhensky, Yu. A.) Преображенский, Ю. А.: *Новая экономика* Moscow, 1926. (English translation, *The New Economics*, Oxford University Press, 1964.) Cf.: Berend, T. I.: A szocialista gazdasági stratégiáról folytatott vita (Debate on socialist economic strategy), *Valóság*, 1967, No. 6.

** The authors collaborating in the work *Political Economy* (on the third Soviet edition of which we have relied here) are: Ostrovityanov, K. V.; Leontev, L. A.; Laptev, I. D.; Gatovsky, L. M.; Kuzminov, I. I. – See: Fundamentals of Marxism–Leninism (Edited by O. Kuusinen), London, 1961, pp. 709–727.

*** *Political Economy, ibid.*

to the theory of socialist accumulation, be reflected in costs too. A systematic decrease in costs of production in socialist enterprises means steady savings in live and embodied labour and is, therefore, an objective economic necessity for a socialist society. The decrease in costs reflects the law according to which the productivity of social labour must constantly rise.* The decrease of costs must ensure the increase of socialist accumulation.

Within total costs, the proportion of the costs of the means of production, increases, whereas the proportion of wages in costs relatively decreases. Costs will decrease but this pre-supposes both a continual improvement in the utilization of the means of production and a constantly improving utilization of labour. In order to decrease the wage input in one unit of production it is absolutely necessary that the rate of increase in productivity be faster than that of the increase in wages. In socialism a decrease in wages input per unit of production is concomitant with a parallel increase in wages. The increase in wages is based on the appropriate increase in the worker's output and on the decrease in the quantity of work per unit of production.**

Needless to say that the decrease of value is not simultaneous and does not take place in an identical line with all goods and services. The value of certain groups of products may increase. The raising of the technical level of products and improvement of quality may also demand a higher input of labour and bring about an increase in the value and in the price of a physical unit of the product, whereas the quantity of labour socially necessary for producing one unit of use-value may decrease and the commodity become relatively cheaper. But these exceptions do not change the general rule that parallel with the development of productive forces (calculated in one unit of their use-value) the value of the commodity produced will decrease.

The theory of socialist accumulation is based on the hypothesis according to which the Marxist theory of decreasing commodity value asserts itself under the conditions of a socialist planned economy too; that is to say, it can be separated from the socio-economic frame within which it was formulated. In spite of this, the following may be worth mentioning:

1. Marx developed the proposition of decreasing commodity value as a tendency prevailing in a free market system when:

- price formation is based on free market forces (market price);
- competition takes place in the form of pushing down prices (price competition);
- commodities are the products of capital, consequently, both technical progress and the allocation of economic resources are regulated by the recovery of capital (price maintenance).

In a socialist planned economy administrative price takes the place of the market price and labour competition the place of price competition, whereas free allocation is substituted by the central distribution of economic resources.

2. Decreasing commodity value in capitalism is supported—in certain cases—by wage decreases, whereas the theory of socialist accumulation demands simply that the rate of increase of the productivity of labour must exceed the rate by which wages are rising. At the same time, the policy of income distribution must be based on the principle of distribution according to work done.

3. The following factors play a role in the decrease of commodity value in capitalism:

* *Political Economy, ibid.*
** *Political Economy, ibid.*

– the cyclic character of development and recurring economic crises;
– the labour reserve army and unemployment;
– the constraint set on the development of productive forces by the need for an increasing return on capital.

As against this, a steady economic growth and full employment must be realized in a socialist planned economy. Besides, a planned and proportionate economic growth will, for objective reasons, break through the limitation imposed on development policy of increasing returns on capital.

Of course, the decrease of commodity value is not a condition of socialist accumulation. Accumulation is ensured by savings, or, more exactly, by society not consuming a part of the national income produced. The savings are invested by society, in proportions determined by the plan, in productive and non-productive branches. Accordingly, the national income will increase even if the commodity value does not decrease and accumulation increases, since the proportions of savings in the national income do not decrease.

In this way, the decrease in commodity value is not a condition of the growth of socialist accumulation. On the other hand—if expectations are realistic—it is, evidently, a better alternative than an unchanged commodity value and particularly better than an increasing one.

The policy of price reductions

The concept of the planned price is based on the assumption that the rise in price levels brought about by an abundance of money and the decrease in price levels caused by a dearth of money are peculiar features of the capitalist free market system. Accordingly, inflation–deflation should be considered anarchic features inevitably springing from market spontaneity, features which have been eliminated in a socialist planned economy. It follows from this quite logically that in a socialist economy changes in price relations can only start from the *commodity side* and that the changes in the value of money reflect only the changes in commodity values.

This has given rise to the following hypothesis of socialist political economics: the continuing growth of socialist production as well as its improvement, the decrease of the socially necessary input per unit of production will bring about conditions under which enterprise prices can be reduced. The reduction of enterprise prices is, at the same time, one of the factors in the decrease of costs. An economically justified reduction in enterprise prices will strengthen independent accounting and create the basis on which retail prices can be reduced.* Investigating more closely the aims of *price policy* to be achieved in the long-term development of the price system of the Soviet Union, Yakovets emphasized the following points:**

1. *The price must be an increasingly precise reflection of the level of the socially necessary labour input.* From this derives the following task: the stabilization of the price level and its gradual decrease, well based economically. Prices consistently decreasing in proportion to the decrease in the socially necessary labour input may provide an exact yardstick for the input. A policy of price reduction gives the possibility of keeping prices in line with the changing levels of socially necessary labour input.

* *Political Economy, ibid.*
** Yakovets, Yu. V.: *Op. cit.*

2. *The strengthening role of prices in encouraging the acceleration of scientific–technical progress,* in improving the quality of products and in a rational utilization of resources. This supposes a more active utilization of the price system in accelerating the rate of scientific–technical progress in increasing efficiency, in renewing and expanding the range of products and in the introduction of new achievements of science and technology as well as in putting new, more efficient products into production, parallel with ceasing to produce obsolescent commodities; technical progress and, as a result of an up-to-date structural transformation of production, the pursuance of a consistent policy of making products relatively cheaper. The basic factors in the decrease in costs in long-term planning are indicated as follows:

– *an increase in the productivity of labour exceeding the rise in wages.* The absolute magnitude of wage costs and the reduction of their share in total costs depend on this.

– *The increase in capitalists' demand for labour and the acceleration of the turnover period of capital* based on a more efficient utilization of management techniques, on a technical reconstruction of enterprises as well as on the increase of efficiency based on new techniques and technologies.

– *The decrease of price levels in the engineering industry* as a result of which a relative cheapening of fixed capital and, consequently, a depreciation per unit of production takes place.

– Saving of materials, of prime materials, fuel and energy and the *decrease of specific material input.*

– *Neutralizing the deterioration of natural conditions;* a rational and complex utilization of natural resources in extractive branches and those connected with them; the acceleration of the rate of technical progress by raising efficiency.

3. The scientific–technical revolution is expressed in the expansion of the range of products and in the acceleration of an exchange of products. *Price policy must affect this process through limit prices.*

The designing and production of new products of low efficiency must be discouraged through the implementation of the limit price in a wide sphere.* When elaborating the technical standards for a new product, the limit price of the new product is also determined. According to approved methods, limit prices are set at the level of the upper limit of the price with a 0.8 "cheapening" co-efficient. This means that the new product must be at least by 20% cheaper for the consumer than a similar article already produced (calculated at an identical use-value).** That is why it has been deemed necessary to substitute for this method more up-to-date solutions in pricing in branches of the engineering industry where the production price is set by the weight of the product. In more modern ways of pricing, technical qualities are taken as a basis.***

Introducing the production of new articles often causes additional costs, because the new product will temporarily decrease productivity, profit decreases and so does the extent of funds for incentives. In the pricing practice of the Soviet Union a system operates under which the costs of introducing new articles into production are covered by a special technical development fund for that purpose. This fund is accrued from contributions provided for in the costs of all products of the branch in question.

With a view to accelerating technical development, Soviet economists deem it a

* (Komin, A.) Комин, A.: Ценообразование в системе хозяйственного управления (Pricing in the system of economic management), *Экономическая газета* March 1974, No. 11.

** Yakovets, Yu. V.: *Op. cit.*

*** (Glushkov, M. T.) Глушков, M. T.: Совершенствование оптовых цен (Modernization of producer prices), *Экономическая газета,* 26 June, 1976.

question of decisive importance that the price level of machines and plant should decrease. In the realization within the CMEA of an international specialization *of manufacture and of production co-operation* this view is voiced more and more strongly. According to this view, the specialization of manufacture and productive co-operation will result first of all in getting rid of parallelism in production and so save some socially necessary input, in reducing the range of commodities produced, raising the magnitude of series to an optimum, in applying the best techniques and technologies and in improving the control of producers.* However, international co-operation is effective only if the domestic price of imported part units and spare parts is not higher than the domestic production price of similar articles turned out by home producers. If this is not so, there is no point in co-operation from the viewpoint of the enterprise or the state. The foreign trade price system must be built upon objectively minimal inputs.**

2. Price trends in the Soviet Union

The increase of the price level

The leading Soviet specialist of price statistics, S. G. Stolyarov, wrote the following: "The examination of ... statistical materials has evinced that prices will change from year to year—if we do not consider the effect of great historic events—relatively slowly, in either direction. However, for long periods the general tendency of these changes has been a constant upward course of prices, which do not return to the level they started from." Then he adds: "... the rise of prices takes place at all times; we think that it will continue to take place as long as prices will exist."***

Stolyarov's work may have surprised those who think that price trends in the Soviet Union are being judged on grounds of the theses of price policy and on the latest pricing of consumer goods. Anyhow, Stolyarov has based his statements on price statistics, which cover several centuries of prices in Tsarist Russia, and pursues price trends in the Soviet Union up to 1965. S. G. Strumilin has set up a price table of the period from the end of the sixteenth century up to 1913 (see Table 30).°

The following comprehensive picture of price trends in the Soviet Union can be gained from Stolyarov's work (see Chart 7).

We are going to present a short characterization of price trends from the October revolution onwards to 1926/27. Supposedly Stolyarov has omitted dealing with this period because he would have had to represent a hyperinflation brought about by emergency conditions. He has chosen as a starting point a time by which state price control could operate more efficiently; a period closer to the launching of the first five year plan in 1928.

No implicit price deflator is constructed in the Soviet Union. The price level comparable to price indices characteristic of capitalist countries is to be found somewhere between the retail price index and the agricultural procurement price index,

* (Grinev, V.-Khromov, V.) Гринёв, В.—Хромов, В.: Эффективность международной специализации и кооперирования производства (Efficiency of international specialization of production and of co-operation), *Плановое хозяйство,* 1976, No. 3.

** (Kormnov, Yu. F.) Кормнов, Ю. Ф.: *Социализация и кооперация производства стран СЭВ-а* (The production specialization and the co-operation of CMEA countries), Moscow, 1972.

*** (Stolyarov, S. G.) Столяров, С. Г.: О ценах и ценообразовании СССР (On prices and pricing in the USSR), *Статистика* 1969, pp. 199–201.

° (Strumilin, S. G.) Струмилин, С. Г.: *Очерки экономической истории России Соцэкгиз* (Economic history of Russia), Moscow, 1960, p. 274.

but anyhow in the proximity of the retail price index. This latter summarizes only the price changes of goods and services supplied by socialist trade (state-owned and co-operative). But, in addition to this, there is also a kolkhoz market, with free prices, and here periodically prices will differ significantly from the state-controlled ones.

Table 30

Price formation in Russia from the end of the 16th century to 1913

Product	Unit	Unit price in kopecks		
		end of 16th century	1720	1913
Rye (grain) (pud)	16.38 kg	2.5	7.5	83
Wheat	16.38 kg	3.5	9.5	110
Buckwheat	16.38 kg	3.8	13.0	184
Beef	16.38 kg	21.0	47.0	740
Mutton	16.38 kg	20.0	45.0	640
Fish	16.38 kg	7.0	10.0	400
Butter	16.38 kg	48.0	160.0	1780
Milk	pail	2.0	13.0	150
Eggs	100 piece	10.0	40.0	300
Honey sugar	16.38 kg	50.0	100.0	584
Sheep hide dressed	piece	4.5	17.0	178
Hemp oil	16.38 kg	20.0	57.0	548
Salt	16.38 kg	10.0	24.0	30
Soap	16.38 kg	300.0	400.0	525
Linen (Russian ell)	0.70 m	1.6	3.0	14
Dyed hand-woven linen	0.70 m	2.0	4.0	15
Cloth (Russian)	0.70 m	3.3	5.0	160
Cow-hide boots	pair	12.0	35.0	544
Iron axe	piece	7.5	10.0	0

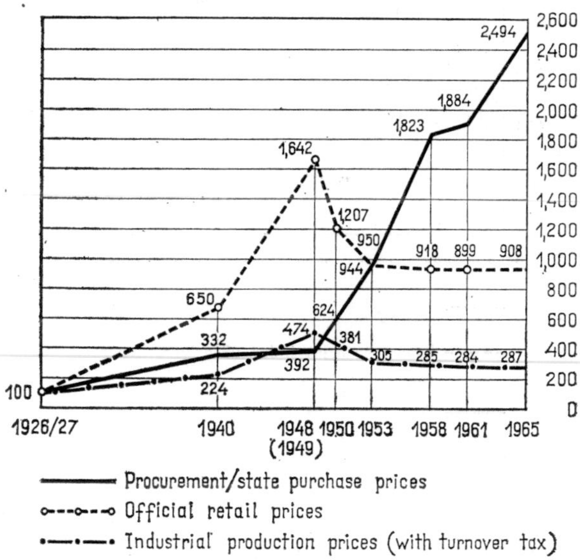

Chart 7. Procurement-state purchase prices, industrial production prices (with turnover tax) and official retail prices in the period 1926/27–1965 (1926/27 = 100)

The seven phases of price trends in the Soviet Union

Yakovets presents price trends in the Soviet Union and, at the same time, Soviet price policy divided into *seven phases*. Drawing on his work we give a short survey of the various phases of price trends, along with the charts by which Yakovets demonstrates price formation.*

The *first phase* (1917–1921) was characterized by a very sharp rise in prices, caused by the economic debacle triggered off by the world war, by the civil war and foreign intervention. From the very beginning the Soviet government endeavoured to hold back prices, or to maintain fixed prices. For this reason the Price Committee of the Supreme Council of the National Economy was established. It began operating in December 1918. But only insignificant quantities of goods could be put on the market at fixed prices, which, thus, were only symbolic. The price level measured by the Central Office of Labour Statistics showed the following picture:

1913	100
1917, Oct.	760
1919, Jan.	16,400
1920, Jan	275,500

In the wake of this, some decrees were issued at the end of 1920, abandoning accounting of prices in terms of money. But within a year's time the distribution of goods and services free of charge was discontinued.

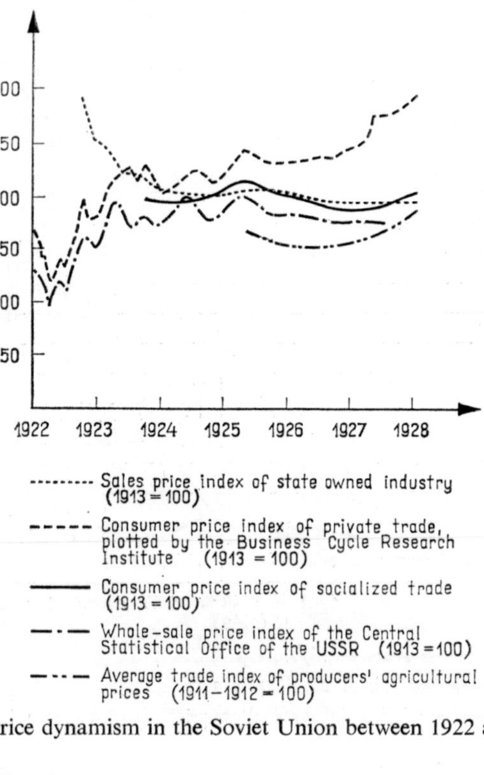

Chart 8. Price dynamism in the Soviet Union between 1922 and 1928

* Yakovets, Yu. V.: *Op. cit.*

The *second phase* (1922–1927) covers the NEP (New Economic Policy) period, up to the first five year plan. Multiple prices were characteristic of price trends in that period. (See Chart 8.)

All efforts of the Soviet Government were directed to stopping price increases and to ensuring a planned reduction of prices. The decision of the Central Committee "On the reduction of producers' and retail sale prices", made at the plenary session in February 1927, having been based on the reports of V. V. Kuibyshev and A. I. Mikoyan, was a general expression of this policy. The concept of a planned price was formulated for the first time on that occasion. "In our economic system the policy of price reductions is the means," we can read, "by which the working class will make efforts with a view to reducing costs ... and by this will create the really healthy sources of socialist accumulation, indispensable for promoting the industrialization of the country."* No doubt, a policy of price stabilization and price reductions is characteristic of the greater part of that period.**

The *third phase* (1928–1940) was the period of five year plans preceding the Second World War. The 'thirties were characterized by a trend towards general and quick price rises. In that phase the industrial production price level rose 2.2-fold, the procurement price level of agricultural products 3.3-fold and the consumer price level in state owned and co-operative trade 6.37-fold. (See Chart 9.)

Having studied various party and government documents, Yu. V. Yakovets has ascertained that these price movements were not planned; moreover, they were not even foreseen. Price policy and pricing were still based on the decisions of the Plenary Session of February 1927, but the tasks set could not be realized.

The *fourth phase* (1941–1950) was the period of the Second World War and of the years following it. At that time the trend of price increases, which had already made itself felt before the war, grew stronger. The procurement price level of agricultural products did not undergo significant changes. But, compared to that of pre-war times, the level of industrial producers' prices rose 2.1-fold and that of state owned retail trade 2.7-fold. (See Chart 10.)

For a better understanding of price trends in later periods it is expedient to refer to the 1949 reform of industrial producers' prices. The price reform was aimed at eliminating the considerable budget subsidy brought about by the increased costs after the post-war reconstruction of the industry. Accordingly, the 1949 reform of industrial producers' prices was based—at least in some branches—on costs which were to decrease inevitably when the reconstruction phase was over.

* Decisions of the Congresses, Conferences and Plenary Sessions of the Soviet Communist Party.

** It seems to be expedient to refer to the investigations conducted under the leadership of S. G. Strumilin in the 'twenties and 'thirties to prove that labour productivity had risen in Russia and in the Soviet Union in the course of three centuries as a function of socio-economic systems. G. Sorokin revived the results of these investigations in his paper "Methodological questions bearing on economic growth indicators" he submitted to the Fifth World Congress of Economists in Tokyo in 1977. The following table is to be found in that paper:

The index of labour input: hour/ton

Period	Coal	Pig iron	Sugar
1. Feudalism	100	100	100
2. Capitalism			
a. Pre-monopoly	62	59	23
b. Monopoly	53	14.3	11
3. Socialism	27	4.0	3.2

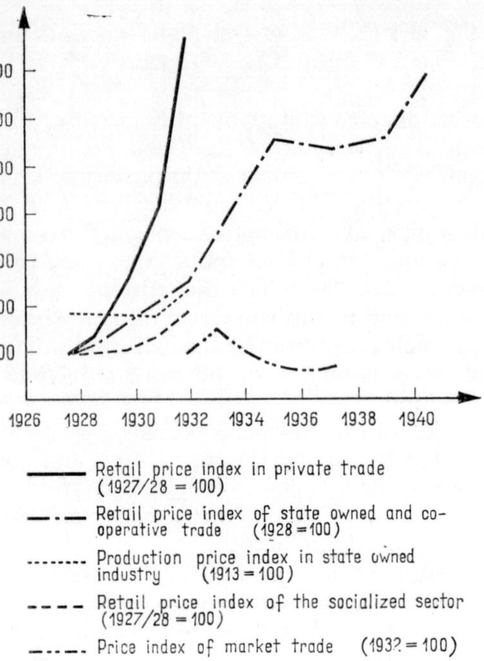

Chart 9. Price trends in the Soviet Union between 1926 and 1940

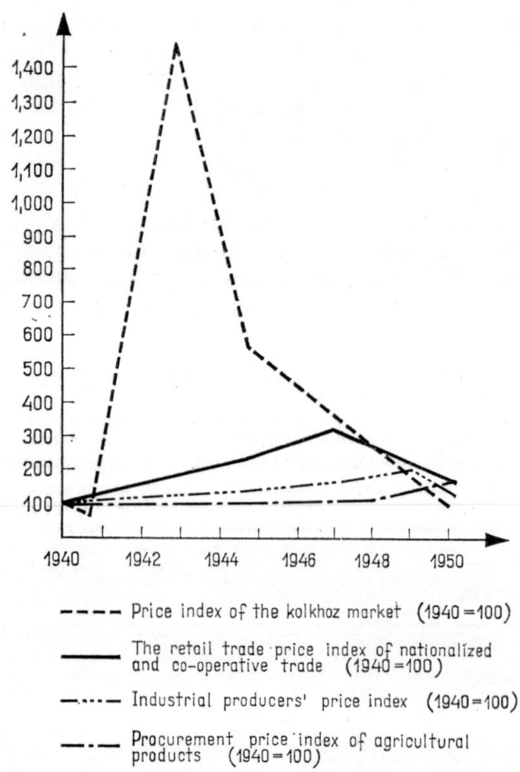

Chart 10. Price trends in the Soviet Union between 1940 and 1950

The most characteristic feature of the *fifth phase* (1951–1960) was a considerable decrease in price levels in general retail trade and in industrial producers' prices. This tendency lasted up to the mid-fifties; then gave way to a general stabilization of all price levels with the exception of the procurement price levels of agricultural products. (See Chart 11.)

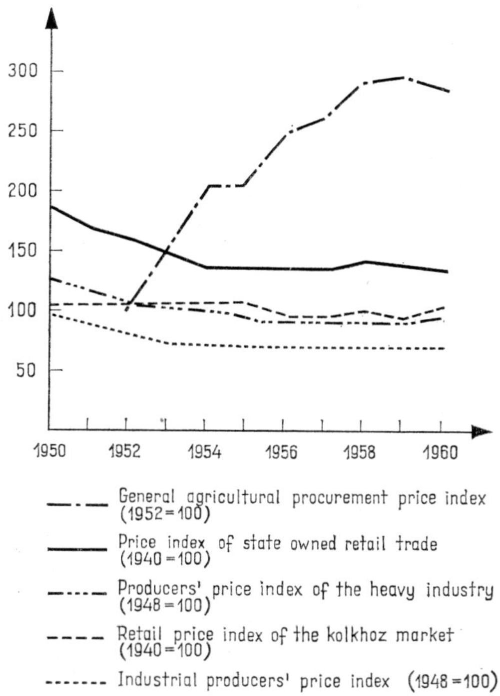

Chart 11. Price trends in the Soviet Union between 1950 and 1960

At that time the raising of state procurement prices of agricultural products was considered only a temporary measure. According to the decision of the 1951 Plenary Session of the Central Committee of the Communist Party of the Soviet Union "further increases in the incomes of kolkhozes are to be covered ... by a considerable increase in gross production and in commodity production, and by a decrease in labour input and input of means per single unit of the product. This will render an increase in the kolkhoz's incomes possible in the future as well as the decrease in procurement prices and thus it will allow the possibility of decreasing retail prices in state owned retail trade..."*

Sixth phase (1961–1970). Against previous expectations the procurement price level of agricultural products was raised several times. In the 'seventies the procurement price level rose 1.7-fold, whereas the industrial producers' price level rose to a lesser extent. Retail prices in state owned trade did not rise significantly; on the other hand the price level of the kolkhoz market increased considerably. (See Chart 12.)

In the early 1970s the *seventh phase* of the development of the price system began in the Soviet Union. "In the present phase," Yu. V. Yakovets wrote, "the central task of

* *Решения партии и правительства по хозяйственным вопросам, 1953—61 гг.* (Party and governmental decisions on economic issues, 1953–61), Vol. 4, Moscow, 1963, p. 432.

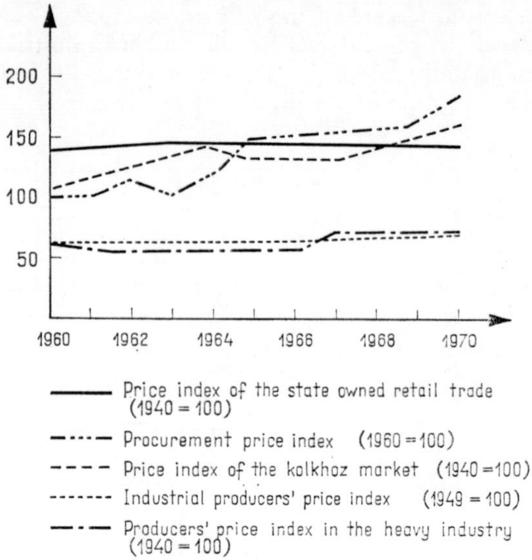

Chart 12. Price trends in the Soviet Union between 1960 and 1970

the planned control of price movements is to ensure the stability of the general price level and to decrease, in an economically reasonable manner, the prices of different kinds of commodities and groups of goods."

Peculiarities of price trends in the Soviet Union

Soviet experience also confirms the law of general price rises. We should add that price trends in the Soviet Union have been fraught with dramatic turns hardly known elsewhere in the history of prices. The October Revolution inherited from the war economy of Tsarist Russia inflation, which grew into hyperinflation. The process was put an end to by the 1924 money reform, which meant a devaluation of the Rouble, on a parity of 50 milliard Roubles = 1 gold Rouble. That is to say the devaluation of the Rouble was established at having been 50 milliards-fold.*

In order to deplete the amount of money inflated in financing the Second World War, a second money reform became necessary in the Soviet Union in 1947. This, however, was of a somewhat different character, the bank-notes having been exchanged at a 1:10 ratio. With respect to savings bank deposits, they were acknowledged at a ratio of one to one up to 3,000 Roubles; deposits of higher sums were devalued by 50%; in case of state loans one new Rouble was given for 3 old ones.** In its external appearance the Rouble was revalorized on the 1st of January, 1960: the Rouble equivalent of 2.27 US Dollars being set at 0.9. In fact a devaluation took place because the prices and wages to be paid in new Roubles were set at a ratio of 1:10 compared to the old ones.

In summary it can be stated that about three decades were needed for Soviet power,

* Atlas, Z.: Pénzforgalom és hitel a Szovjetunióban (Money circulation and credit in the Soviet Union), Budapest, 1951, p. 189.

** Kronrod, Yu. A.: A pénz a szocialista társadalomban (Money in socialist society), Budapest, 1956.

relying on a planned socialist economy, to overcome price phenomena, or, to put it more exactly, to be able to organize a planned process of economic growth under conditions of commodity production by enforcing price stability. The first peculiarity is the fact that between the two world wars prices rose strongly at a time when price decreasing tendencies were appearing in the capitalist world; whereas, after the Second World War, prices were stabilized when inflation became permanent in the capitalist world. This expresses most pointedly *the complete separation of price trends in the Soviet Union from world market prices.*

A country with a trade (convertible) currency and with a market economy—particularly if it has a significant foreign trade—can divorce its domestic price relations from world market (foreign trade) prices only within certain limits, unless it infringes the laws of economic rationality. One of the determinants of inflation which, after the Second World War, has become permanent in the capitalist world, is the importation of inflation. The feedback effect of inflation to countries from the world market is to be seen both through import and export deals. By *import,* because rising prices will increase production costs in the sphere of the means of production and will have a direct effect in case of the price formation of consumption goods. By *export,* because if sales can be effected on the world market only at systematically rising prices, this will render the sale on the domestic market at unchanged prices unadvantageous from a financial point of view; here the export price drives up domestic prices.

In the period between the two world wars the foreign trade of the Soviet Union was, naturally, adjusted to world market prices. The only change that took place in this respect after the Second World War was that new and different criteria of pricing were introduced within the socialist economic integration (i.e. the Council for Mutual Economic Assistance). Here too foreign trade pricing is based on the world market price. The specific feature of pricing in the Soviet Union may be best described as *foreign trade prices not having an organic connexion with domestic prices.* Domestic prices are regulated by price controlling authorities; the difference between controlled domestic prices and foreign trade prices is settled from the budget with foreign trading enterprises. In case of imported goods, which are not produced domestically, price controlling authorities will fix the domestic price of the imported goods by adjusting them to official domestic prices.

The national currency of the Soviet Union, the Rouble, is not convertible. Needless to say this markedly facilitates an autonomous price policy. But let us point out that if the Soviet Union rendered its currency convertible, this in itself would not force it to give up its autonomous price policy. The economic potentialities of the Soviet Union make the introduction of a currency reform of this type possible, without requiring the economic control by the state and, within it, pricing, to be changed. In this respect *socialist ownership relations play a determining role. Both within and outside the sphere of state ownership the price system of the Soviet Union is based on differentiated pricing.* It is in essence a double centred price system. For products within the sphere of state ownership, the basis of prices is costs and for products outside the sphere of state ownership the basis of prices is value.*

Planned pricing of commodities within the sphere of state ownership starts from the principle of the enterprises' own accounting. It is a condition for the undisturbed operation of accounting that, if the enterprise works according to its plan, price incomes should cover the costs of simple re-production. This cannot be a self-financing price, since it exists in a system of economic control where the financial

* (Maisenberg, L. I.) Майзенберг, Л. И.: *Ценообразование в народном хозяйстве СССР* (Pricing in the national economy of the Soviet Union), Moscow, 1953.

resources of development are put at the disposal of enterprises by the budget—free of charge—, by the centralization of social savings and by re-distribution. On the other hand, the production price of the enterprises must contain also some profit since the conditions of production are different in enterprises operating parallel. As a general rule price is adjusted to costs of enterprises operating under average conditions with the addition of some profit.

In case of products circulating outside the sphere of state ownership, the price level must be adjusted to the value level, or else income distribution and re-distribution could not operate. As a general rule the state budget skims from the sphere of commodities circulating outside the sphere of state ownership that part of the income created in the course of value production which is needed to cover the requirements of society as a whole.

The double centred price system is based on the principle that *price changes within the sphere of state ownership do not affect the financial connexion between budget and enterprises*. This is the so-called "zero balance solution". State owned extractive branches of industry may operate with a deficit, whereas processing branches of industry operate with high profits. Under such price conditions the state budget may make up the price income of the former from the profit skimmed off from the latter. If the price of extractive sectors is raised, the budget subsidy of extractive sectors can be eliminated; but, parallel with this, the profit that can be skimmed off from non-extractive sectors will decrease accordingly; the position of the budget remains unchanged. Within the sphere of state ownership, a general raising of the price level cannot increase the budget's profits, because, along with the increased income, the expenditure of the state—as consumer or investor—will also grow.

The specific feature of a socialist economy originates, first of all, in these connexions. "State owned enterprise price" expresses this specific trait. This peculiarity is expressed, among others, in the fact that the producers' price level of state owned enterprises may be lower than the value, either because a part of the costs of inputs are refunded by the budget by means other than prices, or because a part of the input does not appear as the enterprise's production cost, because it is separately treated by the state as a requirement of the whole society and as such is separately financed.

A zero balance can assert itself also in the price control of *commodities circulating outside the sphere of state ownership*. If we take the sector not owned by the state, and/or the population as a whole, it is very easy to take measures which will bring about a zero balance. The agricultural price level can be raised while, at the same time, the consumer price of foodstuffs remains unchanged, and the surplus income of agriculture can be skimmed off in the form of taxes. Under given circumstances such measures can reach a point where zero balances operate in all relations. Such measures do not affect the population, since the consumer prices of foodstuffs remain unchanged. These measures do not affect the budget, since the decrease of the taxes included in the prices of foodstuffs, or subsidized prices become equalized by the raised taxes levied on agriculture. Agriculture, on the other hand, pays in taxes the amount obtained by means of increased prices.

Such measures can be taken in the relationship of consumer prices too. The state may raise the prices of certain commodities and return the income thus skimmed off either by reducing other prices or by increasing wages. This, too, is a step neutral in every respect. The decrease of the prices of commodities reduces the net income included in the prices and subject to skimming off. However, all this is equalized by the surplus income realized in the raised prices. In the form of price reductions or wage rises society will regain everything that has been skimmed off by price rises in certain articles.

But the zero balance is genuine in both cases only on the average of the national economy. For example, in agriculture producers do not enjoy the advantages of price rises in the same proportion as the proportion of surplus taxes they have to pay. Measures which have no effect on the average of agriculture do have an effect on the single producers, putting one in a better situation than the other. Only when the object is differentiation is it worth-while to take such measures. The variant of consumer prices mentioned here as an example can be judged in the same way.

3. Repressed inflation

The price stabilizing policy of socialist countries

In socialist societies the price and wage control of the state comes across in *consumer price stability,* which is indicated in the consumer price index as follows:

Table 31

The annual average extent of the changes of the consumer price index in the period 1960–1973*

Country	Foodstuffs	Other articles	Altogether
Bulgaria	+1.5	+0.1	+0.8
Czechoslovakia	+0.4	+0.8	+0.5
GDR	+0.2	−0.3	−0.1
Hungary	+1.4	+0.6	+1.8
Poland	+1.2	+0.4	+0.7
Romania	+0.7	−0.5	−0.1
Soviet Union	+0.5	−0.6	—

* Because of the different calculation methods and the deviations of the spheres of goods and business, the consumer price indices published in the European socialist countries cannot be compared. With the exception of a few countries, the published price statistics represent the retail trade (or the socialist retail trade) price index.

The socialist countries regard retail price stability as an important element of social stability. It is merely a difference in judgement that causes some socialist countries (the Soviet Union for example) to interpret stability as the stable level of consumer prices, while others (for instance Czechoslovakia) consider a slow price increase of industrial goods, embodying new technologies or new fashion trends, compatible with stability, and others again (for instance Hungary), keeping their prices relatively stable, attach greater importance to the function of prices in maintaining equilibrium.

In socialist countries the stability of the consumer price level is centrally controlled in harmony with incomes in the form of *planned pricing*. Price and incomes policy is institutionally integrated by government control of the economy. Foreign exchange restrictions even render it possible to arrange a relationship between the world market (CMEA contractual) price and the domestic price in a centrally organized way. Yugoslavia is an exception to this rule partly because it is the market price which best suits workers' self-management and partly because the Yugoslav dinar is a trade currency. As a consequence, the effect of inflation on the world market upon the Yugoslav economy assumes the same form as in most market economies.

The *criteria of planned pricing* are different in the field of agricultural procurement, in industrial production and in consumer goods. They vary even from country to country, since in different economic mechanisms the role of prices in planned development is different. In the socialist countries, however, the criteria of price planning are the same. Socialist countries endeavour to proceed with due consideration of the principle of *complexity*. When agricultural procurement prices or industrial producer prices are modified, the effect such modifications are likely to have on the income relations of the productive branches concerned is always taken into consideration. In certain cases price changes must not be permitted to affect the viability of the productive branch in question; in others price changes may be aimed at providing new conditions for enterprise decisions. It is always in the light of such considerations that measures related to prices are linked with modifications to the financial regulators (taxes, subsidies, credit terms, etc.).

Because of its significance *the planning of consumer prices* needs further elucidation. The policy of consumer prices is part and parcel of the *living standards policy*. This policy embraces (1) employment policy, (2) wage policy, (3) the policy of social benefits, and (4) the policy of consumer prices. Planned pricing, accordingly, is more than merely the control of prices. It also includes the control of wages and incomes, in harmony with prices. *In this context the consumer price plan comprises*

– the likely modifications of relative prices regardless of whether they have been brought about by administrative price measures or by market factors (planning of price movements);

– the foreseeable changes in the consumer price level (planning of the price level) through changes in relative prices;

– the differentiating effect of changes in the price level upon the incomes of the different strata of society (effect planning).

Through its effect on the differentiation of incomes, the consumer price plan takes account of other factors in living standard policy. For the policy of wages and social benefits it is important that the price plan quantifies the effect of the foreseeable price movements for each social stratum which is regarded as an independent entity from the point of view of living standard policy. That is to say, what is aimed at is not only to prevent the rising consumer price level from causing a decline in the living standard of any social stratum considered as an independent entity, but to have the real wages (real incomes) of the independent social stratum comply with the plan. In this interpretation the consumer price plan is satisfactory only if it enables the determination of the average and the lowest level of the rises in wages and salaries, if it keeps pensions, family allowances, social benefits, interest on savings bank deposits, etc., at an unchanged or higher level.

Over the last twenty-five years the European socialist countries have regularly *raised the level of agricultural procurement prices*. In addition to their endeavour to improve the self-financing capacity of agriculture they have chosen this way primarily in order to ensure incomes parity between industrial and agricultural workers. In Western Europe this process took place at an earlier period. Historically the gap between agricultural and industrial prices was created in Europe by the low world market price of agricultural products. Under such conditions it would have been impossible to ensure the continuity of agricultural production in Europe.

The industrial price level increased in most European socialist countries, due not only to rising wages but also to changes in socio-economic relations. The creation of a fund for research and development activity, the acceleration of technical progress and environmental protection increased costs. In certain productive branches cheap technologies had to be discarded: the workers were no longer willing to undertake the type of labour these technologies demanded. This, in the first instance, leads to wage rises and, in the second, to an inevitable change in technology. The urgent demand of the masses for commodities and services can sometimes be met by more expensive technologies than the existing ones, etc.

The rise in the industrial producer price level is greater in countries dependent on imported energy and materials, since production costs are also influenced by the *world market price*. Although socialist countries trade with the world market, in their (extensive) trade on the CMEA market the CMEA contractual prices are based on world market prices freed from cyclical elements. From 1958 to 1974 this principle of pricing has been enforced by the correction of the CMEA contract prices every five years. Since 1975 the CMEA has switched over to a yearly correction, on the basis of international market prices during the preceding five years.

To raise producers' (procurement) prices and maintain unchanged retail prices was possible only by means of a significant *budget subsidy* on prime necessities.

Open and repressed inflation

Price stability based on administrative measures does not of course provide full protection against inflation.

Novozhilov* explored profoundly the situation which prevailed in the Soviet Union's economy in the period of transition from War Communism to the New Economic Policy. The policy pursued had been one of low prices adapted to the level of wages paid for the production of the goods concerned. These prices had a very slight effect on the realization of any net social income. Those responsible for price policy in that period strove to open up the market for workers in the lower income brackets. In his analysis of the situation Novozhilov found that *the policy of low prices has a similar effect to that of inflation, replacing price rises by an increasingly acute scarcity of goods.* He termed this situation "credit inflation".

When studying the restrictive economy during the Second World War, Western economists revived the discussion which had taken place in the Soviet Union in the 'twenties. The difference lies only in the terminology: "inflationary gap"** was substituted for "commodity shortage" and "credit inflation" was replaced by the term "repressed inflation".***

Repressed inflation is manifested in disguised price rises, forced purchases and forced savings. These manifestations exist even today in the economies of socialist societies, as a consequence of the fact that excess demand has been institutionally integrated into the economies of most of them. Economists in socialist countries refer time and again to the presence of inflationary pressure, though they generally avoid using the term "inflation". We meet with the following designations: sellers' market,°

* (Novozhilov, V. V.) Новожилов, В. В.: Недостаток товаров (Scarcity of commodities), *Вестник финансов,* 1927, No. 5.

** Keynes, J. M.: *How to Pay for the War,* London, 1940. Lundberg, E.: I kom stutveckling och köpfraftsöverkott under krigwären; Meddelendedn fran Konjukturinstitut, Ser. B: 2, Stockholm, 1943. Salant, S.: The Inflationary Gap, *American Economic Review,* 1942.

*** Hansen, B.: *A Study in the Theory of Inflation,* London, 1951.

° Péter, Gy.: A gazdaságosság és a jövedelmezőség jelentősége a tervgazdaságban (The significance of economy and profitability in a planned economy), *Közgazdasági Szemle,* Nos. 6–8. 1956.

disguised price rise,* delayed demand,** unsatisfied demand,*** non-voluntary savings,° etc.

If the government controls prices, it can be supposed that the functions affecting value relations are taken into consideration; that is to say, control will follow—at least there will be that tendency—price movements determined by supply. Inflationary pressure can then only manifest itself through demand. In other words: repressed inflation is adjusted to the framework of the theory of excess demand. In case of excess demand the differentiation between open and repressed inflation can be explained as a function of free price movements and administrative price control.

The accelerated inflation in industrially developed capitalist countries has drawn attention to a *comparative analysis of open and repressed inflation.* Economists of the Western world who support the free market will consider open inflation a better alternative than a repressed one. The historical background of the theory of repressed inflation will also support their standpoint, since this theory was connected with the critical analysis which followed the measures taken after the termination of War Communism in the Soviet Union. In the Western world the theory has from the beginning been connected with restrictive war economy. This historical background of the theory gives rise to a false judgement concerning the inflationary pressure present in socialist economies.

The theory of a repressed inflation based on a war situation was expounded most thoroughly by Bent Hansen.°° In such a situation the fixing of prices and wages had been complemented by an extensive system of rationing (coupons). Using two basic charts (models for perfect competition and for monopolies) Hansen tried to bring home the significance of the inflationary gap caused by the administrative freezing of prices and wages. This may in part explain the fact that when analysing the inflationary pressure in socialist economies, Western economists are prone to exaggerate its negative effect.°°° According to them a socialist economy should be regarded as one in a state of permanent mobilization; that is, essentially an economy of the same type as a restrictive war economy. However, socialist economy cannot be characterized in this manner.

Even if one bears in mind a war situation, one can detect certain weak points in Hansen's models. Hagger considered the re-examination of these models important also for situations nearer to reality, situations in which a lesser degree of price control

* Csikós-Nagy, B.: *Árpolitika az átmeneti gazdaságban* (Price policy in transitional economy) Budapest, 1958.

** (Portigul, S.) Портигул, С.: Платежеспособный спрос и предложение товаров в социалистическом воспроизводстве (Solvent demand and supply in socialist reproduction), *Вопросы экономики,* No. 12, 1969.

*** (Kaganov, G.) Каганов, Г.: О некоторых вопросах теории и практики товарного и денежного обращения при социализме (On some theoretical and practical problems of commodity and money circulation in socialism), *Деньги и кредит,* No. 1, 1970.

° (Sukhorochkina, Yu.) Сухорочкина, Ю.: Совещания работников статистики семейных бюджетов (Conference of statisticians on family budgets), *Вестник статистики,* No. 8, 1970.

°° Hansen, B.: *A Study in the Theory of Inflation,* London, 1951.

°°° Bush, K.: Soviet Inflation. In: Laulen, Y. (ed.): *Banking, Money and Credit in the USSR,* NATO, Brussels, 1973.

Campbell, R.: Macro-economic Models in Central Price Setting in the Soviet Economy. In: Ghrels, F. et al. (eds.): *Essays in Economic Analysis and Policy,* Bloomington, Ind. 1970.

Garvy, G.: Inflation and Price Stabilisation Policies in Eastern European Countries; mimeographed paper presented to the CESES Conference in Venice, August, 1974.

Grossmann, G.: Gold and the Sword: Money in the Soviet Command Economy. In Rosovsky, H. (ed.): *Industrialisation in Two Systems,* 1966.

is exercised, aimed at the decrease of excess demand.* Polak outlined a war economy price control model in which, though price movements are strictly controlled, the aim is not a price freeze. He distinguished between autonomous market price rises and official price control, the latter of which takes place with a view to compensating —partly or wholly—the effect of the increases of other prices.** This debate dealt with possible alternatives to price and wage control in a restrictive war economy in countries with a free market system.

Socialist countries control prices and wages in a profoundly different situation. In the European socialist countries the consumption of the population is realized in *free trade, without rationing*. As a general rule the only field exempt from the market is the distribution of housing. Rents in socialist countries are low and enable even people in the lower income brackets to live in comfortable flats. Low rents necessarily create excess demand, which makes it necessary that new and empty flats should be centrally distributed. But this does not mean an excess demand on the macro-economic level. It means rather that under socialist conditions—as they are interpreted at present—housing is a transitional category between public and individual products: it has a price but it is not the price that controls distribution.

Administrative price control must thus meet certain definite requirements. If the administratively guaranteed price level becomes too far removed from the equilibrium level it not only restricts the function of money, but also the process of planned pricing as a whole.

Manifestations of repressed inflation

Taking *stabilizing planned pricing* as a basis, the following can be considered inflationary manifestations:

- unplanned rises of the price level,
- disguised price rises,
- forced purchases and
- forced savings.

The possibility of an *unplanned rise in the price level* is created by the mixed price mechanism. Even in those socialist countries where prices are fixed in the widest sphere, this form is comprehensively enforced only on those products and services which are sold or provided by the socialist (state owned and co-operative) enterprises. It goes without saying that there are controlled prices (for public services, etc.) even outside this sphere, but there is a free market too on which small producers sell their goods (for instance the kolkhoz market in the Soviet Union). Furthermore, some socialist countries (Poland, Czechoslovakia, Hungary) permit the pricing for certain non-staple commodities (services) produced (provided) by state owned enterprises and/or co-operatives to be subject to agreement between the enterprises. If, through this system there occurs an unplanned rise in the price level, this must be interpreted as an inflation.

A *disguised price rise* signals a rise in the price level, not indicated by price statistics. This may happen even with the price index under close observation. Price statistics elaborated according to the classic system are neutral to changes in quality and assortment. The price level may rise even without the price of a single product changing, partly by putting commodities of an inferior quality on the market, partly by

* Hagger, A. J.: *The Theory of Inflation*, London and New York, 1964.

** Polak, J. J.: On the Theory of Price Control, *Review of Economic Statistics*, February, 1945.

withdrawing certain assortments from the market and replacing them by new ones only slightly different, but sold at disproportionately higher prices. It is only further processing and commercial enterprises which are in a position to check whether the prices and the quality correspond with official regulations. However, in the case of excess demand, this supervisory function becomes less effective.

Forced purchases indicate that consumer preferences are restricted. The consumer does not find the assortment on the market which he is after. Naturally, no country can rely for her supply upon commodities she does not possess. Neither can a country enrich her assortment of supply by importing to a higher degree than she is capable of, while keeping the international balance of payments in equilibrium. Forced purchases indicate the deterioration of the commodity supply, caused by an imbalance and by inflationary pressure. Furthermore the development of the productive forces, and the rising living standard thereby achieved, transforms the consumption pattern, and this must be followed by a change in the supply structure. Demand for more expensive assortments causes a rise in the average prices of various commodity groups. That is why the rise in average prices is not to be considered as an indicator of forced purchases. In the case of excess demand, on the other hand, the quality factor is combined with the elements of inflationary pressure in the rise of average prices.

Forced savings prove that there is a shortage of non-substitutable products and a definite demand. The consumer is unwilling to spend his money, reserved for certain definite goods, on the commodity available on the market and prefers to save his income in the hope that the desired item will be available later.

In the case of excess demand inflationary pressure makes itself felt *not only in the sphere of consumer goods but in that of the means of production as well.* According to some economists the means of production are not commodities if technical and material supply is centrally organized. Under such conditions money cannot regulate anything, since the means of production can be obtained only for a commodity voucher.* However, all means of production cannot be centrally distributed. Furthermore, in a system of central quotas the specifications (technical parameters) of every product cannot be given in the same detail as they appear in the form of commodities in enterprise relations. Accordingly, control by plan directives had to assume that the most essential criteria of the means of production embodying their use-value will be enforced in the enterprises' contractual relations. This, too, gives free course to manifestations of inflationary pressure.

In the field of the means of production the conditions for disguised price rises induced by excess demand are even stronger, because the authorities can regulate the prices of components, part units, special-purpose machines produced with widely varying technical parameters only indirectly, by normative prescriptions. In the field of the means of production inflationary pressure even appears in additional new forms, of which excessively large stocks of unfinished products, disturbances in the organization of production and investment, delays in the completion of new projects, etc. are typical examples.

Excess demand causes irregularities also in the *labour market*. Excess demand on the consumer market has in itself an adverse effect on labour discipline, as it prevents workers from using their wages freely. Excess demand for means of production creates bottlenecks in the plants; disproportions within individual enterprises impede the

* Such views have recently been voiced by V. Kulizov and N. Shekhet. For studying the problem see (Valovoi, D.) Валовои, Д.: О планомерном использовании товарно-денежных отношений (On the planned utilization of commodity and money relations), *Плановое хозяйство,* 1974, No. 2.

most rational utilization of the available manpower; the result is unemployment within the factory, to a varying degree.

In socialist countries *inflationary pressure* is not only perceived, it is also *regularly analysed* during the elaboration of the yearly plans. Planning, of whatever type, begins with a critical analysis of the actual economic situation, by summing up the experience gathered in the course of the continuous observation of trade in the means of production as well as in consumer goods. The source of information for operative market supervision includes the utilization of capacities, order books, reports on delays in deliveries, changes in stocks, etc. This means that the goal of economic development which planning strives to determine over the medium or the long range on the basis of the system of economic balance, is preceded by an analysis of real processes. It is this analysis which must provide an answer to the question whether the development of the national economy should be pursued under conditions of equilibrium or disequilibrium with the abolition (mitigation) or continuance (or enhancement) of inflationary pressure.

Waste of resources under inflation

Owing to the difficulties of a *quantitative* comparison of open and repressed inflation, analyses have to resort to *qualitative* criteria to be able to draw conclusions. Such analyses are mostly performed in Western countries to "prove" why open inflation is preferable to repressed inflation, the latter of which is prone to introduce irrational elements into the national economy. This hypothesis is clearly reflected in the title "Inflation, Communist Style". According to it irrationality is created by a budgetary policy which keeps prices stable by means of subsidies. According to this hypothesis price subsidies consume capital that could be invested in new plant and modernization, and they make it impossible to satisfy the increasing demands of consumers in socialist countries. Consumers pay dearly for official price stability.*

Let us study the budgetary price subsidy more closely. With state ownership, the entire productive organization of society may be regarded as being "one enterprise" and the aggregate products as being "one product". The state's freedom of decision acts in two directions: (1) the selection of products to determine how the *market and non-market mechanisms* should be interrelated in the mixed system of distribution; (2) the selection of products turned into commodities, to determine *where, in what direction and to what degree prices should deviate from input*. The budget may compensate the incremental costs of one product from the incremental profit accrued by another. The state does essentially the same as an enterprise does in a market economy when, in consideration of the equilibrium prices, it distributes overhead costs among the products according to their cost-bearing capacities.

If the cost level of the gross output is thus planned, there is no difficulty. For price preferences the state will use only such sums as are obtained through dispreferences. This is natural and according to rules since the price level corresponds with the value level and the budget only performs a re-distribution. The same happens when, to avert inflation on the world market, the budget grants subsidies to imports. If the price level of exports and imports (the proportion of goods exchanged in foreign trade) remains unchanged, no problems will arise; the money used by the budget to compensate for higher import prices is equal to the extra earnings of the state, achieved through a rise in the export price level.

* Inflation, Communist Style, *Time*, August 1974, No. 5.

All this can also be formulated in another way. Budget expenditure for price subsidies cannot be set apart from the prices and income relations in which it fulfils its function. The ending of price subsidies will not increase the social capital but will rather diminish it. In fact the state grants budgetary (price) subsidies mainly to keep the cost of living at a low level. In the lower income brackets it is the staples and public services which absorb the major portion of incomes. Under such circumstances budgetary price subsidies could be ended without the infringment of social justice only by an overcompensation of wages.

The only realistic argument would be that, if relative prices do not adapt to relative inputs, economic rationality suffers. But it is exactly this hypothesis that justifies the linking of comparative analysis of the two basic types of inflation with a similar *comparative study of the value systems of capitalism and socialism.* If we regard the optimum as rational and waste as a condition which deviates from the optimum, we shall still have to determine what the optimum is. Bergson pointed out that the optimum state must be determined *as a function of social utility.** The social welfare function introduced by Bergson refers to the ideological aspects of the economy. The notion of social utility in socialism differs widely from the notion of social utility in capitalism. From this it follows that socio-economic systems must be qualified by criteria which are valid for them. The socialist state:

– narrows down the sphere of products which become commodities; it regards part of divisible products as public goods; furthermore

– it grades such products as become commodities (and thus fall under the sphere of action of the market) according to their social significance; it sets consumer prices apart from input according to political preferences and dispreferences.

The sphere of *public goods* is wider than in the free market model because some of the elements of the communist principle of distribution according to needs, do indeed already exist in socialism. The tendency is to organize consumption by society in the sphere of *basic social care.* This embraces child care, schooling and education, health protection and care for the aged. At the same time *many products which are linked with basic social care become commodities.* In this respect it is the task of preferences to minimize the exclusion function of the market. The coverage for all this is provided by dispreferences of those commodities whose consumption is not indispensable, whose excessive consumption is indeed harmful to health—and may be even harmful to society.

Inevitably, the socialist order of values replaces *the consumers' sovereignty by social sovereignty* in order to restrict the supply regulating function of consumer preferences. In the final analysis social sovereignty is expressed in

– socially organized consumption in the sphere of basic social care, whereby the notion of public good becomes separated from the technical criteria of products (from divisibility) and

– in adjusting the relative prices of commodities to their relative social scarcity —more precisely to their relative scarcity on the market, corrected by political preferences (dispreferences).

In the sense of the *Pareto optimum* socialism may be considered to have a lower economic efficiency than capitalism. In this approach there exists a gap in efficiency

* Bergson, A.: *Essays in Normative Economics,* Cambridge (Mass.), 1966.

and it may be said that in socialism there is a waste of economic resources. But if we set out from the *socialist optimum,* we shall arrive at exactly opposite results. This —however strange it may sound—directly follows from the fact that in rationality as well as in waste an ideology is expressed.

It will also be clear that the income re-distributing function of the budget, the separation of prices from value (and among others price subsidies) in themselves are far from being inflation-induced manifestations. This budgetary function would be kept alive by social utility even though state planning would set the goals of economic development as the maintenance of equilibrium. It is also beyond doubt that in the case of excess demand, this budgetary function is complemented with anti-inflationary elements. It is also open to question whether the socialist order of values unequivocally determines the criteria according to which collective consumption is separated from the market and price is separated from value. And if so, whether the state organizes the economy in strict compliance with these criteria.

Obviously, *in either socio-economic system the optimum cannot be enforced beyond certain limits.* In a market economy it is imperfect competition, in a planned economy it is imperfect state control which impedes the attainment of the optimum. Furthermore, in either system, external effects must be taken into account. This, however, will not alter the essential fact that the waste hypothesis implied in the phrase "Inflation, Communist Style" remains devoid of meaning for the Marxist economist.

Looking at the problem from the aspect of the waste of resources, open and repressed inflation should be compared also with respect to the interrelation of the *existence and mitigation of excess demand.* According to some views price rationality caused by excess demand is specific to repressed inflation. Accordingly, approaching the problem of open and repressed inflation from the angle of the waste of economic resources, the two should be distinguished in the following way: whilst in open inflation the price clears the market, in repressed inflation it is the rational function of the price that is repressed. Actually, however, it is only a fiction that in open inflation excess demand ceases to exist. Even in open inflation prevailing demand —writes Lerner—is equal to prevailing supply, prices rising as much as may be needed to clear the market. Yet, this clearing of the market is not an equilibrium except in the sense in which supply is always equal to demand, because it is only the same transaction seen from the other side. There is no real equilibrium. Both under conditions of rising prices and of fixed prices excess demand will prevent the rational classic price mechanism from directing the process of distribution.*

The liberation of price movements would not put an end to excess demand in socialist countries. The transformation of repressed inflation into open inflation would cause matters to go from bad to worse. It is not prices that should be liberated, but excess demand should be abolished. *Inflationary pressure does not necessarily exist in a socialist economy.* It can be abolished or at least minimized if the state (1) determines the resources tied down for development from the national income in harmony with the requirements of equilibrium, (2) creates more direct relations between consumer and producer and, finally (3) ensures harmony between demand and supply in a flexible price mechanism.

* Lerner, A. P.: The Inflationary Process. Some Theoretical Aspects, *The Review of Economics and Statistics,* Vol. XXXI, 1949. It is noteworthy that the Joint Economic Committee of the USA Congress rejected the introduction of a comprehensive price and wage control with the argument that it "...would not be workable at the present time because of the distortions already present in both the wage and price structure, the disparities between U. S. and world prices...". (An Action Program to Reduce Inflation and Restore Economic Growth, Interim Report, 21 Sept., 1974, Washington.)

The debates in the Soviet Union in the 'twenties were significant not only from the point of view of repressed inflation but also for *establishing theoretically an optimally operating social economy*. As early as this Yushkov suggested a system of planned economy in which the "semi-automatic optimum" of the development of the national economy is combined with the maximum operative independence of the units of the economic system.* Ever since then scientific research has played an important role in improving the operation of economic control.

* (Yushkov, L. O.) Юшков, Л. О.: Основные вопросы плановой методологии (The fundamentals of the plan method), *Вестник финансов*, 10 November, 1928.

Chapter Four

COSTS OF ECONOMIC GROWTH

1. The humanization of the economy

The East–West and the North–South problems

The price trends of seven centuries give a good idea of the determinant role on a world scale of secular price movements. We must start from the position of the world economy also when investigating anticipated price trends or when seeking an answer to the question of what price relations around 2000 will be like.

The processes taking place at present in the world economy can best be characterized by pointing to the East–West and the North–South problems. The former expresses the economic relations between countries of different socio-economic systems and the latter those between "rich" and "poor" countries.

The problem of *East–West trade* has been highlighted by the overthrow of the unified economic system of the world, and by the emergence of the socialist system of international economic order. Within the socialist system of world economy seven European countries (Albania, Bulgaria, Czechoslovakia, Hungary, Poland, Romania and the Soviet Union) established in 1947 the Council for Mutual Economic Assistance (CMEA). The German Democratic Republic joined the CMEA in 1950, Mongolia in 1962, Cuba in 1972 and Vietnam in 1978. On the other hand, Albania quitted the CMEA.

Prior to the Second World War economic connexions among European socialist countries were rather loose. Indeed, in prewar times the economy of most of the CMEA countries had developed as part and parcel of the West European economy. The CMEA was a natural outcome of the socialist revolutions that took place after the Second World War, one of its tasks having been to conduct an *economic reorientation*. In this connexion it should also be noted that capitalist countries made use of all possible means of discrimination to overturn socialist economies historically oriented to the West and thus highly vulnerable.

Individually the European socialist countries would have found it extremely difficult to fend off such attacks by the capitalist world. An economic association became essential for preserving socialist achievements, and the possibilities for this were created, first of all, by the natural resources of the Soviet Union. Economic relations established with the Soviet Union enabled productive forces, which had been upset during the Second World War, to consolidate, and large scale development programs to be realized. By stretching to the limit the use of her natural resources, the Soviet Union could satisfy not only her own needs but also a considerable part of the raw material requirements of European socialist countries. At the same time, when shaping her own production structure, the Soviet Union was able to take into account the export potentials of European socialist countries. Thus the political decisions of communist countries were based on realistic economic foundations. Relying on the CMEA, the European socialist countries could develop their productive forces swiftly. So far they have fulfilled large-scale industrialization programs and have diversified their economies.

In international relations the *CMEA is the principal market* of the socialist countries concerned. But the CMEA is not an autarkical association. This market does not ensure all material–technical conditions for the economic growth of its individual member countries. Thus, although different in its extent, the trade transacted on the world market by the CMEA countries individually is significant. Indeed, the significance of these economic relations has grown in the 'seventies owing to the fact that most of the European socialist countries have passed from the extensive *phase of economic development to the intensive* one. In this connexion an ever growing significance is attached to technical transfer. With a view to maintaining the rate of economic growth and *enhancing the intensity of their economies* the European socialist countries are profoundly interested in developing East–West trade. But the possibilities of this trade are limited. The problem is rooted in their *foreign trade commodity structure.*

Table 32

The commodity structure of East–West trade* (1975)

Denomination	Export into capitalist countries	Import from capitalist countries
Basic materials and semi-finished products	64	28
Machines and plant	9	36
Products of agriculture and the food industry	11	12
Consumption goods	16	24
Altogether:	100	100

* Table set upon grounds of commodity groups No. 0–9 of the SITC nomenclature.

Source: Economic Bulletin for Europe, 1976.

The socialist countries chiefly export basic materials and semi-finished goods, as well as the products of agriculture and the food industry to capitalist countries and import from them almost solely machinery and plant or industrial goods. This foreign trade commodity structure presents a distorted reflection of the production structure. With their machinery and plant as well as with consumption goods, the socialist countries can penetrate the capitalist world market only with the greatest difficulty. For this reason East–West trade cannot develop dynamically and even at a development rate lower than is desired, the socialist countries are running up debts in capitalist countries. The so-called *"capitalist balance of payment deficit"* is one of the manifestations of the international structural crisis.

The problem of *North–South trade* has been highlighted by the abolition of the colonial system and, in connexion with it, the transition from old forms of economic subordination to new ones. From the point of view of foreign trade commodity structure it shows features akin to those of East–West trade.

The South exports chiefly prime materials and semi-finished products to the North and purchases in exchange mainly machines and plant, as well as consumer goods. The basic position of Southern countries differs from that of socialist countries by the fact that their distorted foreign trade commodity structure reflects their distorted production pattern. In the framework of the colonial system the production of the developing world evolved, as a matter course, on *oligo-cultural* lines. Having attained their political independence, these countries could develop their economies only in

Table 33

The commodity structure of North–South trade* (1975)

Denomination	Export to the North	Import from the North
Basic materials and semi-finished products	73	28
Machines and plant	2	46
Products of agriculture and the food industry	14	12
Consumption goods	11	14
Total:	100	100

* Table set upon grounds of commodity groups No. 0–9 of the SITC nomenclature.

Source: Economic Bulletin for Europe, 1976.

a subordinate position in the world economy. Thus from the point of view of the South the disadvantage lies in the production structure itself. But the final effect is identical: *a chronic deficit of the balance of payments.*

What is to be understood by the costs of economic growth?

When we wish to obtain a picture of anticipated price (value) relations, we are seeking an answer to two questions. One is the trend of the level of price (value) and the other that of relative prices. Our initial hypothesis is as follows: the East–West problem is primarily connected with commodity value and with its anticipated trend. On the other hand, the North–South problem is connected with the trend of natural (monopoly) rent and with its anticipated international redistribution. This difference cannot of course be deduced from price trends, since the various factors determining prices (value, rent, relative scarcity, inflation or deflation) become synthesized in the market price. But if we want to anticipate price trends, it is necessary to investigate the various factors one by one.

We shall first investigate the problem of the *value level,* and shall apply the classic method of analysing secular price trends, by differentiating between price movements induced from the commodity side and those induced by the money side. In what follows we assume a state devoid of inflation, that is to say, we limit our investigations to price trends induced from the *commodity side.*

If we want to examine anticipated price trends by starting from the commodity side, we have to raise the question as to whether, in the last quarter of our century, the process of economic growth will take place with increasing or decreasing returns. The view according to which, in the long run, the commodity side induces a rise of prices (values) appears to be characteristic. The hypotheses of the costs of economic growth are connected with this very issue.

In the first instance, we must draw attention to the various possible interpretations of the costs of economic growth. Four of these are worth mentioning:

– Costs of economic growth arising from the international re-distribution of incomes;
– Investment costs of research and development surpassing the "normative" level;

– Unquantified costs, on account of which the increased rate of growth of the GNP overestimates the rise of social welfare;

– Specific input increasing with economic growth.

A. K. Bagchi set forth the concept according to which the costs of economic growth are connected with the *international re-distribution of incomes.** This concept can also be interpreted as an analysis of the costs of economic growth regarded from the point of view of the developing world, its essence being that the gap in economic development is partly or wholly the aftermath of colonial exploitation. Bagchi analyses extensively the different forms of exploitation. As a consequence of this exploitation the costs of growth in the developing world are too high compared to the rate of economic growth in these countries, and to the structure in which it is taking place.

The uncompensated costs of economic growth were caused—according to Bagchi—by the grave contradictions arising from growth in the capitalist mode. He indicated three factors: (1) The contradiction between the capitalist class and rentiers and the rest of the population within the country; (2) the contradiction between capitalist ruling classes of different countries and (3) the contradictory nature of the economic processes set in motion by capitalism (cyclical growth, inflationary recession, stagnation etc.). This latter is often regarded as a process of necessary correction of economic processes, while the fact that the costs are mostly borne by the workers is left out of consideration. But the central contradiction springs from the exploitation of the Third World countries by the capitalist classes of the West European countries and of North America.

Some interpretations of the costs of research, development and investment *in a closed system of national economies,* would regard such costs as *exceeding the average international costs* (the so-called normative costs). This view has taken root among Polish economists who have directed attention to the problems of government planning and of the central allocation of resources under conditions of a socialist economy. Under the comprehensive title "How can the costs of growth be reduced?" a series was launched in the Polish periodical *Kultura.* Introducing the debate W. Wilczynski started from the viewpoint that Poland could not but choose, at least in the present period, a relatively capital consuming type of economic growth. In his view input required for increasing GNP has been high in Poland in the past 30 years on account of at least two objective reasons. First: an up-to-date technical infrastructure and productive potential had to be created from practically nothing. Secondly: investments for raw material supply—i.e. such investments as could in a certain sense be saved by countries possessing no raw materials—required stupendous inputs.

Waste is also considered a cost of economic growth.** In this interpretation the relatively high costs of growth are explained by subjective reasons as well as objective ones. In the sphere of "superfluous" costs Wilczynski attributed particular significance to two factors: (1) Wrong investment decisions, in which the chosen investment variant is worse than the optimum; a decision failing to take secondary effects fully into account. (2) Shortcomings of the economic mechanism: the relative inefficiency of means put into the service of ends. Polish economists have explored thoroughly the

* Bagchi, A. K.: The costs of economic growth as viewed from less developed countries. Paper submitted to the Fifth World Congress of the IEA (Tokyo, 29 August–3 Sept., 1977).

** Wilczynski, W.: Jak obnizyc koszty naszego rozwoju? (How can the costs of growth be reduced?) *Kultura,* Warsaw, 24 April, 1977.

shortcomings of socialist economic control and the costs of economic growth connected with them—costs that could have been avoided.*

The *welfare intepretation* of the costs of economic growth has been adopted in a wider sphere. According to it these costs are expressed in the fact that the growth rate of GNP measured conventionally is overestimated as against the actual growth of welfare. These problems are well systematized by F. Modigliani**. According to him growth in measured output is overstated partly on account of measurement errors (bias) and partly on account of externalities. Measurement errors lead to an overstatement of the net output, whereas externalities cause an overstatement of the increment in net benefits received by the consumer. When analysing measurement errors (bias) he refers to W. Nordhaus's and J. Tobin's*** investigations, the results of which show the overstatement of the net output to be due to the following:

- measurement methods fail to take into consideration deterioration in quality;
- they do not reflect structural changes in the course of which the weight of intermediate outputs increases at the cost of the final output;
- economic growth has hidden costs, such as, e.g. the costs of urbanization.

As against this, one could mention the shortening of the legal working week, which again gives rise to the question of how the real value of leisure can be quantified, and, along with it the value increase, arising from the decrease of the legal working week.

Externalities arise both in the sphere of production and of consumption. In the sphere of production one of their main manifestations is the fact that environment pollution exceeds the growth rate of output. In the sphere of production both physical and social (positional) externalities can be shown. Externalities *per se* refer to the fact that from the point of individual productive forces input is lower than social costs and utility measured from the viewpoint of individual consumers is higher than social utility.

F. Modigliani's paper was prepared for the 5th World Congress of the International Economic Association held in Tokyo in 1977, and was based on E. Malinvaud's paper in the debate on costs of economic growth.° S. Tsuru also prepared a paper for the same debate and pointed out particularly the significance of costs connected with the process of urbanization.°°

Finally, the costs of economic growth can also be interpreted as a hypothesis of value increase. In the present writer's opinion this category has economic content only in this interpretation. How does this interpretation differ from the views set forth on grounds of welfare economics, in a complex investigation of changes taking place in output relations? Let us take, for instance, urbanization. As a matter of course, this makes certain kinds of costs (e.g. transport costs) increase more rapidly than GNP. However, this is only an inevitable concomitant of structural change springing from the process of economic growth. Urbanization changes the consumption structure and

* Matysik, A.: Luka w rabekynku i w zarzadzaniu. Jak potanic rozwoj? (A gap in the market and in control), *Kultura*, Warsaw, 7 August, 1977.

** Modigliani, F.: Comments on "Costs of Economic Growth" by Edmond Malinvaud, Fifth World Congress of the International Economic Association, Tokyo, 29 August–3 September 1977.

*** Tobin, J.–Nordhaus, W.: "Is Growth Obsolete?" In: *Economic Growth*, National Bureau of Economic Research, Columbia University Press, New York, 1972.

° Malinvaud, E.: Costs of Economic Growth. Fifth World Congress of the International Economic Association, Tokyo, 29 August–3 September, 1977.

°° Tsuru, S.: Comments on "Costs of Economic Growth" by Edmond Malinvaud. Fifth World Congress of the International Economic Association, Tokyo, 29 August–3 September, 1977.

this reacts upon the production structure. In harmony with it a transformation of the production cost structure also takes place. Accordingly, the fact that certain kinds of costs increase more rapidly than GNP does not necessarily mean the presence of costs of growth. If overcompensated by savings achieved in the sphere of other kinds of costs—there are no costs of the former kind.

No matter how one interprets the costs of economic growth, they will, in one way or the other, be connected with estimated price (value) relations. And yet, if we examine the costs of economic growth from the standpoint that factors raising the level of value (price) emerge from the commodity side, this can only be based on the assumption that the specific input per unit of product increases. This trend can assert itself decisively in connexion with the *humanization of the economy*.

But we must refer to two constraints. One is the increase of *leisure,* while externalities constitute the other. At the present time the most significant manifestation of the social utility of economic growth is the decrease of the legal working week. The discussions are mainly focussed on whether this utility factor can be quantified or not. In one way or another everything can be quantified. In the case of leisure the worker performs this quantification by renouncing his leisure for higher wages. However, quite irrespective of whether we correct GNP by means of such criteria or by others, no such correction is possible in the case of value (price) relations. Temporarily the shortening of the legal working week may compensate or overcompensate the increase of productivity, i.e. it induces a rise of the price level. The argument may, of course, be put forward that in such cases the price rise is offset by the increasing social utility manifested in the increase of leisure. This, however, is outside the scope of our examination. Since externalities are not internal costs, they cannot become factors of value (price) formation, unless the taxation of the production (distribution) process is created in harmony with them.

The quality of life

Economic growth takes place in parallel with structural changes. That is why it seems justifiable to differentiate between two factors of the increase of volume: one is the *quantitative increase* and the other the change of qualitative composition. A quantitative growth always takes place hand in hand with a quality increase. Indeed, in this sense quantity and quality are not opposed. However, if we investigate the movement processes of the world economy in the system of East–West relations, the quality factor of growth should be treated separately. It was the competition of socio-economic systems that focussed attention on the debate about the *quality of life*. New features expected to influence the foreseeable trend of commodity value are also connected with this.

Let us begin from the conditions of *classic capitalism* in which the tendency towards diminishing commodity value asserted itself. That historical period was marked by a large-scale development of productive forces and by a modernization process of the economy. However, at the same time the anti-human features of a market economy also emerged: (1) by means of capitalist private ownership the *exploitation* of man by man could be realized; (2) in the course of capital centralization and concentration the inequality within society grew ever sharper; (3) rationality adjusting itself to the conditions of the battle of competition led to a marked differentiation of incomes; the wealth of a small minority was coupled with the *poverty of the great masses;* (4) the cyclical development of the economy and the recurring crises institutionalized the feeling of a *precariousness of existence;* (5) the function of labour as a commodity in the process of value production was determined by such development tendencies of manufacturing technologies and marketing techniques as were exclusively dictated by the *profit motive*.

Already in the last century the anti-human features of the free market economy gave rise to debates on the *meaning of development* and the *quality of life*. Two aspects of these debates deserve special attention. First of all, it was in the wake of these debates that the idea of socialism gained ground. In the minds of many, ideas about the quality of life came to be identified with a transition from individualism to collectivism, which is a system in which not the consumer's but society's sovereignty determines the movement of economic processes. In accordance with this the idea of a society without exploitation came to be formulated, as a production method more highly developed than that of capitalist private ownership. Secondly, it was in these debates that the socialist point of view became identified with opposition to a market economy of commodity production. In the opinion of many, the market was a particular concomitant of capitalist mode of production, since, relying on the market, capitalism could curb production, maintain the relative scarcity of goods and, when all is said and done, could restrict consumption.

In this model commodity exchange and money economy would disappear together with capitalism. Marx imagined that in the economy of a socialist society the government would organize production directly on grounds of needs. He assumed such a degree of development of the productive forces as would render the unrestricted satisfaction of human needs possible if the profit interest of capitalists did not restrict production.* Engels had the same idea, namely, when society took possession of the means of production commodity production would come to an end and so would the rule of products over producers.**

This was the starting-point in Russia when, after the victory of the October Revolution of 1917, the Soviet Union was established. During the short historical period called war communism the system of barter (money-less) economy was introduced. But it was soon apparent that in this way economic consolidation could hardly be expected. Money, prices, trade, i.e. the categories of a market economy, were therefore restored in the Soviet Union. Lenin gave the reason, most tersely: life has shown that we were mistaken.*** In the present century the *realistic problem* therefore arises that countries, pursuing a socialist course of development, have to solve the tasks of socialist construction within the framework of commodity production.

Adopting commodity production under conditions of socialism *admits only* that the abolishment of capitalist private ownership cannot, of itself, terminate the necessity of economizing on resources. We are forced to manage the economy on account of the scarcity of commodities. By switching over to a socialist planned economy such capacities as served as "dormant" reserves in capitalism can be brought into operation. But the additional accumulation of commodities is only a fragment of what would be needed to meet the needs of society without any limitations. And if, owing to the scarcity of products, consumption must be restricted, it is the market mechanism that can surmount difficulties with least disturbance, by setting into motion the market clearing function of price.

Economists supporting capitalism and those who support socialism will, obviously, formulate the meaning of development and the quality of life in different terms. This constitutes the *ideological aspect of economy*, which, at the same time, lies at the root of

* Marx, K.: *Critique of the Gotha Programme*, New York, 1938.

** Engels, F.: *Herr Eugen Dühring's Revolution in Science*, New York, 1939.

*** Lenin, V. I.: *Tax in Kind*, Moscow, 1965.

the East–West problem. In this way we should also like to study the criteria that determine the movement of values. But, first of all, two comments should be made. To begin with, let us suppose that in the next decades the world economy will develop in an environment of the peaceful co-existence of countries of different socio-economic systems. Secondly, let us suppose that price movements in the world economy will continue to be determined decisively by the changes of value relations in capitalist countries, while criteria characteristic of the economy of socialist societies, will—in an indirect way—play significant roles. Without doubt, the challenge represented by the existence and rapid development of socialist countries strongly influences the economic policy of governments in capitalist countries.

The socialization process

The co-existence of countries with different socio-economic systems is a characteristic feature of our times. What peculiarities of economic processes are due to this fact? When judging this, let us start from the convergence theory formulated by Galbraith. According to it the economic mechanism of a modern industrial society is objectively determined. In his view the development of productive forces and the institutional framework of an economy determined by this development is essential. A *homogeneous picture of modern industrial societies* emerges, but it will not be created by socialist transformation induced by politics, but by the automatism of productive forces as it were in spite of politics.*

As is evident, the convergence theory interprets the essence of socio-economic systems as a *system of economic management*. Seen from this aspect the antagonism between capitalism and socialism appears as a state of contrasts and conflicts between *different economic mechanisms,* or, all things considered, between market and plan. Should this be acceptable, then the convergence theory would be justifiable, since, due to objective reasons, the elements of government planning are becoming stronger in capitalist market economies, just as in socialist planned economies is the role of incentives played by market mechanisms. The sharpening of the anti-social features of economic crises used to lead to an anti-cyclical economic policy in *capitalism,* whereas at present, on account of the structural crisis, the budgetary policy increasingly adopts the forms of government planning. Commodity production took root in *socialism* as a result of the experiences gained during the period of war communism in the Soviet Union, whereas in our own time, in order to achieve higher efficiency and to enhance international competitiveness, a fuller utilization of the possibilities of the market mechanism is encouraged.

But let us point out that there is a difference in quality between a planned economy and the mechanism introduced into capitalism by government planning gaining ground. In the same way there is a qualitative difference between a free market economy and socialist commodity production, however strongly the market mechanism is activated. Moreover, the principal problems of socio-economic systems spring not from the relationship of plan and market, but from *property and class relations.* The question of the economic mechanism touches only the role of the government. On the other hand, class and property relations are connected with the question: in whose interest is control exercised? When all is said and done, what the socio-economic system of a country is like depends on the character of state power and on property and class

* Galbraith, J. K.: *The Affluent Society,* Boston, 1958.

relations. Economic control takes shape on the basis of these relations or, as it were, in their interests.

However, when we take up a stand against the convergence theory, it is actually not convergence as such but the manner of its interpretation we object to. Indeed, convergence takes place for objective reasons, but not outside the systems of capitalism and socialism, or, more exactly, not as an alternative outside these systems but as a shift over from capitalism to socialism. The spread of monopolies in capitalism was characterized by Lenin as a *transition from capitalism into a higher system.* "Competition turns into monopoly. The result is great progress in the socialization of production. Among other things the process of technical development and innovation is also socialized."... "This is something quite different from the old, free competition of scattered entrepreneurs, who do not know anything about each other and are producing for unknown markets. Concentration has developed to such an extent that, one can almost take account of all natural resources ... in the several countries and even ... in world relations. However, the gigantic monopolistic alliances not only take account of these resources but also keep them within their own grasp. These alliances make approximate assessments of the market and "distribute" it among one another on the basis of contracts... Capitalism leads to a general socialization of production and, as it were, plunges the capitalists, without their wanting or being aware of it, into some new social order, which is a transition between a totally free competition and total socialization."*

The socialization process taking place within the framework of capitalism, a process which Lenin stated, arose from the spread of monopolies in the first decades of the 20th century, strengthened further in later decades and was even enriched by new features. This has been recognized by the convergence theory, but has been interpreted as a process outside socio-political systems. Indeed, this is the "antechamber" of socialism, but it is not yet socialism. Property and class relations are connected with this shift of emphasis.

We interpret the socialization of production as paving the way to the humanization of the economy. At the same time, this determines the meaning of development: *the self-realization of man, the unfolding of the personality.* Quite a few people may think that this aim can be achieved more completely by individualism. The circumstance that in a free market economy the consumer's sovereignty controls economic processes is often referred to. On the other hand, we know that sovereignty rests on the inequality of people. If for no other reasons than capitalist private ownership itself, capitalism cannot ensure equal opportunities for self-realization. Besides, in a free market economy the tendency asserts itself that every product should possibly be sold as a commodity. This leads to the other tendency that, while an ever-growing mass of commodities is produced, people become slaves of commodities. In one interpretation this very fact is expressed in the term "consumers' society". The easing of the anti-human features of capitalist production explains why the industrially developed capitalist countries try to adopt such criteria characteristic of the economy of socialist societies as are compatible with capitalist private ownership.

But let us emphasize *that the humanization process in socialist societies is far from having been completed.* First of all we must bear in mind that socialist transformation is gaining ground mostly in moderately developed countries and in the developing world. It is the endeavour of these countries to catch up with the level of industrially developed capitalist countries by raising the level of *per capita* GNP as soon as

* Lenin, V. I.: Imperialism, the Highest Stage of Capitalism, *Selected works*, London, 1944, pp. 80–99.

possible. But they have to defend their socialist achievements as well. These circumstances present problems for both the concrete institutional system and the government planning of economic development.

Marcuse's criticism of society concerning the institutional systems both of capitalism and of socialism is well known.* He ignores the conflict between production and other property relations and judges the existing industrial societies as being uniformly highly rational in developing technological sources, but irrational in putting the results into the improvement of social welfare. According to his hypothesis there is no scarcity: it is only created by a manipulation of needs, and encouraged by the desire for acquisition. According to him automatized production in the United States can already ensure the prime necessities of society; the need for direct productive labour being marginal, direct productive work might be dispensed with. His reasoning leads in the end to the abolition of the compulsion of economic management and thus of the historically evolved system of the division of labour.

In the society of the realm of "freedom" one man cannot dominate another and institutions do not dominate man; violence is reduced to the extent demanded by organized social co-existence; science and technology are utilized to the maximum, which renders the minimization of direct productive work possible; people take part in productive work according to their changing inclinations and abilities.

As we can see Marcuse formulates the humanization of the economy in an extreme manner and takes up an anti-socialist stand by outlining a Utopian picture of society, and he criticizes the conditions that can realistically be created at present. His system of social values is linked with a world outside productive labour. As against him Marx's viewpoint was that the realm of freedom can be realized only outside working time needed socially. This is the time that can be used for enjoyment and rest, for giving free scope to free activity and development. In the case of direct productive work the situation is different, for here the distribution of labour sets limits to the realization of human autonomy.

In what follows we are going to analyse the costs of economic growth, focussing our investigations on the humanization process of the economy. Let us suppose that the process of humanization exerts and essential influence upon the formation of commodity value.

At the present time economic growth impairs efficiency due to objective reasons. Seen from this viewpoint the "Cost of Economic Growth" may be seen as an aggravation of the conditions of economic growth. These costs emerge not from the mere fact of economic growth but from the specific situation concomitant with the humanization of the economy. The processes incurring costs appear on the one hand in the relationship between man and nature and on the other in the relationship between people. They promote man's greater self-realization and a better unfolding of the personality.

2. Wage costs of economic growth

Basic conditions of labour relations

In capitalism the production process takes place in the framework of market relations of the entrepreneur, the capitalist, the landowner and the labourer. It is taken as a matter of course, not only that the worker sells his labour, but also that

* Marcuse, H.: *One-Dimensional Man*, Toronto, 1964.

the landowner in return for the land he has let for utilization, and the capitalist in return for the capital invested, want to share in the surplus value. Under the conditions of capitalism this participation (land rent and capital interest) as well as wages are determined by the market relations of the production factors. Nevertheless, in the sphere of the factors of production labour has a specific character compared to land and capital.

Labourers produce on the one hand value and on the other consumer goods. In the economy their relations in their capacity of producers of value are expressed in production costs (and within them in wages); in their capacity as consumers in prices (and within them in retail prices). Parallel with the humanization process of the economy, the satisfaction of needs, as against labour, is coming increasingly to the fore as a production factor. That is why labour relations could not remain simply in a system of employment agreements between enterprises and workers. Moreover, the collective contracts brought about through the mediation of trade unions have not proved sufficient to determine in an adequately humanized way the general conditions of work.

The humanization of the economy—first and foremost in the interest of workers—pre-supposed the presence of government control in organizing the economy; it also pre-supposed the presence of constitutional guarantees to regulate the participation of society in labour; within the framework of these guarantees the rights and duties of enterprises and workers within labour relations, the participation—conveyed by their trade unions—of the workers' right in controlling their living and working conditions, and further in developing and supervising the enterprise's activity.

However, it is only in *socialist countries* that legal measures of a normative character can be consistently integrated into the general system of the economic order. In these countries the right to work is decreed by the constitution of socialist society and the regulation of participation in the work of society, the basic rights and duties of workers and of enterprises as well as their guarantees, are, as a general rule, laid down in the Labour Code as well as in specific laws connected with it. But in capitalist countries too labour law has been established or is being established; their governments' feeling of responsibility for the regulation of basic questions of labour relations in harmony with ethics is increasing.

The subject-matter of labour law varies widely according to countries. This is not the place in which to go into details. Nor is this necessary. It would seem to be sufficient to investigate the principal forms of the general order of participation in the work of society, the forms that are most important from the point of the humanization of the economy, and formulate a general tendency regarding the main direction of development on a relatively wide international platform. Three guiding principles appear as main tendencies.

1. *Ensuring the right to work.* Regarded from the point of view of the trend of commodity value this seems to be the most important change taking place as against 19th century capitalism. Constitutionally this right has in general been ensured by socialist societies only. But, by implication, it has been obtained in quite a few industrially developed countries too. We have in mind the countries in which the paying of unemployment benefits has been institutionalized.

As a matter of course the right to work is different from an institutional system of unemployment benefit. In the former case the obligation is to ensure an opportunity to work for every person of working age. In the latter case the obligation is binding only with respect to persons already employed.

The principle of *full employment* has been introduced into economic policy by the right to work. But consistently this right was only ensured in socialist countries.

In capitalist countries employment policy is shaped as a function of anti-inflationary policy; unemployment also plays a part in stabilization policy.

In socialist countries the principle of full employment has led to a differentiation between the extensive and intensive phases of growth in the development of productive forces. In the extensive phase of growth—when there is as yet no full employment—the creation of new jobs is the main criterion of development. The intensive phase of growth starts when full employment has been achieved and the lack of new labour is the chief obstacle to growth.

It is evident that conditions are less favourable from the standpoint of production costs in the phase of economic growth in which partial employment is transformed into full employment than in the phase when production is to be increased in a state of full employment. In the former phase it is the social motive that plays the leading role in structural policy and in the latter phase it is the economic one. But both phases differ basically from conditions on the competitive market.

2. *The legal order of participation in the work of society.* Because of humanitarian considerations the government limits the right to free choice of work. The most important manifestations of these restrictions are as follows:

a. It sets *the minimum age limit* (the completion of one's 14th year), at which a person is entitled to enter into employment.

b. It establishes the *legal working week* (e.g. 48, 44, 40, 36 hours per week). In this situation special cases have to be designated on account of which

– longer working time than the average can be set in certain sectors, because the nature of work renders this inevitable (e.g. in transport, in seasonal agricultural work, etc.),

– in other sectors the legal working week can only be shorter than the average, e.g. in factories or plants where production is continuous or takes place in three shifts, or else in jobs particularly harmful to health (e.g. in places where radioactivity may prove harmful).

c. The humanization process leads to a *shortening of the legal working week.* The importance of leisure increases and this time is less and less regulated by the rules of labour re-production and increasingly by man's self-realization. The changes taking place in this relationship of society and economy indicate most markedly the labourer's function as a producer of value and as a consumer.

Nevertheless the time actually spent at work is longer than the legal working week. In certain cases *overtime work* is inevitable. If the legal working week has been established by the provisions of law, the conditions of overtime work must also be set by the provisions of law.

d. It grants special protection to women and minors (e.g. to such as have not completed their 18th year yet) when they enter employment.

The law can prohibit the employment of women and minors in labour that may have harmful consequences for their physique and for their development, respectively. In many countries the employment of minors, particularly of young people under 16 years of age, for night work and for overtime work is prohibited. This refers to pregnant women and mothers of infants too.

e. Workers must be given the opportunity to eat (breaks in work), they are entitled to one day of rest every week and holidays in every year spent in employment (e.g. 12 days); furthermore additional holidays are due to them after the total time they have spent in employment. In addition to this—as a general rule—laws regulate days to be kept as holidays.

3. *The principle ensuring the safe and healthy performance of work.* The demand that the factory or any other establishment should ensure that work can be done under healthy and safe conditions in using machines, materials or other equipment belongs to the question pertaining to the general conditions of work. Dangers arising in work must be minimized, first of all, by improving technical conditions and by the correct organization of work. If necessary, appropriate protective measures have to be taken. Accordingly, in many countries rules have been implemented under which protective equipment and garments, as well as protective food and drink must be supplied.

Only enterprises can determine wages and other payments in all their details. Where the proper conditions can be created, enterprises use a system of payment by results or a system of piece rates. This justified the government's regulating *basic questions of setting and treating of work norms that serve as a basis for payment by results.* Where this is taking place, the government generally introduces work norms that can be fulfilled by

– a labourer of average ability, with appropriate skills and biological qualities (intellectual and physical) and possessing the necessary experience;

– norms that can be realized in the prescribed daily working time under appropriate conditions of technology, organization, health and safety, while meeting all quality and economic requirements.

Equality and income distribution

Income distribution based on the principle of equality under the conditions of full employment is another chief requirement of the humanization of the economy. Equality and *egalitarianism are different things.* It is in the nature of things that the different quantity, quality, social utility of work done should differentiate incomes. The salary of white collar workers exceeds the wages of labourers. Due to objective reasons

– the salary of white collar workers is differentiated according to their qualification, their sphere of activity, the time spent in employment;

– the wages of labourers according to the level of their skill and the conditions under which their work is to be done.

However, in addition to these objective criteria, factors that originate from the *unequal position of the members* of society also differentiate incomes. These factors are mostly connected with the operation of the market mechanism. The essence of the problem can be best illuminated by conjuring up the period of classic capitalism. In that period the unequal position of the members of society led to very sharp differentiations of incomes.

1. Workers were in a disadvantageous position compared to *capitalists,* and this was most clearly reflected by the distribution of wealth, but was expressed in incomes distribution too.

2. Labourers were in a disadvantageous position compared to *white collar workers,* a situation created by the manner of their participation in the work of society and by the hierarchical structure on which the distribution of work was based. This led to a differentiation of incomes to a greater extent than was justified.

The class structure of society, and stratification within it, institutionalized pauperism. The wealth of the few and the *destitution* of the masses were concomitants of 19th century classic capitalism.

3. Agricultural labourers were in a disadvantageous position compared to industrial ones. This was caused by the differences in productivity of work in the two economic sectors.

4. Workers engaged in the several branches of production were in an unequal position, because of the different technical development (profitability) of the various branches of industry, and, in agriculture, decisively by the different qualities of the soil.

5. Women and minors were in a disadvantageous position compared to male labour and this was reflected in the low level of wages of branches where female labour was predominant.

It is a natural concomitant of equality that no disadvantageous discrimination according to sex, age, nationality, race and origin of the workers be exercised when labour relations are established and the rights and duties prescribed in employment are determined. Under the conditions of classic capitalism this could not be ensured. Thus, those who favoured equality had to take up, at the same time, an anti-capitalistic stand.

In enforcing equality, there are elements connected with socio-economic systems and others that are independent of them. The inequality springing from capitalist private ownership can be abolished only by the socialization of the means of production. That is why socialism is a precondition of the enforcement of *total equality*. At the same time the socialization of the means of production in itself will not put an end to all forms of inequality. Characteristics of the incomes distribution inherited from capitalism will become rigid in socialism too and can be abolished only gradually by means of a purposeful incomes distribution policy. However, up to a point, the same can take place in capitalism too. And what is more, if we consider the humanization of the economy an objective process, this assumption also indicates that the government's incomes distribution policy—interpreted in this way—inevitably comes into force.

The incomes distribution policy we have in mind can—owing to the above outlined peculiarities of incomes differentiation—be characterized as a policy of the *levelling of incomes*. In pursuing this, governments will avail themselves both of direct and indirect instruments.

Governments will levy both direct and indirect taxes on personal incomes. The differentiation of direct taxes (e.g. incomes tax) from indirect ones (e.g. excise duty) is based on this. The view used to prevail that *incomes re-distribution adjusted to the requirements of production policy was characteristic of capitalist countries, whilst incomes re-distribution adjusted to the requirements of social policy was characteristic of socialist countries.* The two income structures were counterposed as belonging to the basic characteristics of the two socio-economic systems. But the difference of the incomes structures characteristic of socialist and of capitalist countries is rather rooted in the fact that *socialist societies have not in general emerged in industrially developed countries.* And if the society of a country brings about a socialist revolution at a relatively low level of the development of productive forces, socialist production conditions will, as it were, inevitably enforce an incomes policy subordinated to the principles of social policy. This throws light upon the difference which—without any reason—is identified with the difference of the two socio-economic systems. Socialism and social policy are two different things. If approached realistically *incomes policy is inevitably always taking shape as a dilemma from the point of view of production policy and of social policy.*

There is a certain connexion between *the stage of development of productive forces and the system of incomes re-distribution.* A country in the initial stage of industrialization can hardly start capital production without imposing customs barriers and a turnover tax, particularly if there is no influx of capital—or if it is insignificant—and if the savings of the population are also insufficient. Customs duties mean an income for the government and favourable price conditions for industrialization, whereas the turnover tax may ensure the conditions for government financing of the economy. In such a socio-economic structure taxes levied on value produced in agriculture have a special significance; however, in most countries this is realized in an indirect way, by the channels of the industry and wholesale; for instance by turnover tax.

And yet we should not consider income tax and turnover tax as basically different elements of income regulation systems. In a developed economy income tax and turnover tax are not a case of *either – or,* but of *both – and.* Either of them performs specific functions and is, thus, indispensable. One cannot replace the other. Both taxes correct the market distribution—income tax corrects money incomes and turnover tax corrects commodity demand. It is one of the important tasks of income tax policy to correct the income structure emerging from the market mechanism. Apart from some exceptional cases turnover tax cannot perform this function, since its task is the correction of the consumer price structure.

In an industrially developed society production and income relations can be regulated satisfactorily only in a *multi-channel* taxation system. At the same time indirect instruments in themselves are not enough *to enforce the principle of equality in income relations.* In these countries *direct* instruments must also be utilized. In this connexion it is worth-while to recall the ECE Seminar held in Stockholm between 3–7 December, 1973 under the sponsorship of the Economic Commission for Europe, or rather the round table conference held on the first day of the Conference at which, under the chairmanship of Eric Lundberg, a group of economists discussed the factors and conditions of long-term economic growth.* In common with other economists E. Lundberg emphasized that along with taxation economic growth had not solved the problem of equality as had been previously believed. B. Horvat added that in industrially developed capitalist countries the potential of taxation for levelling incomes had been exhausted and yet the differences in incomes were striking.

Although in most industrially developed capitalist countries *direct* instruments are also used, striking differences in incomes remain. *Government price control in agriculture* has been introduced chiefly with a view to creating, maintaining or approaching incomes parity between agrarian labourers and industrial ones. Moreover, in numerous countries minimum wages are set by provisions of law. In addition to this, the humanization process of the economy leads to an increasing role of the government in regulating prices and wages.

Workers are paid wages for their work and they are also granted social benefits. Benefits in addition to wages are differentiated in different countries depending on the system of *social insurance.* Where social insurance free of charge has been decreed, workers and members of their families are entitled, in case of illness, to medical care, hospitalization, medicaments and therapeutical equipment. In case of inability to work, workers get sickness benefit. During pregnancy and at childbirth, working women are entitled to a grant; and if the worker dies his dependents get a death allowance. In case of industrial injury and of occupational diseases, workers are

* Participants of the round table debate were: E. Lundberg; L. P. Blanc; B. Horvat; E. Mason; C. T. Saunders; J. R. N. Stone and J. Tinbergen. UN: Factors and Conditions of Long-Term Growth. Seminar on Factors and Conditions of Long-Term Growth, Stockholm (Sweden), 3–7 December, 1973. New York, 1974.

given extra social insurance care. The comprehensive system of social benefits can be highly varied. This is characteristic of countries where workers are given a family allowance for their dependents; where having reached retiring age or suffering from disability workers are entitled to a pension; and, should the worker die, his dependents, too, are covered by a pension. These benefits may cover social and cultural fields too.

The changing relationship between prices and wages

If we regard price as a pure market category, we must also suppose that labour has a market value. According to this, the market value of commodities regulates wages. Or, in other words, by means of price relations the market controls both employment and wage relations. This is one of the hypotheses of perfect competition. And it is the model to which classic capitalism has approached most closely.

In our own time—at least in economically developed societies— the situation is different. Labour has invariably remained a production factor, but its specific character divorces it basically from land and capital. In order to make it operate, a special mechanism is demanded which in capitalism differs from that in socialism. However, they have a common tendency: the role of prices in regulating wages has weakened. Indeed, if we consider the trend of the course of wages, we gain the impression that wages, as it were, "externally" are integrated into costs. In a downward direction prices are regulated by the market's value-judgements of commodities, whereas in an upward direction prices are regulated by the autonomous laws of wage movements. If we consider price from the point of view of the commodity market, it can only be an equilibrium price, at least as long as it is made to operate as a market price. However, if we regard price from the point of view of the labour market, it is a welfare price, at least within the framework determined by the government's incomes distribution policy and by the trade unions' wage policy, which must be observed in the wage regulation of enterprises.

Seen from this viewpoint, price has a Janus face. On the one hand, it keeps demand in harmony with supply and as such performs a market clearing function. On the other, it keeps wages in harmony with prices in a co-ordinated income structure. In this capacity prices serve the living standards policy. But, in this connexion, some complementary remarks should be made.

1. The price that can be so characterized is showing a tendency to emerge both in capitalism and in socialism, the difference being that within the changing relationship of prices and wages, different elements have a priority. In a capitalist market economy the changing relationship between prices and wages is coupled with the preservation of the market price system. Accordingly, the market clearing function of prices enjoys a definite priority. On the other hand, in a socialist commodity economy the government pursues an active living standard policy and the realization of distribution according to work done enjoys priority.

2. The changing relationship between prices and wages is emerging gradually in close connexion with the process of economic growth. A levelling of incomes can also be undertaken at the incomes level already reached. In this case certain classes of society (branches of occupation, etc.) attain surplus income at the cost of others. But the levelling of incomes brought about in this way causes social tensions. Such tensions can be best avoided if the levelling of incomes takes place by means of distributable income surpluses in the course of economic growth.

3. The changing relationship between prices and wages leads, as a matter of course, to a transformation of the price mechanism. Prices developing in this direction run

more and more counter to the mechanism created by the free market. For objective reasons indirect—and, in certain cases, direct—government price regulation becomes inevitable, by means, *inter alia,* of activating the incomes re-distribution function of the budget. The assumption is that the budget must fulfil such a task not only by the taxation system but also by the price system.

The changing relationship between prices and wages can also be considered as a decrease of social mobility, as a manifestation of a gradually growing rigidity of society. Wages escape the direct control of prices—or the tendency of prices to be regulated by means of wages ceases—because the development of social consciousness increases the social expectations of government regulation to limit significant incomes differentiations brought about by spontaneous market processes.

Interpreted in this way, the decrease of social mobility creates new conditions for price movements as a matter of course. It is a concomitant of the incomes structure that, in market system economies, the relative price rises first of all in the sectors where the phases of work can only be partly—or not at all—mechanized, or where the productivity of work lags behind the average.

Reasoning abstractly, one would suppose that in certain sectors, among others in the sphere of services, the relative price would rise in the case of a stable, or perhaps even of a decreasing price level, since in other sectors, where the productivity of work rises more than the average, this is expressed by the diminishing of prices too. But, in fact, we have to judge the changing relationship of prices and wages in the complex system of processes comprehensively characterized by the humanization of economy, a system in which a government induced demand-pull is also realized. That is why the change of relative prices would be coupled with the rise of price levels even if the humanization of the economy did not cause an increase of the specific production costs.

A true appraisal of the changing relationship of prices and wages demands the dispelling of a false belief. In industrially developed societies wage costs stand at about 10% of gross output. This may create the impression that the changing relationship of prices and wages could not exert too significant an influence on price (value) formation. In fact the components of price (value) are wages and net incomes. Material costs, depreciation etc. are only forms of expression for previously performed labour processes. In this connexion it might be advisable to recall here what has been written in Chapter One.

3. Technological costs of growth

The costs of environment protection

The production, distribution and consumption of certain commodities causes damage to the environment: the *human environment* becomes polluted or damaged in a way that changes its natural qualities unfavourably, or impairs the living conditions of man. The soil, water, air, the countryside, the living world and the environment of towns and villages can suffer equally in consequence of these harmful effects. These effects derive from the production, storing, transport, handling or utilization of biological, chemical or radioactive material which impair or endanger the human environment by a single accident or by cumulative pollution.

The endangering of the *earth* may mean damage to the soil, to the rock bed or to mineral deposits. It occurs when the user—depending on the proposed use or character of the area—fails to maintain the fertility of the soil, or fails to employ the methods, means and regulations destined to prevent damage of the soil brought about by forces of nature (erosion, exhaustion, sodification, or by its becoming either arid or water-logged). The same effect may be brought about if those pursuing geological research, mining or other such work, having finished their work, fail to restore the area or to make provision for its further utilization. The earth can be polluted by waste materials as well as by other means.

Endangering the *water* may refer to surface and subterranean water (mineral and medicinal waters), as well as to river beds. The contamination and harmful pollution of water are the chief manifestations. This pollution occurs if measures to prevent the contamination of water are not taken when certain kinds of material are transported by water, or are stored, handled or used near water. The operation of machines, ships and oil rigs, may also contaminate or pollute water.

Harmful pollution of the *air* may occur in the course of mining, industrial, construction, agricultural or other activities, unless a method or process has been used which prevents air pollution or reduces it to a tolerable level. There are kinds of fuel, motor vehicles, machines, heating and other equipment whose operation particularly endangers human environment. It is characteristic of them, that they emit large quantities of air-polluting substances (gas, chemical and radioactive material, dust, soot, smoke, etc.) and stench.

It is natural that man should endeavour to save his environment from all kinds of damage that may harm his health or impair his general well-being. Moreover, society expects governments to lay down basic rules to protect human environment in order to protect man's health, and to bring about a systematic improvement of the living conditions both of the present generation and of future ones. It is the task of *environmental protection* to promote the defense of human environment, to recognize the causes of pollution and other damage, to establish and to enforce the means and conditions by which harmful effects can be prevented, reduced or eliminated in order to protect the interests of society.

The significance of environmental protection is also indicated by the attention paid to it by the UN. The decision made in 1970 about "International Development Strategy" emphasized that national and international efforts should be intensified "to arrest the deterioration of the human environment and to take measures towards its improvement, and to promote activities that will help maintain the *ecological balance* on which human survival depends."* In 1972 the UN staged a conference on questions of human environment.** In the same year the United Nations Environment Programme (UNEP) was set out and in 1974 a foundation was established.*** In 1976 a conference was held on human settlement.° It should be added that the 1976 UN report on "The Future of the World Economy" (the so-called Leontief model) was also based on a paper dealing with the environmental aspects of future world economy.°°

* International Development Strategy: Action Programme of the General Assembly for the Second United Nations Development Decade. United Nations publication, Sales No. E. 71. a.2, para. 72.

** Report of the United Nations Conference on the Human Environment. United Nations publications, Sales No. E.72. II.A.14.

*** International Habitat and Human Settlements Foundation. General Assembly Resolution 3327. XXIX.

° United Nations Conference on Human Settlements (Habitat). Assembly Resolutions 3001 XXVII and 3128 XXVIII.

°° The Future of the World Economy. United Nations, 1976. Department of Economic and Social Affairs. The Report was prepared by a research team lead by A. P. Carter, Wassily Leontief and Peter Petri.

The Leontief model is an experiment to establish the costs of environmental protection on a world-wide basis. Basically, the model establishes the costs according to regions from the point of view of their economy. Table 34 offers information on the proportion of environmental protection investments within total investments, while Table 35 gives information about the share of the GDP costs taken up by environmental protection.

Table 34

Capital stock of abatement sector (CAB) and its share in total capital stock (% CT)

	1970		1980		1990		2000	
	CAB	%CT	CAB	%CT	CAB	%CT	CAB	%CT
North America	77.5	3.4	121.9	3.4	156.0	3.0	191.7	2.5
Latin America Medium	0.0	0.0	4.3	1.5	8.8	1.3	38.4	2.3
Latin America Low	0.0	0.0	0.0	0.0	0.0	0.0	6.0	1.0
Western Europe High	35.9	2.7	67.2	3.2	107.9	3.1	160.6	3.2
Western Europe Medium	1.2	1.1	2.4	1.1	5.6	1.1	21.3	1.8
USSR	9.9	1.3	38.9	2.8	87.4	3.1	125.3	2.6
Eastern Europe	3.5	1.2	13.8	2.7	28.8	3.1	40.8	2.9
Asia Centrally Planned	0.0	0.0	0.0	0.0	0.0	0.0	0.0	0.0
Japan	8.6	2.8	23.7	3.6	45.9	3.9	70.0	3.9
Asia Low	0.0	0.0	0.0	0.0	0.0	0.0	0.0	0.0
Middle East	0.0	0.0	1.9	1.2	0.0	0.0	39.8	1.9
Arid Africa	0.0	0.0	0.0	0.0	0.0	0.0	0.0	0.0
Tropical Africa	0.0	0.0	0.0	0.0	0.0	0.0	0.0	0.0
Southern Africa	0.3	0.9	0.6	1.2	1.3	1.1	5.8	2.0
Oceania	1.7	2.1	4.0	3.1	8.9	3.6	10.4	2.5

Table 35

Current costs of abatement and their share in GDP ($ billions)

	1970		1980		1990		2000	
	Share	%	Share	%	Share	%	Share	%
North America	8.5	0.80	13.5	0.877	17.2	0.829	21.2	0.780
Latin America Medium	0.0	0.0	0.05	0.244	1.0	0.245	4.1	0.461
Latin America Low	0.0	0.0	0.0	0.0	0.0	0.0	0.6	0.198
Western Europe High	3.9	0.533	7.2	0.690	11.5	0.709	17.2	0.793
Western Europe Medium	0.1	0.179	0.3	0.194	0.6	0.216	2.3	0.399
USSR	1.1	0.247	4.2	0.554	9.4	0.683	13.4	0.670
Eastern Europe	0.4	0.229	1.5	0.538	3.1	0.641	4.3	0.635
Asia Centrally Planned	0.0	0.0	0.0	0.0	0.0	0.0	0.0	0.0
Japan	0.9	0.465	2.5	0.678	4.9	0.830	7.5	0.895
Asia Low	0.0	0.0	0.0	0.0	0.0	0.0	0.0	0.0
Middle East	0.0	0.0	0.2	0.149	0.0	0.0	4.3	0.436
Arid Africa	0.0	0.0	0.0	0.0	0.0	0.0	0.0	0.0
Tropical Africa	0.0	0.0	0.0	0.0	0.0	0.0	0.0	0.0
Southern Africa	0.0	0.164	0.1	0.222	0.1	0.219	0.6	0.418
Oceania	0.2	0.421	0.4	0.671	0.9	0.858	1.1	0.689

The following points should be made about the costs of environmental protection included in the table. Pollution of the open seas is left out of consideration. It is further assumed that 1970 USA standards can serve as a model. Accordingly, in every region where the gross product *per capita* (at 1970 value) is over $ 2,000, the US standards of 1970 are to be applied. In these regions pollution is to be reduced to the level obtained in the USA in 1970; thereafter abatement activities should be increased in such a way as to keep net emissions of pollutants down to the 1970 level. The regions falling into this category are North America, Western Europe, Japan and Oceania.

It was assumed that for regions in the $ 700 to $ 2,000 *per capita* income bracket, which in 1970 included all other developed and medium income regions, the proportion abated ought to be equal to half of the USA figure for 1970. According to the study, two of these regions, namely the Soviet Union and Eastern Europe, would reach US abatement standards by 1980; in the other regions concerned progress in pollution abatement would be significantly lower.

For regions with a gross product of less than $ 700 *per capita*, no environmental protection costs were envisaged. This was based on the assumption that pollution does not, as a rule, present serious problems at the stage of development in question, except for certain industrial and urban centres. Should any country at this level of *per capita* income feel it necessary to proceed with pollution abatement, it would have to consider the trade-off between less pollution and faster development. In 1970 all of the developing regions fell into this purely hypothetical "no-abatement" category. It was found that some of them, mainly the oil producing countries of Latin America, the Middle East and Africa would have to introduce pollution abatement activities as early as 1980.

Wastefree technologies

When evaluating the Leontief model, it should be borne in mind that pollution abatement equipment is not always completely efficient. Not all pollutants would be eliminated in the processes of abatement. The authors of the paper point out that the processes aimed at eliminating pollution from air and water at present leave 1 per cent pollution in air and about 20 per cent in water. Although technologies for pollution abatement are being developed rapidly, no abatement processes are as yet commercially available against many pollutants (e.g. sulphur, nitrogen oxides, hydrocarbons, etc.).

A. Arakelyan has drawn attention to the complexity of the problem.* So far, he writes, attention has been focussed only on the abatement of industrial mass gases, the most important pollutants (ashes, sulphur-anhydride, flue gas), although such pollutants as ozonoxide, sulphides, organic detergents, aldehyds, which ,though becoming more and more invisible and imperceptible, are much more dangerous, ought to be fought against. Numerous bacteria (among them harmful ones) grow and survive in hot, concentrated acid solutions and even multiply in them. At the same time it is impossible to dissolve or disperse certain substances which enter environment. Inevitably they accumulate and their accumulation alters the environment in a way harmful to human beings. The danger lies not only in the increasing concentration of certain pollution elements in the environment, but also in the collective effect of some compounds. The interaction of the different substances forms them into new compounds of incomparably greater toxic effect.

It is partly on account of these elements that A. Arakelyan considers it of basic importance that the enormous and constantly increasing input invested in the building

* (Arakelyan, A.) Аракелян, А.: Научно-техническая революция и биосфера (The Scientific-Technical Revolution and Bio-Environs), *Вопросы экономики*,1976, No. 5.

of pollution abatement equipment should be reduced by seeking for and applying such ways of industrial development and laying down such conditions for the purity of the bio-environment as will bring this about. Under the conditions of the scientific–technical revolution the cardinal solution to the problem of the protection of the bio-environment is to change over to technologies based on new principles, technologies that eliminate waste and result in a complex utilization of raw materials.

Although in the West debates are in progress about the radiation damage of nuclear power plants, A. Arakelyan cites nuclear power plants as "clean" in order to prove that the scientific–technical revolution will create the conditions under which the pollution of the natural environment can be conquered. Energy plants all over the world consume a tremendous amount of oxygen and emit into the atmosphere 200–250 million of airborne particles and sulphur-anhydride. By 2000 the amount of such waste will have risen to 1.5 milliard tons and 400 million tons respectively. Nuclear power plants do not require oxygen, nor do they pollute the environment with slag, sulphur and other waste materials. Moreover, he writes, several years' experience gained during the operation of the Novovorezhen nuclear power plant has demonstrated, by means of monitoring the content of the atmosphere within a radius of 50 km, that radioactive concentration within the zone of the nuclear power plant is on the admittable level of radioactivity and has not reached even 1% of what is considered "safe" for those working at the power plant.

In general A. Arakelyan considers that plants built on the principle of wastefree technologies will become the plants of the future. He considers this important also in relation to the elimination of the waste of natural resources. He points out that, e.g. in non-ferrous metallurgy (even in case of the richest ores) 99% of the extracted rock is discarded. Moreover, losses are inevitable during the further processing of the extracted metals (copper, molybden, etc.). The finished industrial product represents only 2% of the weight of the raw material, i.e. 98% of this material is not utilized but becomes waste, and as such pollutes the environment.

The only debatable point in A. Arakelyan's argument is in relation to the costs of the new technology. According to him, the enterprises working with wastefree production technologies as well as the complex processing of raw materials can bring about a considerable increase in the efficiency of investments and reduce the cost of constructing valuable pollution abatement equipment. A complex processing of a raw material within one enterprise is always cheaper than the manufacture of the same raw material by different enterprises producing the same products. Moreover, wastefree technologies will do away with the danger of environment pollution.

If this is so, the spread of wastefree technologies should be carried out more vigorously. However, "traditional" technologies are subject not only to the compulsory construction of expensive abatement equipment, but environmental protection also raises barriers to an economical location of industry. Remedies designed to protect the *environment of settlements* are continually being suggested. They provide increased protection for all areas where human beings live and work, and they are intended to provide an environment which is both aesthetic and suited to proper use. Where such protective measures are enforced, works or establishments can be constructed or may continue to operate only if they do not have a harmful effect on the life of the population. That is to say, it is forbidden:

– to cause harmful or dangerous noise and other vibrations (light, percussion), radioactivity, heat, etc.;

– to operate machines, engines, motor vehicles and other means of transport which cause harmful noise or produce dangerous vibrations.

– The operation of motor vehicles and other means of conveyance can be restricted;
– waste is to be stored, handled, treated, etc. only in places and ways specifically provided for the purpose.

These restrictions mean that environments that would otherwise be considered most economical locations for new industries have to be left out of consideration; or else that plants can only be established in such locations if technologies that increase specific costs are applied. It is also to be borne in mind that when "settlement environment" is given greater protection, usually protective zones or protective distances are also created.

The question also arises in cases when profitability, taken in the narrow sense, regulates the applied technology, whether slag could be thrown into the pit-tip or chemicals could find their way into the air through chimneys, etc., if their utilization were profitable under the given price (cost) conditions. It is hardly conceivable that this would be allowed to continue. On the other hand, if wastefree technologies are to be introduced because of increasing environmental pollution, then the demand to establish price relations in accordance with this is fully justified.

Humanized technologies

The introduction of wastefree technologies is a significant advance not only from the point of environmental protection but also of the humanization of the production process. This is so, because the more serious cases of unskilled labour are connected, *inter alia,* with handling material within the plant. Of course the task of humanizing production in plant and in business organization is a much more comprehensive one. More and more attention is being devoted to these questions by different countries.*

The most important elements in the self-realization of man can be summarized as follows: the need for creative work, continuous training, development of all sides of one's personality, abundant opportunity for contact with nature and for widening one's horizons. This can be achieved throughout society if such new communities can be created in the places of work as will react dynamically to the requirements of social development and so induce the members of the community to develop. However, this form of community can predominate only when society has created the adequate conditions needed for a cultured way of life, when leisure time has grown considerably, when elementary and higher education is available for everybody, and when hierarchical forms can be disregarded.

Once man has succeeded in devising the complex techniques required to deal with problems of environment pollution, progress may be made towards humanizing technology, so that work may be carried out creatively and without danger to health. It goes without saying that the processes of mechanization and humanization do not necessarily go hand in hand. The trend of technical development may on occasions be to the advantage of the labour force, but in some instances it may be adversely affected.

* Various analyses are pursued in Hungary within the framework of the National Committee for Technical Development. Most of the papers are prepared under György S. Szakasits's coordination. Cf. in particular the following papers of the NCTD: A tudományos-technikai forradalom és társadalmi feltételei (Scientific–technical revolution and its social conditions), 1971; A hosszú távú gazdaságfejlesztés műszaki politikájának irányelvei (Guiding principles of the policy of technology in long-term economic development), 1973; A munkaerő alkalmazkodása az új technikához (Adaptation of labour force to new technologies), 1976. In the following we rely mostly upon these papers.

In general, the *conveyor belt system of production* has a negative effect upon workers. Rigid specialization compels the worker to perform a single, repetitive action over a prolonged period and this is harmful both to his physical and psychological health. Any type of mechanization which causes increased boredom and nervous tension and which demands continuous concentration is abhorrent to the worker.

The humanization of technology can be brought about by a *complex process of mechanization,* by the use of *automation* and the introduction of *computers.* The effect upon labour of complex mechanization and automation is basically favourable; these methods reduce, or in many cases eliminate, the need for manual labour. They integrate work processes and crafts and bring to the fore occupations requiring multiple skills and advanced training. They enlarge the worker's sphere of activity and gradually cause the worker confined to a narrowly specialized field to be replaced by the all-rounder. A further advantage of automation is that it not only increases the safety of the individual worker, but is beneficial also to the safety and efficiency of the whole organization. All the above relates to the introduction of computers, when, in the first instance, routine work and routine decisions become computerized. Once technology has been humanized, man is needed only at the stage when decisions are to be made in the knowledge of human and social requirements.

However, as far as one can see, complex mechanization, automation and computerization do not entirely remove the chief obstacle to the humanization of man's relationship with technology, and that is the plight of the unskilled worker. Technical development which takes place in this way will increase the creative character of work for only a section of the workers; the remainder will still be condemned to non-creative, monotonous, routine work, which is often both physically and mentally taxing. In addition, automation creates certain new elements of alienation. It separates workers from the work process and from one another. The distance between places of work increases, and it becomes more difficult to establish contact between workers, thus arousing in them a feeling of alienation.

Some additional comments should be made at this point.

1. A. Arakelyan has drawn our attention to the possibilities inherent in the radical transformation of technologies. As a result of the scientific–technical revolution, labour-consuming processes will gradually be transformed into electrophysical, electrochemical, ultrasonic, electron radiation, biological and other up-to-date technologies. Nevertheless it cannot be said that all questions relating to the humanization of production have already been clarified. It is fallacious to suggest that the technical sciences have already reached the stage necessary for such a transformation and that the only impediment is the "capacity" of the economy.

It is not at all easy to create harmony between man, machine and the natural environment.

Ergonomy, *the science of the rational use of energy,* requires not only technical expertise and practical experience but must also draw on the knowledge of the social scientists. In principle every working tool is produced for the use of man, with the intention of making man's life easier. From this point of view technical development may be said to be for the benefit of humanity. But one must not ignore those aspects of technical development which are profit-oriented and which may be harmful to human beings.

2. At present and in the foreseeable future the main trends of technical development will be dictated by the struggle *between capitalism and socialism.* In the nature of things socialist societies will tend to lay emphasis on those aspects of technical development which will be beneficial to the workers. At the same time they are anxious to attain the economic level of the industrially developed capitalist countries.

This means that they cannot forego the application of manufacturing technologies which ensure relatively quick economic growth; nor can they entirely ignore the evolution of technology in industrially developed capitalist societies. In other words, for some time to come, the trend of technical development will be dictated by the need to increase commodity production. These trends will be largely determined by the profit motive except in those instances where governments choose to pursue fiscal and economic policies contrary to that motive.

3. In the nineteenth century the extent of mechanization was regulated by the framework of commodity production and by the maximization of profit. These were the criteria which controlled both the choice of development strategy and the pace of its advance. This must always be borne in mind when judging the effect of mechanization on production costs. It is not technical development *per se* that reduces specific input but rather that the competition inherent in a market economy requires that even technical development be considered from this standpoint. One imagines that in such a case there is considerable social mobility and that the economy is capable of adapting to changing conditions.

If the emphasis is on the human aspects of mechanization, the picture obtained is quite different. Under conditions of commodity production efficiency, that is to say profit, is the most important criterion of technical development—and this criterion does not necessarily coincide with the principle of humanization. If technical development is approached from the point of view of social need and the increasing demands of society, priority may be given to those trends of development which have been ousted by the profit motive from consideration as realistic possibilities. It is not surprising therefore that those who consider humanization the most important element in the development of the process of production may reach a point where they will discard commodity production itself. And, indeed, if, in the production process, products are to be manufactured as commodities, if demand is to be met by means of commodity exchange, then those technical developments on which the process of humanization depends cannot be consistently achieved.

To avoid any misunderstanding, it should be emphasized that it has been in commodity production that the tendency towards complex mechanization, automation and computerization has emerged. Moreover, the possibilities commodity production can offer are as yet far from being exhausted. At the same time, humanization in the sphere of production pre-supposes the presence of such stabilizing factors as cannot be ensured by market processes alone. Thus government market control and a conscious constraint of market automatism based thereon seem to be important.

The development of man–machine systems within the general process of the scientific–technical revolution can be controlled by various means. One method is to define the four phases of development as follows:

- simple, manual systems;
- single circuit systems at a basic level;
- closed-loop control systems;
- machine systems with automatic computerized control.

If one considers the situation from this standpoint, it is clear that the scientific–technical revolution is only in its initial stages in the industrially less developed countries. The trend is mainly in the direction of a change-over from simple, manual systems to single-circuit ones at a basic level; the introduction of semi-automatic technologies is much less widespread. Variations among the industrially developed countries will only be found in the degree of progress achieved.

It appears that the solution of problems of ergonomy will become of paramount importance rather in the twenty-first century than in the twentieth. One is forced to draw this conclusion particularly if one believes that humanization is an all-embracing process which covers both the institutional system of social economy and the question of the relationship between human beings. One is thus led to consider the hierarchical structure of society and, inevitably, the process of bureaucratization, which it is difficult to reconcile with human self-realization.

It is not intended to suggest that consideration of the problems of the humanization of technologies is untimely, but one must put the problem in a realistic framework. Those who are dealing with problems of technical development and plant organization are aware of a progressive increase in social expectations, and also of the fact that time and again this process produces new demands. In consequence of the rising expectations of society a host of problems, varying from production under the shift-system to labour safety, require to be kept continually in mind and dealt with in a manner acceptable to society. Specific input is increased by the need to re-assess these problems with the advance in technology. It is, however, assumed that these additional costs can be met due to the increased efficiency brought about by technical development.

4. Improving the prospects of future generations

Rationality and wasteful management

Millions of decisions are made in economic life every day. Most of them are routine decisions ensuring the smooth flow and continuity of economic life. But there are also *critical* decisions which must be distinguished from the others. These decisions are meant to alter the established course of economic processes in one way or another. These vital decisions exert their effect on the economy in the long, short or medium run.

At the same time decisions made in the past are a constraint on present decisions, because of the *commitments* which ensue from them. It is, of course, possible to alter previous decisions. Indeed, important decisions taken at present are to some extent a means of adjusting the economy to the changing conditions of development, since action always takes place in a socio-economic environment, whose processes of development are regulated by decisions made at different times and levels, in harmony with—or perhaps even contradictory to—one another. This background must be taken into consideration when new decisions are made.

In the following paragraphs we shall direct our attention to important long-term decisions, and in particular to those which have a bearing on the relationship *between generations*. We are considering the relationship between generations as part of a system of long-term decisions, although in economic life the transition from one generation to the other takes place gradually. This interpretation is justified in at least two respects: (1) In individual families the shift of generations is adjusted to the life-cycle and depends on whether the previous generation has bequeathed goods to the new one and if so to what extent. (2) In the system of state and social institutions the transition from one generation to another is based on differentiating between the present and the future. Whoever takes part in decision-making bearing on the future, and in particular on the remote future, is aware of the fact that he is determining the course of economic processes for generations to come.

The concept of *rationality* expresses both the *lex minimi* and the requirement that the present generation should not achieve economic results at the expense of future generations. In its capacity as *lex minimi*, economic rationality treats productive factors so that they will ensure maximum results for a given total input. Accordingly, we assume that the production factors (labour, land, capital) can be substituted one for the other in the production process and we assume also that those who are interested in results will bring about the association of production factors by minimizing costs. But the requirements of rationality can be met by minimizing costs only if the relative price of factors of production provides an appropriate environment for economic decisions. In this case minimum specific costs are equated with optimum social benefits. Elements of irrationality will appear in an economy managed less efficiently.

Irrationality indicates that society gives up a part of the utility it could have achieved if the *lex minimi* had prevailed. The impression is thus given that irrationality is the responsibility of the generation that has committed the mistake. Indeed, this is often the case if today's irrationality impairs future prospects. But when we investigate the harmful effect of present-day irrationalities on future generations, we think of the specific manifestations that can be best brought to a common denominator by wasteful management.

Wasteful management results from enforcing the principle of the *lex minimi* by wasting the factors of production that are at the disposal of society. In one way or another present irrationalities will have an adverse effect on the economic conditions which future generations will inherit. And yet, if we are thinking in terms of rationality in the long run, we distinguish, within all the scarce productive factors available to society, the unrenewable *natural resources from all the others*. When reference is made to wasteful management within irrationality, the implication is that the present generation is wasting exhaustible natural resources.

Of course the borderline is not so clear. We cannot narrow down possible cases of wasteful management to the sphere of minerals. For instance, it would be considered wasteful management if, e.g. in forestry, woodfelling were carried out more quickly than afforestation could produce new growth. In the sphere of non-renewable natural resources anything which disturbs or indeed undermines the biological balance is considered wasteful management. These examples of wasteful management call attention to elements of irrationality, which, through *biological processes,* eventually cause damage that may not be reversed at a later stage.

Economic growth and its possible acceleration are of utmost importance in decision-making on economic policy. This is so not only because the developing nations are intent on catching up with the industrially developed countries, but because the antagonism and struggle between capitalism and socialism also cause priority to be given to these objectives. The socialist countries want to catch up with and to leave behind the industrially most developed capitalist countries, in terms of both *per capita* production as well as in the level of the efficiency of labour. On the other hand, industrially developed capitalist countries want to retain the advantages they have gained in the past in the development of productive forces, and, if possible, even to increase them. We are living in an era of challenge, which concentrates powers, never known before, upon developing productive forces both quantitatively and qualitatively.

Arising out of all this the need for natural resources has steadily increased and the demand for these resources grows year by year. This gives rise to the question as to whether we are not exhausting too quickly these natural resources which cannot be regenerated.

A manifesto signed by "A Natural Scientist" and entitled "A Blueprint for Survival" appeared in the January 1972 issue of *The Ecologist*. It states that unless economic growth and population increase are halted, famine, pollution and the exhaustion of raw material reserves will ruin the world. The manifesto was based on the results of

Dennis Meadows's research.* Its essence can be summarized as follows: if the present world trends of population growth, pollution and raw material consumption continue, a collapse of the economic system of the world will be inevitable by the middle of the next century. One of the reasons for this is the *exhaustion of non-renewable raw material resources.* According to the Club of Rome the situation would be the same even if all known reserves of raw materials could be doubled, or if, by perfecting the methods of recycling materials, the quantity of raw materials needed for one unit of industrial production could be reduced to a quarter under conditions of exponential utilization of raw materials. All this could only delay the debacle by a matter of years or perhaps decades. That is why they advise mankind consciously to restrict growth, the "0 growth" considered to be a state of equilibrium.

Robert Malthus already foresaw the disaster of over-population more than a century and a half ago. His law is as follows: mankind is increasing at the rate of geometrical progression (1, 2, 4, 8, etc.) whilst food supply at the rate of arithmetic progression (1, 2, 3, 4, etc.)** However, most of the economists have rejected the theory of the Club of Rome, in the same way as they earlier rejected Robert Malthus's hypothesis.***

Maximization of long-term returns

Whatever one's opinion of the theses of the Club of Rome is, the extent to which present-day economists "re-discover" land, as a factor of production, to be reckoned with as a barrier to economic growth cannot escape attention. G. M. Heal° explained this by poiting out that in the 1930s, when the theory of decision alternatives emerged, attention was focussed on the wrong utilization of the labour potential at the disposal of society. Later, during the war and in the post-war period, a relative scarcity of capital appeared to be the most substantial barrier to economic growth. In this century, particularly in its first third, natural resources, especially supplies of minerals, did not seem to be an important problem for industrialized countries. They either possessed their own resources or else could import unlimited quantities from developing countries: initially because they controlled these countries as parts of the colonial system, and later because—although these countries became independent—they needed foreign exchange so badly that they could not do without unlimited export to their principal—and often only—export partners.

H. Hotelling's paper demonstrates the great importance of land in processes of income distribution in the 18th and 19th centuries.°° At the time of the industrial revolution decisions of settlement, etc. in England were greatly influenced by natural factors. In general it would have been unthinkable for anyone in the 19th century to

* Supported by the Club of Rome, Dennis Meadows convened in the M.I.T. a group of scientists and scholars to study for two years long-term global problems. Their work resulted in three books:

The Limits to Growth, Universe Books, New York, 1972 (by D. H. Meadows–J. Randers–W. Behrens);

Towards Global Equilibrium, Wright-Allen Press, Cambridge, Mass., 1973 (co-edited with D. H. Meadows);

The Dynamics of Growth in a Finite World, Wright-Allen Press, Cambridge, Mass., 1974 (co-edited with D. H. Meadows).

** Malthus, Rh. R.: *An Essay on the Principle of Population,* 1803.

*** Baade, Fr.: *Der Wettlauf zum Jahre 2000,* Gerhard Stalling Verlag, 1961, 2nd edition.

° Heal, G. M.: Economics and Resources. Economics Seminar Paper Series, 1975/11, University of Sussex.

°° Hotelling, H.: The Economics of Exhaustible Resources, *Journal of Political Economy,* No. 4, 1931.

discuss economic dynamism or to analyse the process of production without paying particular attention to natural resources. And yet, this was the very thing economists of the 20th century did for several decades. To summarize: the change in economic and social conditions directed attention in the 19th century to land; in the first four decades of the 20th century to labour; in the two decades following this to capital —whereas, in our own time natural resources are again coming to the fore.

In the light of all this, we must find the answer to the question: what can be considered *the optimum rate of extraction?* This is clearly necessary from the standpoint of *the economics of business* management. When a new source of mineral supply is discovered, two questions must be clarified. The first is whether or not the mineral can be extracted. This can be examined by comparing costs and world market prices. The other is to determine the extraction capacity. The capacity yields the optimum by which in the long run maximum global results can be reached. This can be calculated nominally and by discounting.

Long-term results calculated by discounting express the annual nominal results with a determined factor (rate of interest) in terms of its *present (in situ)* results. Or, to put it more precisely, long-term results can be calculated nominally or with discounting and, in the latter case, with a lower or higher rate of interest. In their function the *in situ* value of a given mineral resource is different. The value is highest if the long-term results are calculated nominally; or, in other words, the higher the interest rate of discount, the smaller the value.

Miklós Tóth dealt in great detail with *in situ* value calculations and with questions of economic rationality connected with it.* At the author's request Miklós Tóth prepared the economic model shown here. Say, we have four sources of identical capacity and useful life, but, on account of differences in natural endowment, extraction takes place with differing results (profits). (For simplicity's sake the sources are grouped in twos):

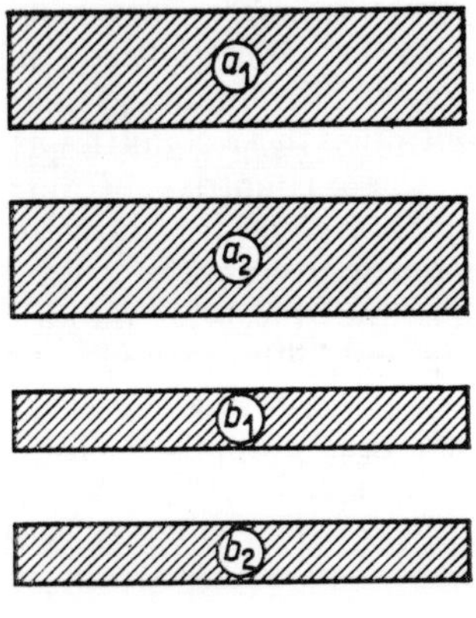

Suppose that in order to meet demands, two sources are always to be utilized at a time; suppose further that the utilization of the resources—irrespective of time—occurs at an identical technical level in every case—that is, that the technical level does not influence the annual profit of the different sources; then the following three basic combinations of utilization are possible:

* Tóth, M.: Az ásványvagyon-gazdálkodási és ásványvagyon-védelmi döntéselőkészítések rendszertani alapjai (Foundations of the taxonomics for preparing decision-making for management and protection of mineral resources), *Bányászat*, Budapest, No. 7, 1975, pp. 449–456.

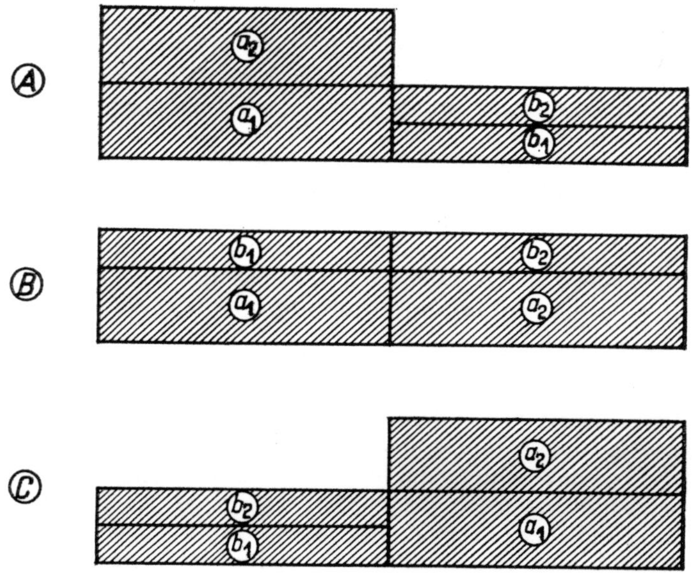

By comparing the three combinations we can observe the following:

1. The nominal value of every possible global result is similar in all the three combinations.
2. Whatever the discount factor we calculate with, combination *A* ensures the maximum result at present values.
3. The higher the discount factor with which we calculate the present value of all possible global results, the more favourable, relatively, combination *A* will be.
4. Common sense will discard combination *C* as a matter of course.
5. If we want to use half of the result that can be achieved in the first period according to combination *B* for consumption in case *A* too, then—as demonstrated by the model—about 65% more can be devoted to the technical development of sources b_1 and b_2, whose turn comes in the second period. Thus they may even achieve results surpassing the present result of sources a_1 and a_2. But in case of the *A* combination, even if half of the higher profit attainable in case of *A* is used for consumption—as we should do in case of combination *B*— considerably more (over 30% more according to the model) can be spent from the higher profit upon the technical development of sources b_1 and b_2.

Whether we calculate nominally or with discounts, the optimum utilization of natural resources is gained if we make use, first of all, of the *favourable endowments of natural resources.* If the *present generation* proceeds in this way, it will not in any way discriminate against *tomorrow's generation.* To utilize favourably located natural resources is not only the present generation's right, it is also its *duty* because in this way it will be able to create the technical basis by which to overcome the problems associated with natural resources which are less favourably located.

Finally, there are two conditions on which one may presume optimum exhaustion. One is that an earlier extraction of favourably located natural resources should not destroy the possibility of later extraction of resources worthy of exploitation.

The second is that the rate of extraction should not exceed the optimum for the location in question. This is generally 1/30 per year of the quantity suitable for extraction. If one or other of these two conditions is not fulfilled it may happen that the discounted value of the long-term global results will be higher if the more favourable resources are given priority. This may occur chiefly when calculations are made at a high discount rate.*

But what is the answer on a macro-economic level? At any rate one requirement can be formulated: priority should be given to all investments that promote rationality in processing and utilization as against investments devoted to expanding extraction, in case the costs of the former are smaller than the marginal costs of the extraction of natural resources which may be expected in the long run.

The optimum rate of accumulation and its pattern

There is not always freedom of decision with respect to discounts. If the owner of a bill of exchange wants to obtain money before its maturity, he can achieve this only by discounting. The discounting bank will calculate the interest for the time till its maturity from the amount indicated on the bill of exchange. When debts bear interest, the amount of this interest is capitalized and added to the debt, and the figure calculated in this way is reduced according to the discounted interest rate. What applies on the creditor's side applies also on that of the debtor. Economic decisions based on borrowed money can—as a general rule—only be based on the assumption that by using the borrowed money—or even independently of it—the position of the debtor will improve in a manner that will enable him not only to repay the money but also to pay interest on it.

Quite independent of this is the other question of how to evaluate future results in comparison with those of the present. This is no longer a creditor–debtor relationship but the relationship of society with future generations or else the individual's relationship with his own future. The responsibility of any generation to the future is, when all is said and done, not connected with discounting but with the *saving of a proportion of income*. The improving economic prospects of succeeding generations are based on the fact that previous generations have reserved a part of the value produced, or have spent it on developing productive forces—that is to say on future, consumption—instead of consuming it.

Ramsey's paper about a mathematical theory of saving is worthy of attention.** Ramsey's mathematical model examines the optimum share of saving, or, more exactly, seeks to find the answer to the question how the *optimum share for accumulation and for consumption from the national income can be established*. The mathematical formula is based on the following hypothesis: the rate of saving multiplied by the marginal utility of money should always be equal to the amount by which the total net rate of enjoyment of utility falls short of the maximum possible rate of enjoyment. In his opinion: the more we save, the sooner we shall reach happiness. In conformity with this view is Ramsey's opinion of excessive consumption, which arises when the

* To study the optimum extraction rate see also:
Beckman, H. J.: A Note on Growth with Exhaustible Resources.
Dasgupta, P. S.–Heal, G. M.: The Optimal Depletion of Exhaustible Resources.
Stiglitz, J. E.: Growth with Exhaustible Resources, *Review of Economic Studies*, Symposium on Exhaustible Resources, January, 1975.
Rawls, J.: *A Theory of Justice*, Oxford University Press, 1973.

** Ramsey, F. P.: A Mathematical Theory of Saving, *The Economic Journal*, Vol. XXXVIII, 1928, pp. 543–599.

accumulation desired cannot be ensured. There is no necessity to give a critical analysis of the simplified suppositions under which Ramsey formulated his mathematical theory. It is even questionable whether it is possible to quantify the optimum saving rate unequivocally on the basis of the model he expounded.

Opinions about the optimum rate of savings may differ, depending on which factors among those which determine the rate, we give priority. The probable increase of population constitutes a reason for increased saving, as does the possibility that future inventions will increase happiness to a degree not envisaged at present. On the other hand, the probability that future inventions and improvements in organization are likely to make income obtainable with less sacrifice than at present is a reason for saving less.

When all is said and done it matters little whether the individual saves when he is young to provide against reduction of income in old age, or whether he saves in order also to leave something to his successors. The essential point is the peculiar pattern of the productive organization of society, which from the outset harmonizes the present lower level of consumption with its future higher level. The management of economy cannot be separated from social savings; economic policy (or the interest rate) can only influence their extent.

When one comes to study the capitalist market economy and the socialist planned economy in regard to the optimum measure of saving, it is clear that they differ. In a capitalist market economy the interest rate determines the rate of savings, assuming a balanced development of the economy. In a socialist planned economy the government can restrict the function of prices and thus also the role of the interest rate in determining the proportion in which the national income is divided between consumption and accumulation. The savings rate is determined by government planning, in which priority is given to political considerations. In the interest of the future, political considerations may cause restrictions to be imposed which are independent of the individual's inclination to save or of the economic criteria on which individuals make their economic decisions. One must bear all this in mind when discussing the problem of the savings ratio in comparing different socio-economic systems. It is characteristic of socialist societies in particular that, in the course of the development of the productive forces, there is a general tendency for

– the share in the total quantity of production of sectors manufacturing means of production to increase as does

– the share of costs allocated from the national income to research and development.

The sciences (the training of cadres and the technical–research basis) are productive forces. Investigations conducted by UN and by other international organizations have established the connexion between effective economic growth and the efficient allocation of inputs to research and development. In the period before the Second World War the average annual economic growth in West Europe was 2%. In the decades following the Second World War it was about 5% and this rate only declined in the 1970s. The acceleration of economic growth is explained by the fact that, prior to the Second World War, countries spent only a few per mille of the national income on research and development, whereas after the Second World War this amount rose to 2–3%. One may assume from these calculations that research and development activities together account for about 50% of economic growth.

Input for research and development is higher than is indicated in the budgets of various countries. These figures do not contain the "external" costs of the manufacture of individual machines, although considerable intellectual and innovative activity lies behind their production and, indeed, the manufacture of individual machines represents a considerable share in the output of the engineering industry. Nor do reports indicate accelerated depreciation, although accumulation and the process of modernizing production appearing in this way is considerable.

Countries are attempting to create and maintain a research and development basis suitable

- for research into international scientific–technical progress on a large scale;
- for adapting such advances as can be integrated into the national economy;
- for spreading research and development culture;
- for maintaining and even strengthening the competitiveness of their industries on an international scale.

In the nature of things, the spread of research and development activity brings about certain changes in the relationship of research work to the organization of production. The foundation of research activity is threefold: basic, applied, and development research. These are connected partly directly and partly indirectly with production. Not even in the sphere of applied research can the input be exactly assessed according to products. It is in general difficult to consider research costs as production costs, unless research is pursued within the enterprise itself or in research establishments financed by it (designing bureaux, experimental laboratories, etc.).

Mineral supply

Both the improving mineral supply and the systematically improving conditions for the extraction of minerals demonstrate that the present generation manages the economy efficiently not by austerity but by an optimum accumulation of the national income produced, using appropriate means to achieve this end and paying increasing attention to the establishment of the research and development basis. Mankind seems to have been able to avoid grave mistakes in this field so far. But how can we judge the future of mineral supply?

In spite of a marked increase in consumption, the known stocks of most raw materials have increased greatly since 1950:

- that of iron ore eleven times;
- that of chromium six–seven times;
- that of crude oil 5.7 times.

In spite of the fact that the earth's crust contains relatively little tin and lead as compared with other ores, the known stocks will last 20 years, just as they were expected to do 40–50 years ago.*

N. Sazykin provides a valuable survey of the minerals available in the earth. According to it, stocks—if the level of extraction and utilization of the mid-seventies is maintained—will in general be sufficient for 30–40 years, but certain minerals will last for several hundred years. There are only a couple of materials of which a scarcity (bottleneck) might appear in the 20th century.**

* B. Varon: Enough of Everything for Everyone, Forever? *Finance and Development*, No. 10, 1975.

** (Sazykin, N.) Сазыкин, Н.: Минеральные ресурсы, проблемы и перспективы (Mineral resources: problems and perspectives), *Вопросы экономики*, No. 1, 1974, pp. 26–36.

The technologies of mining, of enriching and processing mineral raw materials are systematically improving. By this means the production costs of mineral raw materials decrease, and the efficiency of extraction and utilization improves. A good example of this is the trend of open-cast mining and that of technical development of mining in very deep locations—methods that are basically different from traditional ones. As a consequence of the basic development of mining and processing technologies, the quantity of the raw minerals in question may increase substantially in such cases.

The development of the technology of alumina production may, e.g. bring into the range of aluminium ores materials which contain much less aluminium than bauxite, but can be produced—along with shales—in large quantities and with a low input. The fact that materials for nuclear fission may be obtained from desert sands and from sea-water, as well as the circumstance that the uranium isotope 238 can be released, may augment the resources of energy carriers of the world to an almost boundless extent, let alone the possibilities of the utilization of solar energy. Also to be included among the benefits derived from technological development are a complex utilization of certain mineral raw materials and a fuller utilization of certain components, which make extraction more economical.

In the 1970s copper metal was produced from copper resources containing 0.5% ore at lower costs in real value (i.e. compared to the prices of other products) than in the 1850s when the ore content was 5–7%. Why should we suppose that future technical development will not counterbalance the deteriorating quality of extracted raw materials as it did in the past?*

Nor is it certain that the tendency towards deterioration in the quality of raw materials will continue throughout the world in the coming decades. It should be borne in mind that in the past prospecting for and discovery of raw materials was carried out by industrially developed countries. Prospecting is still at an initial stage in the territories of the developing countries.**

According to G. Sazykin barely 5% of the possible stock of a number of minerals has so far been discovered. As regards potential reserves, he emphasizes the following: The perfecting of the methods and technologies of open and of deep level mining, as well as the development of geology and branches of science related to it (particularly physics and chemistry) are consistent with a radical transformation of the whole geological service, which will render possible the finding of further rich deposits. A great many scientific institutions in many countries are engaged in studying the *utilization of the vast resources of the seas of the world.* There is an enormous quantity of iron–manganese particles—their diameter being 0.05–200 mm, or bigger—in these seas. In addition to iron–manganese particles, they also contain copper, cobalt, nickel. Some American experts believe that, in spite of these particles being at great depths (4–5 km), they can be extracted in such a way that the costs of extraction will be no greater than the inputs required for extraction on land.

Of the underwater resources at present only crude oil is extracted in large quantities. At the present time reserves of crude oil at wells in the sea are estimated at 60–150 milliard tons—a quantity which is substantially greater than the stocks of crude oil which have so far been discovered on land. Prospecting in the deep seas is in progress.

* Radetzki, M.: Metal Mineral Resource Exhaustion and the Threat to Material Progress: The Case of Copper, *World Development,* Nos. 2–3, 1975.

** Dobozi, I.: A nemzetközi kitermelőipar szerkezeti változásainak előrejelzése, *MTA Világgazdasági Kutató Intézeti Közlemények* (Forecasting of the structural changes of the international extracting industry. Bulletin of the Research Institute for World Economy of the Hungarian Academy of Sciences), 1976.

Ten years ago drilling for crude oil was carried out to a depth of 15 m; today wells are 180 m deep and progress is being made with experiments for drilling down to a depth of 300 m.

In spite of the fact that vast reserves of mineral resources are available in the seas and oceans, the rise in the rate of extraction from now until the year 2000 will not be rapid except in a few cases. It is doubtful if they will play a considerable role in the world economy with the exception of the extraction of crude oil, natural gas, manganese and bromine, since, basically, extraction of resources on land is less costly than extraction from the sea.

The trend towards improvement in the supply of natural resources will be accelerated by the scientific–technical revolution of the present age. This is a general law of development. The acceleration of development is convincingly demonstrated by the hyperbolic decrease of its duration in prehistoric ages (stone age, copper age, bronze age and iron age). But, an accelerating rate of technical development is also rendered probable by the fact that, whereas mass utilization of coal took place only after several thousand years of heating with wood, mass utilization of hydrocarbons in the supply of energy took only 150 years from the beginning of the use of coal, and scarcely 50 years after hydrocarbons came into general use, nuclear fission is being employed to supply energy.

Labour input—market value—price

In the light of all this, how can one describe the world the present generation will leave as a heritage to the one which follows? A comparison of the present with the general political, social and economic relations of the 19th century seems an obvious starting-point. Basic and manifold changes have taken (and are taking) place.

– World economy today follows more and more a poly- rather than an oligo-centric pattern.

– The economy of nations is developing under conditions of an antagonism and struggle between different socio-economic systems.

– In the competition for accelerated technical development the time factor plays a more important role than the economical use of resources.

– The scarcity of natural resources has brought about a transformation of rationality, which renders possible the minimization of inputs coupled with a waste of resources.

– Policy has rendered the price category more and more to serve levelling; this is the way in which an international re-distribution of national incomes in favour of the developing world may be achieved.

– The relationship between society and economy is changing and this reduces mobility.

– The demand for full employment and a proportionate development of incomes is becoming stronger.

– The expectations of society (the protection of workers and of the environment, improved working conditions, etc.) have altered the demands made upon technology.

The view that the trend of value (price) cannot be determined in this century on the basis of criteria relevant to the previous century, appears justified.

1. *The role of demand in regulating price formation has grown weaker*. An equilibrium price can no longer be considered as a competitive price, as a price on which supply does not exert an influence and the government cannot be considered an exogenous

factor in the economy, indifferent to processes taking place in economic life. New features in the background of value relations could not be explained in the medium of perfect competition devoid of policies. Thus, *a priori* two things are to be supposed: one is that supply enjoys an advantage over demand in the market. The other is the fact that governments, relying on the budget and on its incomes re-distribution function, are not only able to influence price relations in other respects but will actually do so.

The change of the role of the government in becoming an endogenous factor of economy, where previously it was an exogenous one, is one of the main characteristics of the change in the relationship between demand and supply. In socialist societies this new function of the government is an objective concomitant of the nationalization of the means of production. But even in capitalist societies the challenge of socialism makes systematic economic growth and full employment a demand the government has to meet. In the service of these aims economic policy has the effect of enhancing demand and this leads in the first instance to the superiority of supply to demand in the economy.

2. *The connexion between supplementary costs of economic growth and the decrease of the specific costs per unit of product has weakened.* The most important factors in this change are the following:

– The nineteenth century trend towards the spread of the 48 hours' working week has been ousted by a tendency towards a working week of 40–44 hours, or even less.

– In the nineteenth century there was an organic connexion between the productivity of labour and the increase of wages. According to this, wage differentials existed between branches of production, between groups of workers and between occupations. The cheap labour of women and children was a reserve. By contrast, at the present time differentiation of incomes is decreasing and the disparity between industrial and agricultural or between male and female labour is diminishing or being eliminated. There is a growing tendency towards distribution according to work done. It is becoming more and more difficult to bring capitalist private ownership and capitalist economy in general into harmony with these tendencies.

– In the nineteenth century the whole course of technical development was determined by the reduction of specific costs. In our time the emphasis is on a systematic extension of supply and technical development in order to humanize production, even though this increases specific costs in production.

3. *A structural transformation of the GNP is taking place as a result of which the proportion of public goods is increasing and so is that of only partly divisible individual products.* In this connexion the sphere in which the social value of products takes the form of market value is decreasing and in the sphere of products a divergence of market value from social value is becoming apparent.

Only in a socialist society can this structural transformation definitely assert itself, since there the change of commodities into public goods is not based on technical criteria but on criteria of need. And yet, even in capitalist societies one can observe a tendency for socially organized consumption to be extended into spheres (public education, health services, etc.) in which, from a purely technical point of view, the market too, could perform distribution.

The market can evaluate commodities only in relation to participants in the market (producers and consumers). In this sense it is often stated that the market can reflect "internal" effects only and no "external" ones. In the case of wholly divisible commodities the producer's (internal) input coincides with social input, whereas the consumer's (internal) profit corresponds to the social utility of the product. That is, in addition to fully divisible individual products and indivisible public goods there are also products that become commodities, although they are only partly divisible. But the market cannot evaluate only partly divisible commodities in harmony with their social value.

Specialists in the techniques of economic calculations have often drawn attention to the unfavourable position of commodities in this respect. When, e.g. the competition between railways and road traffic is discussed, it is frequently mentioned that in railway traffic the building and maintenance of the rail network are internal factors, whereas in road traffic they are external. It is also well known that in industrial centres industrial capacity can be created with less capital input than in agricultural regions. This is so, because, among other things, the infrastructure is already there in the former, whereas in the latter it can be created only with a certain amount of industrial collaboration. Town planners frequently draw attention to the fact that in over-crowded industrial areas the additional infrastructural investment required for the creation of a new, productive working environment may be several times higher than the investment in the factory itself.

One of the conditions of the concept of socially necessary labour input is that it should reflect the social input of commodity production at the producer's end. This condition is met, if, in the course of producing the product of labour, the use of the social product free of charge does not lead to an exclusion of others, or, if all elements that are preconditions of production are included in the input. These conditions are not always complied with. *Seen from the standpoint of input, external effects are increasingly apparent in the development of productive forces, especially as a result of the scientific–technical revolution.* Under an active research and development policy, acceleration of technical progress is taking place. This activity is supported both directly and indirectly by the government. The more typical this is, the more probable it becomes that the market value of commodities which require basic research will be lower than their value, simply because part of the social input is covered by the budget and does not become part of the production costs.

The partial divisibility of commodities is also expressed in the external effect of utility. When production causes environmental damage, the commodity

– seen from the producer's point of view becomes under-valued (because the input required for environmental protection has been neglected);

– seen from the consumer's point of view its utility becomes over-valued (because social damage has been disregarded).

A condition of the concept of socially necessary labour inputs is that *the product does not reduce the use-value of free goods.* If this condition is not met (because investments in environmental protection have not been made, or else because of a lack of awareness of techniques of environmental protection), the social costs do not correctly reflect the social utility of the product. If an expansion of production leads to an increase in environmental damage, the increase of social utility will lag behind the rate of development as calculated in terms of GNP.

The market value approach to the socially necessary input pre-supposes an adequate foundation of cost interdependencies between economic units. The principle should prevail that nothing should be available in production free of charge which demands a sacrifice on the part of society. However, it is impossible to eliminate external effects completely. These external effects will appear in different degrees depending on the various commodities. That is why the order of importance created by the socially necessary input differs from that which relates to actual labour input; this again differs from the order determined by market values.

As we have seen, the nineteenth century trend towards the decrease of commodity value was connected in many respects with such criteria of the economy as—at least in their pure form—could assert themselves only under conditions of classic capitalism. Consequently, the evaluation of future trends of commodity values cannot be based on this tendency. It is more probable that the value level will rise rather than decrease in the coming decades.

Chapter Five

THE PRICE OF NATURAL RESOURCES

1. The new international economic order

Crisis of the monetary co-operation

Marx analysed the law of value on a national basis, but at the same time he also examined those factors which modify the law of value on an international scale. That is to say, he took into consideration the historic process of the regional expansion of the market. Economic development created national markets by integrating local markets, and international markets came into being through economic co-operation between countries. In every country there exists an average intensity of work and if for the production of certain commodities the time consumed exceeds the socially needed average, this additional work cannot be considered value-producing labour. Only the degree of intensity above the national average changes a country's magnitude of value.

Since single countries are integral parts of the world market, a different situation prevails in the latter. In world trade—to borrow a term from Marx—commodities unfold their value on a world scale. The average intensity of work changes from country to country. These national averages form a flight of steps where each step represents the average unit of universal labour. National labour of higher intensity produces more value during the same time than less intensive labour.

In order to comprehend more easily the idea of the national and international value of commodities, it is particularly important to keep the following in mind:

a. International value is the weighted average of national values of products turned over by foreign trade. Thus international value is a category derived from national values.

b. On the national market the socially necessary labour input is determined in accordance with national conditions. This national magnitude of value changes in foreign trade into international value. The interaction between these two orders of value takes place without differences between the two magnitudes of value becoming involved.

c. The tendency towards integrating national markets on an international scale differs from product to product. Gold is, for example, a typically world trade commodity. There are, however, products limited to national (or local) markets. The latter have therefore no international value.

d. Where products are subjects of international trade, only that part which is turned over in foreign trade represents international value.

All these factors make it clear: *one cannot speak about national values "becoming absorbed" in international values; the independent existence of national values cannot be denied, national values cannot be set against international ones.* All this would lead to a wrong foundation of the price phenomenon from the viewpoint of the theory of value.

The local, national, international and world markets can be considered co-existing markets which have established contacts with each other.

From what has been said hitherto it follows that the socially necessary labour input concerns one or another "field" which has become an economic unit as a result of the social division of labour. In the interrelationship between different economic units only the investigation of relative values is of importance.

Economics, which has developed into an independent science, characterizes society as the culture, and economic culture in particular, of creative people and groups of people; the culture of groups of people, which—though not equally developed—is based on identical principles and is of an identical character. If we accept this, we can speak about the economic culture of the peoples of Europe and North America and of that of regions outside Europe. Therefore the boundaries of society seen from the aspect of economics extend over the same area as do regular economic contacts between peoples. Accordingly, the frontiers of countries cannot be considered as economic dividing lines. Nevertheless the societies of Europe and of North America are to be distinguished from all other societies.

This concept of society expressed the power structure prevailing until the end of the First World War. This was the social framework that determined economic rationality and regulated the conditions under which the law of value could assert itself. This old *oligo-centric world economy,* relying on the colonial system, was based on free world trade and assumed the controlling role of multinational enterprises and military intervention in the last resort. The distribution and re-distribution among countries of values produced by labour were thus regulated in the oligo-centric world economy.

The first world trade conference of the UN took this traditional mechanism as a basis when, in 1948, the Havana Charter was formulated. *The system of international economic co-operation established by the industrially developed capitalist countries after the Second World War* was based on the following principles:

– Every country is interested in the *general development of productive forces.* Due to the international division of labour economic stagnation in any country has an adverse effect on the economy of the other countries.

– Every country is interested in the *convertibility of national currencies.* If the currencies of all countries are convertible, this promotes multilateral international relations.

– Every country is interested in the *equilibrium of the international balance of payments.* If any country becomes insolvent and is therefore compelled to introduce foreign exchange and import restrictions, this diminishes the export possibilities of the other countries.

– Every country is interested in *currency co-operation* to ensure equilibrium in the balance of payments by an internationally harmonized foreign exchange policy, interest rate policy, gold and credit policy. The equilibrium of the international capitalist monetary system would become less secure if these questions were considered the autonomous business of national economic policies.

Thus currency co-operation and free trade have become the two main principles of international economic order in capitalist world economy. The former was sanctioned by the Bretton Woods conference of the UN in 1944; at the same time the *International Monetary Fund* was established. Its foundations were laid by the World Trade Conference of the UN held in Havana in 1948 and were formalized in GATT (General Agreement of Tariffs and Trade). The objectives of GATT were to abolish the obstacles hampering the free play of economic forces.

With the interests of industrially developed capitalist countries in mind, both the monetary co-operation based on the *Bretton Woods* agreement and the conventions of GATT protected the economic structure of these countries upon which their economic superiority relied. They wanted to create an economic model for an obsolete political *status quo*. With the establishment of the Soviet Union, a secular transformation had in fact already begun after the First World War. It was enhanced by the unfolding of the socialist system of world economy and by the cessation of the colonial system.

In spite of all this, the *industrially developed leading capitalist countries were able to keep operating for decades the mechanisms that had sprung from and developed on the basis of an oligo-centric world economy*. Here three factors played a role. (1) The *relationship between the state and the economy* in the leading capitalist countries underwent a change. A switch-over to the Keynesian economic policy opened up new chances for the manifestations of state power, and, indeed, countries availed themselves of this possibility whenever disturbances of the market mechanism made themselves felt and threatened their positions on the world market. (2) The CMEA pursued for a long time the *policy of economic isolation*. This rendered it easier for the industrially developed capitalist countries to organize world trade in the traditional institutional fashion. (3) *New forms of economic dependence* came into being in the former colonial territories, i.e. in developing countries. The integration into the framework of a market economy of even those developing countries which had chosen the socialist course of development was thereby made easier.

Thus, when creating the system of international economic co-operation after the Second World War, they left out of consideration the *two new elements of the development of international trade,* which in many aspects appeared organically intertwined:

– one was the *process of socialization,* which in a group of countries led to the nationalization of the means of production and to a state monopoly of foreign trade;

– the other one was the process of the *diversification of foreign trade,* an inevitable concomitant of the transformation of an oligo-cultural production structure into a poly-cultural one.

The traditional economic mechanism and the basically changed power structure first brought about and then aggravated the structural crisis of the economy. In the period when the traditional international economic order was still viable, the structural crisis may have seemed to be a specific problem of the socialist and developing world, a crisis which could be diverted by industrially developed capitalist countries. But the new phenomena of the 'seventies (the currency crisis and the acceleration of inflation) indicated that the general system of international economic co-operation had to face a crisis. No wonder that in the industrially developed capitalist states attention was focussed on structural transformation and on the related questions of economic policy.

Economic challenge

Our age is that of a transition from capitalism into socialism. Movements in the world economy cannot be divorced from the antagonism between capitalism and socialism. This was the standpoint of the socialist countries when, in the early 'sixties, they suggested the convocation of a world trade conference which, in contrast to the Havana Conference, could give an answer to the new great questions of our era. Accordingly, the socialist countries would have considered it natural if the first Conference on Trade and Development (UNCTAD) convened by the UN in Geneva in 1964 had brought into the focus of attention the questions of trade among countries of different socio-economic systems, and had approached the specific problems of the developing countries as connected with these questions. Instead this the First UNCTAD discussed East–West trade only as a specific question of foreign trade policy, indeed as a side issue to the more general one of the developing world.

The developing countries soon realized that their economic goals would only be acknowledged if they put their international economic policies on a common platform and represented this policy jointly. This was achieved at the first UNCTAD convened by the UN in 1964 and held almost exclusively in the spirit of a fight for the *economic emancipation of the third world.* The material of the Conference was R. Prebisch's report "Toward a New Trade Policy for Development", which reflected the views of 77 developing countries.*

The UN declared the decade of the 'sixties a *development decade.* According to this, the annual increase of the developing countries' national income must reach 5% at least. Up to the time of the 1964 Geneva Conference, the average annual rate of economic growth was under 4%. The rate of growth, though lower than the minimum requirements, led to an imbalance of foreign trade. Under the given conditions it seemed to be objectively impossible for most of the developing countries to reach even a 3–4% rate of growth relying on their own sources of capital. The accumulation capacity is small, because—according to Nurkse—real incomes are low. Low incomes reflect low productivity, this latter, however, is the consequence of the lack of capital; but lack of capital is a consequence of the small capacity for accumulation. Thus even a rather solid development program can be implemented only with an international aid program, that is to say, by incurring debts.**

The Prebisch report advocated a system of international co-operation in which the developing countries would be able to put an end to the imbalance of their foreign trade even while accelerating the rate of their economic growth. The report emphasized that modern technologies offered stupendous possibilities. As a matter of fact the developing countries would not have to wait as long as industrially developed countries did to terminate poverty and the evils linked with it. Nor can they wait for such a long time. The pressure exerted by the masses with a view to improving their living standard is strong and will become the source of increasing tension, both domestically and on a world scale, unless a powerful economic and social development policy is introduced in which international co-operation is to play the leading role.

That is how the 1964 Geneva Conference became the first important phase of the dialogue between the "rich" North and the "poor" South. As a preparation for the Second UNCTAD, held in New Delhi in 1968, the developing countries co-ordinated their tactics in the so-called *Algiers Charter,* which was a unified document expressing their demands. On the one hand, the Algiers Charter repeated the wishes indicated by the developing countries at the First Conference and thereafter, on the other, they complemented them with some new, or newly formulated demands.

The Algiers Charter divided the world into North and South, into central and perimetric countries, into rich and poor ones, and traced back international economic problems to those of rich and poor. It replaced the antagonisms and fights of capitalism and socialism by the thesis of fights and antagonisms between developed and developing countries: the developing world stood unified against the developed one. The alternatives of capitalism and socialism appeared only as divergences in the

* Prebisch, R.: *Toward a New Trade Policy for Development,* UN, New York, 1964.
** Nurkse, R.: *Problems of Capital Formulation in Underdeveloped Countries,* Oxford, 1953.

methods of adjusting to the peculiarities of the economic systems. Thus this Charter confronted

– the majority of countries, where 70% of the population of the earth lived, but which possessed less than 20% of capital

– with the smaller groups of countries, which participated in the international division of labour, in a privileged position.

The developing countries worked out a *global economic strategy,* which, as a new policy of international co-operation, was to ensure equilibrium in the balance of payments, an annual economic growth of at least 5% in the third world. This complex program has two corner-stones: (1) The re-distribution of national incomes produced on a world level in favour of the developing countries. (2) Preferences granted to the products of developing countries on the markets of developed ones, without an obligation of reciprocity. For this reason, this global strategy can be characterized as an economic policy of challenge.

Essentially, the second UNCTAD took place as a dialogue of West–South at a time when the West was not yet under pressure and could consider the Conference organized by the UN as a forum suitable for easing political social tension. In the 'seventies this situation has undergone a change. At first it was the currency crisis and then the acceleration of inflation that weakened the economic stability of the industrially developed capitalist countries; then the oil price explosion, triggered off by the oil exporting countries, disturbed the price structure of the world market and, finally, it was the socialist countries that created new conditions for promoting East–West trade.

UNCTAD has remained an important forum of the North–South dialogue. The third Conference was held in Chile in 1972 and the fourth in Nairobi in 1976. The foundations of this latter were laid by the Manila Declaration of the developing world. In the document "New International Economic Order" the developing countries formulated their strategy for the reform of the international economy submitted to the UN in 1974 and the spirit of its declaration of the "Economic Rights and Duties of Countries" became a decision of the UN.

In seeking an answer to the question why the North–South dialogue *overcame* the East–West problem we can refer to three circumstances: (1) the developing world is more organically connected with the capitalist world economy; whereas East–West trade accounted for only 5% of international trade in 1975; the developing world represented 23% of capitalist world trade; hence the material supply of the developing world is a major factor in keeping the productive forces of the industrially developed capitalist countries operating and in ensuring economic growth; (2) within the socialist system of international economy the integration of the CMEA has provided the mechanism for co-operation with a material and technical basis, in which price and monetary considerations can only play a secondary regulatory role; the developing world has no economic mechanism separate from the capitalist international economic system and thus only its transformation can solve its problems within the framework of the capitalist world economy; (3) the problem of "poor" and "rich" can be more easily handled politically by the industrially developed capitalist countries than an ideological debate. The former can simply not be evaded at all, whereas the latter can be superseded by discrimination.

New principles of economic co-operation

In 1974 the United Nations General Assembly made a resolution about the Establishment of a New International Economic Order, based on equity, sovereign equality, interdependence, common interest and co-operation among all states, which shall correct inequalities and redress existing injustices, make it possible to eliminate the widening gap between the developed and the developing countries and ensure steadily accelerating economic and social development. To that end the UN General Assembly declares that

1. the remaining vestiges of alien and colonial domination, foreign occupation, racial discrimination, *apartheid* and neo-colonialism in all its forms continue to be among the greatest obstacles to the full emancipation and progress of the developing countries; the benefits of technical progress are not shared equitably by all members of the international community; the developing countries, which constitute 70% of the world's population account for only 30% of the world's income: it has proved impossible to achieve an even and balanced development of the international community under the existing economic order;

2. irreversible changes in the relationship of forces in the world necessitate the active, full and equal participation of the developing countries in the formulation and application of all decisions that concern the international community;

3. the political, economic and social well-being of present and future generations depend more than ever on co-operation between all members of the international community on the basis of sovereign equality and the removal of the disequilibrium that exists between them;

4. the new international economic order should be founded for the main following principles:

– the right of every country to adopt the economic and social system that it deems to be the most appropriate for its own development;

– full permanent sovereignty of every state over its natural resources and all economic activities; to safeguard these resources each state is entitled to exercise effective control over them and their exploitation by means suitable to its own situation, including the right to nationalization or transfer of ownership to its own nationals, this right being an expression of the full permanent sovereignty of the state; no state may be subjected to economic, political or any other type of coercion to prevent the free and full exercise of this inalienable right;

– the right of all states to restitution and full compensation for the exploitation and depletion of, and damages to, the natural resources and all other resources of those states, territories and peoples;

– regulation and supervision of the acitivities of transnational corporations by taking measures in the interest of the national economies of the countries where such transnational corporations operate on the basis of the full sovereignty of those countries;

– just and equitable relationship between the prices of raw materials, primary products, manufactures and semi-manufactured goods exported by developing countries and the prices of raw materials, primary commodities, manufactures, capital goods and equipment imported by them to bring about sustained improvement in their unsatisfactory terms of trade and the expansion of the world economy;

– ensuring that one of the main aims of the reformed international monetary system shall be the promotion of the development of the developing countries and the adequate flow of real resources to them;

– improving the competitiveness of natural materials facing competition from synthetic substitutes;
– preferential and non-reciprocal treatment for developing countries, wherever feasible, in all fields of international economic co-operation whenever possible;
– securing favourable conditions for the transfer of financial resources to developing countries;
– giving to the developing countries access to the achievements of modern science and technology, and promoting the transfer of technology and the creation of indigenous technology for the benefit of the developing countries in forms of and in accordance with procedures which are suited to their economies;
– the need for all states to put an end to the waste of natural resources, including food products;
– the strengthening, through individual and collective actions, of mutual economic, trade, financial and technical co-operation among the developing countries, mainly on a preferential basis;
– facilitating the role which producers' associations may play within the framework of international co-operation, and assisting them in the promotion of the sustained growth of world economy and accelerating the development of developing countries.

2. The relative price of natural resources

Terms of trade

In judging the developing world the *world market price* (foreign trade price) is to be treated as a normative category. The world market price must meet definite political–social expectations. In a world economy organized on the basis of the market mechanism this is a quite new approach to international economic co-operation.

While the world market price emerges as a result of demand and supply factors, this, of course, is a sufficient explanation for the relative price of a certain product being what it is and for the changes undergone by this relative price. We then consider price an objectively given magnitude, independent of us, upon which we cannot exert any influence. Under such conditions all a country can do is to abstain from the import of products whose world market price it considers too high, that is if it can do without the product, and to abstain from the export of a product whose world market price it considers too low, if it can do without the foreign exchange it could obtain for it.

As soon as we interpret the world market price as a normative category, the situation changes. In this case an answer must be given to the question of what relative price is "equitable" and "just". The Manila Declaration approached this question from the unfavourable position determined by the oligo-cultural structure. The "global economic strategy" of the developing world deems it a basic interest to re-valuate upwards natural resources, leading to a solution of the financial problems of accelerated economic growth and to an economic levelling between different countries.

But the developing world can catch up economically only by a diversification of its productive forces. That is why industrialization, and the ensuring of favourable conditions for the industrial products of the developing world is an important element of the Manila Declaration. It is here that the *contradictory character of the "normative"* price structure is most striking. No attempt has been made to measure at what price industrial semi-products, capital goods and industrial consumption goods can be manufactured if the price of natural resources is raised to the level that is deemed desirable by the developing countries. By upgrading natural resources a point can be reached at which only the processing of the raw materials within the country is rational, that is to say, at which the ownership of natural resources becomes the chief determinant of economic development. Although no one takes this seriously, it is necessary to draw attention to this possibility in order to demonstrate that a concept which may be justifiable within realistic limits may be turned into its opposite.

In world trade the relative price of natural resources is expressed as terms of trade, i.e. the price-ratios of goods exchanged in foreign trade. In the past fifty years the ratio between products of extractive and of non-extractive branches in foreign trade was the following:

Table 36

Trends of terms of trade in extractive and non-extractive branches (1950 = 100)

Year	Extractive	Non-extractive	Ratio of exchange
1928	87	129	146
1938	34	62	182
1948	100	121	121
1958	98	123	126
1965	102	136	133
1970	105	149	142
1975	317	271	85

In the past half century there have been two periods in which the price trends of the extractive branches appear to be extraordinarily favourable. The first was the period 1950–1952 in the wake of the Korean war, the other the period 1974–1975, in the wake of the oil price explosion. The really favourable period for products of the non-extractive branches was during the Second World War, but after it the demand in products of the extractive branches rose more powerfully than their output. In consequence of this, prices in the extractive branches grew faster than in the processing industry. The prices of products of the extractive branches reached their peak in 1951, in the Korean boom. From 1952 on, the terms of trade moved again in favour of the processing industries, while a turn-about was caused by the oil price explosion in 1973.

Factors of demand and supply will induce price movements of different directions in the sphere of natural resources on the one hand and of industrial semi-finished and finished goods on the other.

Table 37

Intensity of dispersion around the average price

Period	Extractive branches	Non-extractive branches	Average
1950–1959	8.7	5.7	7.5
1960–1969	2.2	0.9	1.0
1970–1975	25.8	5.9	17.5

Among products entering into foreign trade, raw materials and agricultural (tropical) products are subject to peculiar price movements. In contrast to machines and industrial consumer goods their adjustment to general price trends is governed by exceedingly intense periodic fluctuations. As a result of an increased demand, caused by war or natural disasters, the price of natural resources will immediately rise and then new investments or the over-production induced by these conditions will cause a sudden fall in price. Short-term price fluctuations introduce *elements of instability* into the economy. This instability has grave disadvantages.

– *When prices fall,* the exporting country loses the income in foreign exchange it had expected to use to further its development policy. The disadvantage is particularly great if it affects developing countries with an oligo-cultural production structure.
– The *intense and sudden rise of prices* causes unexpected additional foreign exchange expenditure for the importing country and upsets the equilibrium of the international balance of payments.

Indeed, the consequences are identical for both: the equilibrium of the balance of payments is disturbed. Consequently, on one point at least, exporting and importing countries have an interest in common price stability. This could lead to the assumption that a common interest lay in the conclusion of international commodity agreements ensuring price stability. Yet this assumption evades the issue of diametrically opposed interests. It is in the exporting country's interest that price stability should be achieved on as high a price as possible, whilst the importing country wants to have a low price. We may gain some insight into the problem by noting that the search for an institutional solution to the problem of price stability always gained ground when the price of raw materials and agricultural (tropical) products was low on the world market, but never when their price had suddenly risen. In 1902 low prices resulted in the conclusion of the first sugar agreement in Brussels. It was an agreement of major producing companies, similar to a cartel. Nor is it due to chance that the endeavour to conclude international commodity agreements was most powerful for the first time in the 1929–1933 crisis of world economy. Common characteristics of the International Wheat Agreement of 1933 and of the International Sugar Agreement of 1937 were that they came into being under the aegis of the League of Nations; the importers were also admitted as members and finally, contrary to former practice, these agreements were concluded on a governmental level.

These references to events that occured several decades ago seem to indicate that *the chief initiators of international trade agreements are* the exporting and not the importing countries. Neither is it coincidental that the system of international commodity agreements was created in the 'fifties and 'sixties, after the boom brought about by the Korean war (1951–1952). The fall in the prices of raw materials and agricultural (tropical) products caused a marked deterioration in the foreign trade balance of the developing countries. (See Table 38.)

These price trends are chiefly explained by three factors:

a. The United States and the industrially developed West European capitalist countries, the principal export markets for the raw materials of the third world, have significantly increased the domestic bases of their foodstuff and industrial raw material supplies. Traditional raw materials were replaced by synthetics on an ever growing scale.

b. The development of science and technology not only created the bases of synthetic materials in these countries but also resulted in a significant decrease in the specific input of materials. Therefore the demand for traditional raw materials grew more slowly than did production in the processing industries.

c. After the Second World War, the monopolies of the capitalist great powers increased the raw material producing capacities of countries dependent on them,

Table 38

Price scissors in the economic connexions of developed and backward capitalist countries (1953 = 100)

Year	Developed countries	Backward countries	Price scissors
	foreign trade price level		
1938	107	75	143
1948	101	90	112
1950	98	106	93
1956	99	102	97
1959	104	96	108
1961	106	95	112
1964	107	94	114
1967	108	93	116

Source: Two Sorts of Nation. Labour Research, 1962. II. U. N. Digest of Statistics.

Yearbook of International Trade Statistics 1972–73.

to meet the demands of the militarization of the capitalist economy. Their first consideration was raw material requirements for military use, but they kept in mind the need for stock-piling too. Nuclear weapons and remote control missiles created revolutionary changes in military techniques, which affected both the raw material needs of the military and the quantity and range of raw materials deemed necessary for stock-piling. This has led to a permanent crisis on the markets of raw materials.

The position of colonial, semi-colonial and industrially less developed countries in the capitalist world market was also aggravated by the substantial stocks of raw materials accumulated in the industrially developed capitalist countries. They were used in the interest of the consumer countries.

International commodity agreements

The chief measures for stabilizing markets within the framework of international commodity agreements are the following:

a. *Price zones by agreement:* The members agree to keep within the jointly established upper and lower price limits accepted in the agreement when trading in the commodity.

b. *Export quotas:* The participants regulate the supply of the given commodity by dividing among them the total quantity of exports. The quantity, (to be exported by a country) strictly fixed in the agreement, is its quota (e.g. the Coffee or the Sugar Agreement).

c. *Buffer stocks.* The producing (exporting) countries keep stocks, created partly from their own products and partly from their imports. By means of sales or purchases concluded at the right time, they can offset short-run price fluctuations (Tin Agreement).

d. Outside the sphere of trade, the agreement based on *production restriction* regulates supply, whereas the agreement based on *import control* regulates stocks.

e. *Diversification funds.* By creating and using such monetary funds, commodity agreements endeavour to change the oligo-cultural economy of developing countries, also for the purpose of avoiding over-supply (e.g. in case of the Coffee Agreement). Diversification has, of course, other effects too (the possibility of industrialization, the easing of dependence on certain articles, etc.)

According to the first UNCTAD the solutions applied in commodity agreements must be adapted to the characteristics of the commodity in question. In addition to the above, agreements may also contain the following expedient measures:

– measures to liberalize trade;
– guaranteed minimum quotas of imports;
– long-term contracts and import projects;
– long-term sales contracts;
– skimming off systems in the developed importing countries, whose utilization would ensure the return of skimmed off amounts to the exporting developing countries;
– suitable systems of incentives, which would open up new raw material markets for the exporting developing countries.

The market regulated by commodity agreements comprises about a fifth part of the export of the developing countries. On the other hand, Commodity Study Groups operate in a wider sphere, and there are also semi-official agreements.

The *International Commodity Study Groups* represent the first step in regulating raw material problems. Generally they operate within the framework of the UN, under the supervision of FAO and UNCTAD and deal with one or other of the more important raw materials, prime materials or agricultural products. Their activity is of an advisory character. They work in statistics (working up data, introducing definitions of standards); they pursue the market position of the commodity in question (production, consumption, export and import trade, and changes in its world market price); they investigate the means of market stabilization; they give regular information on the position of demand and supply; they prepare papers on various problems of the given commodity and, in some cases, initiate concrete steps with the governments of the member countries or of countries concerned to solve some critical situation. They study the technical–technological problems of production of the given commodity or of materials suitable for replacing it. They survey the possibilities of bringing about inter-governmental agreements and draw up their plans. By their total activity they contribute to a thorough knowledge of the markets for the commodity in question.

Informal arrangements are, so to say, a transitional phase between study groups and commodity agreements and have, in most cases, come into being as a result of the preparatory work of the respective study group. In general, hard market conditions, similar to situations preceding the conclusion of commodity agreements, induce countries to make informal arrangements. They are more advantageous, in so far as they are very flexible, than formal commodity agreements, which are binding. Owing to their informal character, they are established more easily than commodity agreements. In the spirit of such informal agreements the members seek a way out of their difficulties within the framework of semi-official international talks. It is a basic principle of these talks that they take place with the active participation of the producing and the importing countries.

The Manila Declaration, which provided the basis for the fourth UNCTAD, in a complex way formulated the problems for the developing countries of increasing incomes from raw material exports, of the diversification of production and of the improvement of conditions for penetrating the markets of developed countries. At that time the developing countries could already rely on the Declaration on the Establishment of a New International Economic Order and on the action program adopted by the sixth special session of the UN. One of the most important central elements of this Declaration was raw material trade. At the time of the fourth UNCTAD the world market prices of some raw materials were falling from the peak they had reached in 1974.

Table 39

World market price trends of some raw materials (1970 = 100)

Product	1971	1972	1973	1974	1975
Crude oil	127	143	196	641	651
Raw materials and agricultural products covered by commodity agreements					
Tin	96	103	130	219	189
Aluminium	100	91	91	124	141
Wheat	104	116	201	290	258
Coffee	87	98	125	132	147
Cocoa	87	99	166	251	219
Sugar	112	162	205	579	410
Olive oil	104	134	196	302	328
Products outside the sphere of commodity agreements					
Rice	98	110	192	321	231
Maize	99	100	155	190	191
Fruit	123	123	165	173	226
Wine	98	116	180	172	178
Crude rubber	80	81	168	176	136
Copper	78	78	122	144	91
Nickel	103	103	119	134	161
Manganese	121	115	142	216	261

Source: Monthly Bulletin of Statistics, Sept. 1976.

One cannot draw an unequivocal conclusion from the table whether international commodity agreements were able to regulate the market. The price trend of products covered by commodity agreements does not appear to differ from the price trends of those outside the agreements. Anyhow, commodity agreements were concluded at times when there was an over-supply, i.e. in a situation quite different from that of 1973/74. Furthermore, the bulk of articles under agreements were agricultural products, the price fluctuations of which compared with those of other products had been greater up to the end of the 1950s–1960s, due to natural factors even irrespective of the price explosion.

A significant part of the turnover, actually an increasing part during the price explosion, of products under commodity agreements or subject to other attempts to regulate the market, was concluded outside the commodity agreements. UN statistics, on the other hand, show the price trends of the total turnover. The movement of prices under the agreement and in the free market cannot be pursued separately from statistical sources. However, it is a fairly well-known fact that the free market price of aluminium is usually higher at times of price rises and lower at times of price decreases than the so-called "club price". Or in the case of coffee: African producers did not join the agreement for a considerable time, because in this way they were able to increase their share in the market as against traditional South American coffees of relatively higher prices. As can be seen, the role of commodity agreements is rendered rather difficult for products for which there is no regular and formal commodity agreement, such as e.g. copper, although the attitudes of producers, and in other cases of consumers, are partially co-ordinated.

The fourth session of UNCTAD adopted an integrated program for commodities. The commodity coverage of the Integrated Programme should take into account the interests of developing countries in bananas, bauxite, cocoa, coffee, copper, cotton and cotton yarns, hard fibres and products, iron ore, jute and jute-products, manganese, meat, phosphates, rubber, sugar, tea, tropical timber, tin, and vegetable oils, including olive oil, and oil-seeds.

With a view to improving the terms of trade of developing countries and in order to eliminate the economic imbalance between developed and developing countries, concerted efforts should be made in favour of the developing countries towards expanding and diversifying their trade, improving and diversifying their productive capacity, improving their productivity and increasing their export earnings, with a view to counteracting the adverse effects of inflation, thereby sustaining real incomes. Accordingly, the following objectives have been stated:

1. To achieve stable conditions in commodity trade, including avoidance of excessive price fluctuations, at levels which would:

– be remunerative and just to producers and equitable to consumers;

– take account of world inflation and changes in the world economic and monetary situations;

– promote equilibrium between supply and demand within expanding world commodity trade.

2. To improve and sustain the real income of individual developing countries through increased export earnings, and to protect them from fluctuations in export earnings, especially relating to commodities.

3. To seek to improve market access and reliability of supply for primary products and the processed products therefrom, bearing in mind the needs and interests of developing countries.

4. To diversify production in developing countries, including food production and to expand processing of primary products in developing countries with a view to promoting their industrialization and increasing their export earnings.

5. To improve the competitiveness of and to encourage research and development on the problems of natural products competing with synthetics and substitutes, and to consider the harmonization, where appropriate, of the production of synthetics and substitutes in developed countries with the supply of natural products produced in developing countries.

6. To improve the market structures in the field of raw and basic materials that are important from the viewpoint of the exports of the developing countries.

7. To improve marketing, distribution and transport for the commodity exports of developing countries, including an increase in their participation in these activities and their earnings from them.

In accordance with the Integrated Programme, Commodity Agreements were to be concluded by the end of 1978. Within the frame of these agreements the desirable price of the given commodities was to be established and so were the principles and methods according to which this guiding price is set; the instruments and rules that might ensure in principle that the actual world market price remains within the limits of the price zone agreed upon.

The intricate problems to be solved when harmonizing the contrasting interests of producers and consumers come most conspicuously to the fore in talks about the Integrated Programme. Relying on past experiences, the *consumer country* can point out that under market conditions favourable for the *producing country* the world market price will suddenly rise and the commodity agreement would not ensure protection against this for the rightful interests of the consumer country. Every price fluctuation expresses some average, and it would not be difficult to reserve, in case of high export prices, a part of the additional income and use it for income supplements when the export price is low. In the same way the consumer may skim off the low import price to be able to subsidize imports when prices are high. In the case of price stabilization the producer wants to stabilize high prices and therefore it is rather difficult to come to terms with countries interested in consumption. These latter would view as important stabilization at prices considered equitable by the consumer.

The Leontief model

Now we call attention to the work commissioned by the UN about the future of world economy which was carried out by Wassily Leontief and by his collaborators. The Leontief-model* analyses world economy divided into 15 regions. The chief basis for breaking down into regions was *per capita* income, as the yardstick of economic development, and the share of industry in GNP. The formation of homogeneous groups was attempted according to these indices. A further breakdown was carried out in relation to characteristics considered important by the authors, such as the grouping together of developing countries rich in oil, or the division of Africa into arid and tropical parts.

Developed market regions:

1. North America
2. West Europe (high income)
3. Japan
4. Oceania

Developed centrally planned regions:

5. Soviet Union
6. Eastern Europe

Developing market regions:

7. Latin America (medium income)
8. Latin America (low income)
9. Middle East and African oil countries
10. Asia (low income)
11. Africa (arid)
12. Africa (tropical)
13. Asian centrally planned countries

* *The Future of World Economy*, United Nations, 1976. Department of Economic and Social Affairs. The Report was prepared by a research team, headed by A. P. Carter, Wassily Leontief and Peter Petri.

Medium income regions:

14. Western Europe (other than 2 above)
15. Southern Africa

The purpose of the world model is to reveal the possible directions of international economic processes. The model compares the 1970 situation with the hypothetic conditions of the world economy in 1980, 1990 and 2000. The most essential conclusions appear as belonging to the North–South problem. Thus the Leontief model has taken the widely accepted UNCTAD convention, according to which the problems of economic backwardness can be grasped adequately only in their totality.

The growth targets set by the International Development Strategy (IDS) for the Second United Nations Development Decade, as a whole, are 6% per annum for GNP and 3.5% for GNP *per capita,* assuming an average 2.5% annual growth of population.* The IDS does not set targets for growth in developed countries. However, if previous long-term trends in these countries were extrapolated—according to the Leontief model—they would mean an annual growth of about 4.5% in GNP and 3.5% in GNP *per capita*. From all this, however, it follows that the incomes gap of a ratio of 12:1 having existed in 1970 between the developed and the developing countries would not diminish. According to the Leontief model, in order to be able to decrease this incomes gap, the basic hypothesis *(I)* should be corrected *(C)*.

Table 40

Two hypothetical variants of the development of world economy

		Developed countries	Developing countries
Rate of growth (%)			
GNP	I	4.5	6.0
	C	3.6	6.9
Population	I	1.0	2.5
	C	0.6	2.0
GNP *per capita*	I	3.5	3.5
	C	3.0	4.9
Incomes gap in 2000			
	I	12:1	
	C	7:1	

The assumption is that the intended rate of growth in developing countries can be realized gradually and that in the developed countries the rate of growth of gross national product *per capita* will decrease. Calculated at 1970 prices a 4% *per capita* growth would be realized in the group of \$ 3,000–4,000 *per capita* income, 3% in the \$ 4,000–5,000 group, 2.5% in the \$ 5,000–6,000 group, etc. Even under such conditions the average gross national product *per capita* in the non-oil producing regions of Asia and Africa would only amount to approximately \$ 400, while the other regions would enter the \$ 1,000–2,000 group. The equalization between developing

* International Development Strategy, Action Programme of the General Assembly, Second United Nations Development Decade, paras 13, 14, 15 (United Nations, N. Y. 1970 ST/ECA/139).

countries will probably be realized only in the beginning of the next century, but only if those developing countries facing unfavourable conditions were given more efficacious international aid.

Based upon the generalization of the specific inputs of the USA, the so-called Leontief model, which represents the future of world economy, supposes that, in case of a constant price level, the price of minerals will rise in the period 1970–2000, 2.6-fold and that of agricultural products by 14%, and accordingly, the price of finished goods will decrease by 6.8%. (See Table 41.)

In Yu. Yakovets's view similar tendencies can also be predicted in the Soviet Union. According to his paper, the wholesale price level of heavy industry was 9% higher in 1973 than in 1940; but, within it the price level of the coal industry rose 4.71-fold, that of ferrous metallurgy 2.42-fold and of the building material industry 1.73-fold. Regarded in a long-term perspective, the costs of products of the mining industry will rise even more markedly, because, in consequence of accelerated extraction, the natural conditions of production deteriorate. There will have to be development of new sources, poorer in quality and more remote.*

Let us examine the Leontief model somewhat more thoroughly. According to it, agricultural production is to be raised 4.3-fold (5% per annum) in the developing world within thirty years (1970–2000) if the annual 5% increase in GNP is to be achieved. The agricultural demands of developed countries will rise by 60% in thirty years. There are *plenty of land reserves* in the developing zones *that can be put under cultivation,* and there is no physical obstacle to a 30% increase of arable land by 2000, i.e. by 229 million hectares (calculated on a 1970 basis). Agricultural productivity must be raised at least threefold. All this demands radical political measures, among others in the field of soil amelioration and irrigation, of investment credits, of mechanization and labour management. Foreign aid and technology transfer are also needed.

The success of the new revolution in agrarian technology makes necessary land reform as well as other social and institutional changes needed to overcome the non-technical barriers to the intensive utilization of the soil and increased productivity. The creation of an economic milieu favourable for economic development is also of major importance for the encouragement of soil utilization and of the efficient use of labour and technologies.

According to the Leontief model the *raw material and energy demand arising from accelerated development will not encounter the obstacle of absolute scarcity in our century.* However, the utilization of less productive and more costly sources must be taken into account along with more intensive use of new ones, particularly in regions which, as far as we know at present, do not abound in natural resources. In this way differences in sources of raw materials and energy in different parts of the world may decrease. This, however, will inevitably lead to an increase in costs of extraction and prices.

In the Leontief world model, changes in the relative world market prices of products had to be predicted, because this model is a special input–output balance of world economy and covers economic regions of different grades of development, investigating the trends of their trade and payment balances between 1970 and 2000. The model indicates that by 2000 the price of mineral raw materials will rise 2.9-fold compared to the price of processed products (price scissors) and that agricultural products will be 20% dearer than in the basic year.

These indices have been based on unchanged (1970) price levels, disregarding

* (Yakovets, Yu. V.) Яковец, Ю. В.: Движение цен минерального сырья (Price movements of mineral raw materials), *Вопросы экономики,* No. 6, 1975.

Table 41

The estimated world trade prices of the Leontief world model from 1970 to 2000 (1970 = 100)

Sector	1980	1990	2000
1. Cattle	97	108	112
2. Oil-seeds	98	119	126
3. Grain	91	113	121
4. Tuber crops	92	104	108
5. Other agricultural products	88	100	104
6. Copper	87	86	223
7. Bauxite	81	78	94
8. Nickel	82	112	187
9. Tin	81	107	188
10. Lead	78	76	173
11. Steel	81	82	82
12. Crude oil	127	277	312
13. Natural gas	140	496	689
14. Coal	80	73	73
15. Mining (others)	101	100	101
16. Foodstuff industry	100	95	93
17. Crude oil processing	101	94	93
18. Metal processing	109	103	102
19. Textile industry	98	90	89
20. Timber	103	101	100
21. Furniture	95	85	84
22. Paper	99	94	94
23. Printing industry	93	94	97
24. Rubber industry	98	104	108
25. Industrial chemicals	100	99	98
26. Fertilizers	109	128	135
27. Chemical industry (others)	107	122	128
28. Cement	94	90	91
29. Glass	106	105	105
30. Road vehicles	101	96	95
31. Shipbuilding	94	82	80
32. Aircraft building	98	89	89
33. Metal mass products	107	103	103
34. General machine production	95	87	86
35. Electrical machines	98	89	92
36. Scientific instruments	93	82	81
37. Clocks and watches	96	87	88
38. Services	105	102	95
39. Transport	101	97	96
40. Water, electricity	102	99	98
41. Construction	96	93	94
42. Commerce	97	90	90
43. Communication	104	103	102

the inflation problem; the table only indicates the expected changes in the relative valuation of products.

The technique of determining such prices involves the solution of the dual task of the input–output system given the technologies and the value added proportions of the respective years. The changes in relative prices thus reflect the expected shifts in the techniques of production, in labour productivity, and also in the cost of resource extraction expected to occur between 1970 and the years in question. This technique was applied for one region only (North America) and it was assumed—for the sake of illustration—that the relative prices obtained would be representative of price changes prevailing in world trade. Considering that this area produces and absorbs a substantial part of the world's total marketable output, this can be considered a reasonable first approximation to the actual situation.

3. The law of diminishing returns

Average profit and rent

Let us consider the view that variations in prices of natural resources have historically caused price trends to favour industrial semi-finished goods and end products. V. Kollontai, relying on various sources, stated that a 80–90% disparity could be found between the relative productivity of labour and relative foreign trade prices in the second half of the 1950s.* He based his statement upon the concept that, compared with the 1870s, productivity had risen 2.5–3-fold in the industrially developed capitalist countries, whereas in the developing countries productivity had not risen to any notable extent. If price trends had adjusted to the changes of value relations (which latter can be inferred from the rise in productivity of labour), the export price level of industrially developed capitalist countries ought to have decreased by 50% compared with the export price level of developing countries. In actual fact a price change of 30–40% took place in favour of the industrially developed capitalist countries.

However, V. Kollontai's hypothesis can be criticized. One thing is sure: there can be no permanent price disparity between extractive and non-extractive sectors in a market system at a given level of economic development, because it would bring about a distorted production structure, or the extractive sector could be maintained and developed only with government subsidies. In market economies this tends to occur only in agricultural production. At the same time the participation of industrially developed countries in the production of minerals is considerable.

We can obtain information on the mining values of the world, of their distribution according to countries and of the share of different minerals from F. Friedensburg's work.** The 1956 official data of the USA Mining Statistics were taken as a basis of his investigations. This had been justified by several circumstances. The USA is the most important mineral producing country. The Bureau of Mines of the USA has elaborated extraordinarily detailed statistics for several decades. And finally, 1956 was a relatively normal year, when prices approximately reflected value relations. (See Table 42.)

The value of mining output expressed in terms of these equivalents amounted to $ 1,318 million in 1860 and to $ 56,831 million in 1962. The average annual increase is 3.8%, which, according to Friedensburg's calculations, is tantamount to an annual increase of 4.5%, if we leave out of consideration the two world wars and the years immediately following them.*** The annual growth somewhat lags behind that of the rate of increase in industrial production; and this can be traced back to the improve-

* (Kollontai, V.) Коллонтай, В.: Прибыль империалистов от эксплуатации слабо развитых стран (The imperialists' profit originating from the exploitation of less developed countries), *Мировая экономика и международные отношения*, No. 6, 1959.

** Friedensburg, F.: *Die Struktur des Weltbergbaus und die Rangordnung der Bergbauländer*, Wochenbericht des Deutschen Instituts für Wirtschaftsforschung, 1957.

*** Friedensburg, F.: Die Entwicklung der Bergwirtschaft der Welt in den letzten hundert Jahren, *Glückauf*, 6. Jan. 1965, pp. 63–77.

Table 42

Relative values of the most important minerals
(based on the 1956 evaluation of the Bureau of Mines of the USA)

Mineral	Unit	$ value
Hard coal	t	5.31
Brown coal	t	1.86
Crude oil	t	19.39
Natural gas	10^6 m^3	3.78
Gold	kg	1,125
Silver	kg	29.1
Copper	t	936
Tin	t	2,230
Lead	t	346
Zinc	t	302
Nickel	t	1,421
Uranium (U_2O_2)	kg	33.7
Iron ore	t	7.63
Manganese ore	t	48.3
Wolfram ore	t	3,639
Chromium ore	t	46.3
Bauxite	t	7.89
Sulphur	t	26.1
Native salt	t	6.21
Potassium (K_2O)	t	41.8
Phosphate, raw	t	6.12
Asbestos	t	126.5
Diamonds	carat	8.02

ment in the specific input of materials, and to the continual development of the process of improving materials. The ratio is set at 3.8:5 by Friedensburg.

However, for the purpose of our present investigation, the participation of the different minerals and of the different countries in the total value of minerals is of greater significance. With regard to these problems Friedensburg's paper offers the following information (see Tables 43 and 44).

This shows that two thirds of mineral values consisted of energy carriers in 1962.

Due to the shifting of the energy structure from coal to hydrocarbons, the share of Great Britain in the value of extracted minerals decreased, while, at the same time, the developing world acquired a major role through the oil exporting countries. Among the economically developed countries the USA maintained its leading position, the Soviet Union rising to second place and catching up.

Concerning the Soviet Union it is possible to argue that in the structural policy of planned development the price structure does not play a determinant role. However, in the USA, with a free market economy, the profit motive has always played a decisive role in investment activities.

Table 43

Share of the more important minerals in the mineral value of the world

Mineral	1860	1913	1962
		%	
Crude oil	0.1	8.1	41.4
Natural gas	—	0.5	3.9
Coal	54.1	52.4	21.4
Energy carriers	54.2	61.0	66.7
Iron ore	10.4	10.6	7.1
Copper	4.4	7.4	7.5
Gold	19.6	6.0	3.1
Zinc	2.0	2.7	1.9
Lead	5.0	3.3	1.5
Agriculture	—	0.9	1.2
Uranium (U_2O_2)	—	—	1.8
Native salt	—	0.3	1.0
Nickel	—	0.4	0.9
Tin	2.1	2.3	0.8
Sub-total	43.5	33.9	26.8
Others	2.3	5.1	6.5
Total	100.0	100.0	100.0

Table 44

Share of different countries in the mineral value of the world

Country	1860	1913	1962
		%	
USA	13.8	37.9	24.3
Great Britain	42.5	13.3	2.2
Soviet Union	3.3	4.5	17.2
Industrially developed countries	28.9	22.3	11.9
The developing world	11.5	22.0	44.4
Total	100.0	100.0	100.0

Marx's interpretation of the transformation of surplus-profit into ground rent reveal specific features of the pricing of natural resources. According to him, if the agricultural utilization of an area of land ensured the average profit rate, only the owner of the land could cultivate it. Any contract of lease pre-supposes that the price ensures not only the average profit rate but also an absolute ground rent. That is why the price of agricultural produce is regulated by the production conditions of the poorest soil under cultivation in the capitalist mode. This should hold good also for mining.*

After the Second World War these circumstances became modified essentially only

* Marx, K.: *Capital*, Vol. III, Moscow, 1966, pp. 614–802.

in one respect. In consequence of *European agrarian protectionism* the price level of agricultural products is lower than it would be if the governments did not grant budgetary assistance to producers cultivating land in unfavourable natural conditions (mountainous land, etc.) and if they did not subsidize certain agricultural products, or, if they did not encourage intensification (investment, up-to-date agro-technologies), and grant credits etc. To summarize, it can be stated that

– the price level of non-extractive branches is regulated by the average profit rate,
– the price level of extractive branches is regulated by the average profit rate, including land rent (and royalties); whereas
– the price of products produced under particularly favourable natural conditions also includes monopoly rent.

Let us take the world market price of crude oil as an example. Towards the end of the 1950s this price decreased twice to a considerable extent. When it was at its lowest point one barrel of crude oil could be bought for $ 1.76 (f.o.b. Near East port). This led in 1960 to the establishment of OPEC; at that time only a defense against price fluctuations. But even at its lowest level the world market price of crude oil included a monopoly rent. At the approximate time when the OPEC was founded the cost and price conditions could be characterized as follows:

Table 45

The 1961 costs of crude oil

Country	Share of capitalist world production[1]	Costs[2]	
		$/barrel	USA costs = 100
USA	38%	1.63	100
Near East	30%	0.17	11
Venezuela	16%	0.68	42

[1] Petroleum Press Service, January 1962.
[2] La Coopération économique européenne. Troisième rapport de l'OECD, Paris, 1962.

Developing countries suffered from the fact that many had been colonies and also from their dependence on the industrially developed countries. This dependence brought about and maintained their oligo-cultural structure. Secondly, the enterprises of industrially developed countries utilized the greater part of their natural resources. Thus these enterprises accumulated—partly or entirely—ground rent and monopoly rent. And, finally, the price policy of multi-national enterprises was directed, as we shall discuss later, in the interests of the industrially developed countries.

Diminishing returns of land

The historical price disparity between extractive and non-extractive sectors is not widely accepted. On the other hand, based on Ricardo's hypothesis on the diminishing returns of land*, it is accepted that the relative price of products produced in the extractive sectors (agriculture, forestry and mining) must rise in the long run.

* Ricardo, D.: *Principles of Political Economy and Taxation*, London, 1817.

Put into general terms the concept of diminishing returns is the following: an increase in some inputs relative to other fixed inputs will cause total output to increase, but after a point extra output resulting from the same additions of extra inputs is likely to become less and less. Economists usually consider diminishing returns a fundamental law of economics and technology.* But if we consider the laws of socio-economic *development,* this hypothesis is open to debate.

It is well worth recalling Lenin's dispute with Bulgakov in which Lenin pointed out that if labour and other inputs invested successively into new land did not yield diminishing returns, then there would be no sense at all in extending the area of arable land. This is the usual argument for the 'universal' law. But if one reflects but a little bit on this, one must immediately see that this argument is the most inane abstraction, which leaves out of consideration the most important points: the level of technology and the condition of the forces of production. Lenin also pointed out that "additional input in itself presupposes changes in the method of production and in techniques. Of course, supplementary investments of labour and capital are possible (and do occur) on a relatively small scale, at a given, unchanged level of technology; in this case the law is applicable... (but) the unchanged condition of technologies will enforce relatively very narrow limitations to supplementary investments of labour and capital investment. Thus, instead of universal law we have an exceedingly relative 'law'..."**

But Ricardo formulated the doctrine of diminishing returns on land in connexion with the extension of the area under cultivation. He supposed that, parallel with the increase of needs, mankind would be obliged to avail itself of areas that can be cultivated with an ever decreasing efficiency. The share of land less productive than the average, and farther from markets, would increase. Similarly, in mining the share of minerals that can be extracted only with a greater input than the average, due to unfavourable natural conditions, would increase.

The hypothesis on the increasing returns on capital and the diminishing returns on land laid the foundations for the thesis on the rise of the relative price of natural resources. This hypothesis has also taken root in technical sciences and has gained particular importance in economic calculations upon which the efficient utilization of mineral raw material relies. In the following we present the system of criteria for price forecasting established by the Hungarian National Commission for Mineral Resources.***

1. Since natural conditions do not directly influence production conditions, labour inputs into the manufacture of finished goods depend almost entirely on the technical level of production. Thus the cost of products, in general, decreases according to a hyperbola in the function of time.

2. It follows from the limited character of mineral resources and the fact that they cannot be renewed, that whilst at first discoveries obtainable under favourable conditions are being exploited, in the course of time deposits under increasingly unfavourable natural conditions will be utilized. After a certain time this circumstance will

* Samuelson, P. A.: *Economics,* 5th ed., New York–Toronto–London, 1961.

** Lenin, V. I.: *The Agrarian Question and the "Critics of Marx". The Iskra Period 1900–1902.* Book 1, New York, 1929, pp. 184–185.

*** A hazai ásványi nyersanyagbázis hatékony hasznosítására vonatkozó határozatok végrehajtásával kapcsolatos feladatok és ásványvagyon-gazdálkodásunk néhány alapvető elvi kérdése (Some basic questions of principle arising from the implementation of the decisions on the efficient utilization of Hungarian mineral raw materials and the management of the country's mineral resources). Document of the Hungarian Ministry of Heavy Industry, Budapest, 1977.

offset or more than offset the decrease of costs due to the development of extracting techniques.

3. In case of raw materials utilized in a relatively great measure in comparison with mineral resources (e.g. that of hydrocarbons), the hyperbola of costs in the function of time may change into such a parabola whose upward line may dissect the cost hyperbola of the mineral (of coal in the present case) preceding it historically. The huge coal resources of the world render not only a selective extraction but also considerable technical development possible. In case of energy carriers of equal natural conditions, which are available in unlimited quantities (e.g. energy of nuclear fission), the cost curve can, of course, only be a hyperbola in the function of time.

4. In all probability, the cost curve of extraction and utilization depending on natural conditions of mineral raw materials, will change more slowly than that of the finished products of the processing industry.

5. Price ratios between extractive and non-extractive products—as a general rule—will increase in the same direction in the function of time. Deviations from it spring from the transitional lack of harmony between production possibilities and needs, from the fluctuations of demand and supply, from events of world history and chiefly from a transitory failure of natural and economic laws to assert themselves.

The basic model, which can be considered classic, representing the formation of exchange ratios of extractive and non-extractive sectors, shows the following picture:

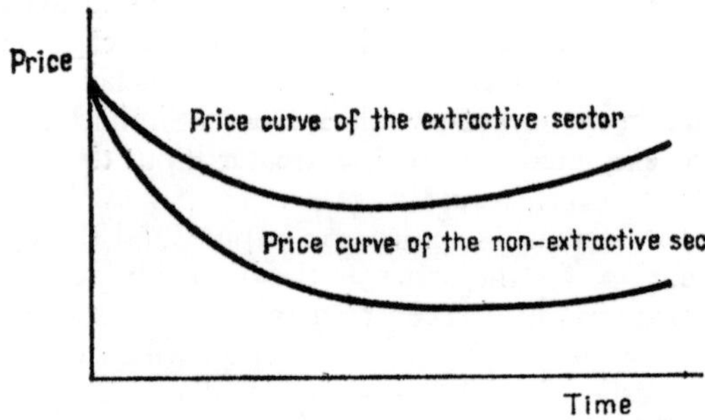

Chart 13. Thesis of the rise of relative prices of natural resources

If, as a general rule, the course of the cost curve in the function of time is parabolic in the extractive sector and hyperbolic in the non-extractive sector, then—whichever point of time we take as basis—the price scissor must open in the long run. If we accept the hypothesis of the laws of returns, these are only the consequences of relative inputs and do not imply income re-distribution.

Only recently have economists started to pay attention to J. Barnett's and Chandler Morse's work published in 1962, in which they analyse the price–cost relations of the USA in a survey of the period 1870–1957. The study was published by the Association of Resources for the Future*. The authors wish to demonstrate the decrease of the relative value of natural resources, i.e. increasing returns.

Some remarks can be made on the investigation methods of Barnett and Morse. The comparability of index numbers for a period of nearly a century can well be queried. The industrial price level and, within it, the average prices of extractive and

* Barnett, H. J.:–Morse, Ch.: *Scarcity and Growth. The Economics of Natural Resources Availability*, Baltimore, 1962.

non-extractive sectors in particular, can be realistic only to a limited extent. In the course of so long a period the production structure undergoes radical changes; new products appear and old ones become obsolete. It is inevitable that the evaluating weights should be changed repeatedly, and this causes "breaks" in price index calculations, which lead to distortions. These can be particularly significant if we perform value, price and cost analyses of the relationship of extractive and non-extractive sectors. However, this is no reason why we should *a priori* deny the fact that long-term trends of value, price and cost relations can be quantified, or the possibility of analyses performed in this way. It is worthwhile picking out two tables of their work (see Tables 46 and 47).

Table 46

Indices of labour–capital input per unit of extractive output in the USA (1920 = 100)

Period	Total extractive	Agriculture	Mining	Forestry
1870–1900	134	132	210	59
1919	122	114	164	106
1957	60	61	47	90

Table 47

Relative input of extractive branches compared with non-extractive ones in the USA (1929 = 100)

Period	Extractive branches	Agriculture	Mining	Forestry
	compared to non-extractive branches			
1870–1900	99	97	154	37
1919	103	97	139	84
1957	87	89	68	130

The evidence mainly shows increasing, not diminishing returns. The cost per unit of total extractive product fell by half during the period and that of mining by even more. Only forestry gives evidence of diminishing returns; cost per unit of product rose from the Civil War to the First World War. But after the First World War the returns of forestry were approximately constant (or slightly increasing).

Thus US experience does not support the hypothesis of an increasing scarcity of natural resources. The hypothesis is not even confirmed by the data of forestry. The increase of unit cost occurring up to 1919 elicited three effects: an introduction of cost reducing innovations, conversion of wood wastes into usable products, and a shift to wood substitutes. The first and the second stabilized cost per unit. The third reflected the effect of previous cost increases on other areas of the economy.

It was Ricardo's hypothesis that the decline in resource quality will partly offset the effect of economy-wide technological advance; and that costs of a unit of goods will, therefore, rise relative to unit costs of non-extractive goods. However, with the exception of forestry, the unit costs in the USA in the period under investigation decreased in the extractive sectors as against those of the non-extractive ones.

We know that in the USA the market motives of development have always been most powerful. Apart from times of war, capital investments for the extraction of domestic natural resources were only made when this proved to be more profitable than the export of capital.

In studying the course of value relations in the USA, it is useful to pay some attention to the conditions under which the law of the diminishing returns of land came into being. Ricardo formulated the law relying on the situation created in Britain in the wake of the Continental blockade ordered by Napoleon. It was a unique situation, which, in itself, was not a sound foundation on which a "universal" law could be built.

Price effects of substitution

An up-to-date industrial commodity structure is characterized by

- a wide assortment of commodities,
- a quick product replacement, and
- comprehensive complementarity and substitutability.

With the widening of the commodity assortment, the question of price relations of allied or substitute products is gaining increasing importance. The great multitude of products has virtually resulted in the prices of the different goods being in a mutual relationship with one another, not in respect of prices of specific products but of the price system. Given this industrial structure, there is an even stronger tendency towards evaluation based on the utility principle in making the prices of related products proportionate. The utility of the product, its evaluation according to its properties deemed important from the point of view of the consumer (user), are attributable to the fact that the consumer is willing to pay more for one product than for another if its utility is superior to that of the cheaper product. Thus, today's commodity pattern gives rise to a certain re-arrangement of product prices, new criteria come into being, which integrate the products of a given industry (related products) into a uniform price system.

The development of product prices into an intricate price system can also be witnessed in the extracting industries, caused by steadily increasing needs and a variety of utilization. Rising demand expands the range of raw materials extracted, and the varied uses to which they are put creates a closer relationship between quality and price through a more accurate grading. What has been observed in the extractive industries occurs to a much greater extent in the manufacturing industries. The expansion of assortments is a natural concomitant of rising living standards and of the mass demand for more sophisticated consumer goods. Technical development is accompanied by the introduction of new products and new varieties. With technical development substitutability and complementarity come increasingly into prominence.

In a modern economy, there is hardly any material that could not be replaced by another kind of material. According to the field of utilization, aluminium, cement and synthetics can be used instead of steel. Zinc-plate can be substituted by glass, or even by paper. More and more concrete is used in the construction industry instead of timber; modern building materials of low specific weight instead of traditional ones. In the furniture industry processes for substituting wood are extensively employed. Synthetics have penetrated nearly all branches of production. Substitution has created competition between products, when the different products are sold by enterprises that would otherwise enjoy a monopoly position.

Two effects of substitution on the price system may be discerned: the regulation of relative prices and of the price level.

1. The effect on the relative price is due to substitution by the consumer. When evaluating the materials that can substitute for one another in industrial processing, the method of stating the so-called *industrial value* is employed. For example, for iron ore it is established how much of its different kinds, or in identical kinds of iron ore, how much of iron ore of different contents of iron, is to be used for producing the quantity of one unit of crude iron.

The industrial value of different kinds and qualities of raw materials is thus established. Various processes, methods of measuring and statistics, mathematical formulae, can be used to establish the industrial value of different qualities of the same product and of different kinds of products that can substitute one another. In the case of raw materials the common feature of these methods is that they fix the use-value, or rather the relative use-value by reference to the effect they have on the cost of the product obtained by their processing.

2. The *price level effect* is the regulation of substitution performed by the producer. Inputs for different raw materials connected with one another, by substitutability, are different with respect to use-value per unit which may be equal from the consumer's viewpoint. If the substitution is complete and the cheaper material does not oust the more expensive one, because there is a demand for the whole quantity, then, in accordance with the principle of marginal cost, the input of the dearer material regulates the joint price level. In the same way, land rent is integrated into the price system through monopoly rent.

Under such conditions the relative price of natural resources can, of course, be judged only if we take into consideration the effects of substitution. The question is intricate, because (1) each of the different materials has manifold possibilities of application: (2) any given kind of raw material can substitute for a very wide variety of materials in the course of its utilization: (3) in the case of every material there is a field of use, where there is no substitute. All this only indicates how many facets economic life possesses, each of which is to be served by the price system. The trend of the relative prices of exhaustible natural resources connected with the replacement effect was the centre of the debate the present author had with G. Heal at the Fifth World Congress of the International Economic Association held in Tokyo in 1977.* Reproduced in Chart 14, *the competitive price curve drawn up by* G. Heal gave rise to the debate.

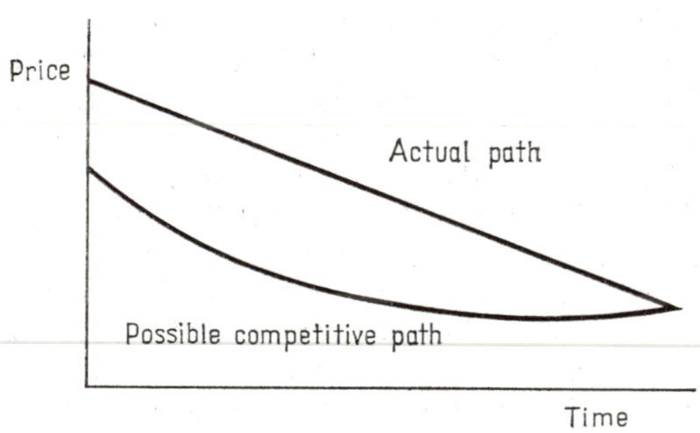

Chart 14. Competitive price curve of natural resources constructed by G. Heal

* Papers submitted to the Fifth World Congress of the International Economic Association held in Tokyo between the 29 August and 3 September 1977 were the following:
Heal, G.: *The Long-Run Movement of the Prices of Exhaustible Resources.*
Csikós-Nagy, B.: *Past and Prospective Price Trends of Natural Resources.*
My consultations with Miklós Tóth were most helpful in my preparations for the Congress. It was also Miklós Tóth who, at my request, drew up Chart 16.

G. Heal set out from various suppositions, three of which are of major significance.

1. If the actual price of some mineral is lower than that set by the "competitive price path" this must be considered "under-pricing" and over-consumption of the material in question.

2. The original price of the mineral must, as a function of the exhaustion of resources, always approach the price of the substituting product. At the time the resources are exhausted, the two prices must tally.

3. Production of the substitute material is costlier than the price of the material it is to replace. Thus the "competitive price path" is a parabola.

This picture would hardly be debatable if the "competitive price path" could be interpreted as one of the possible alternatives in the energy supply situation of the 1970s. However, in Chart 15 G. Heal gives the impression that, in an economy without inflation, the price of minerals can only rise.

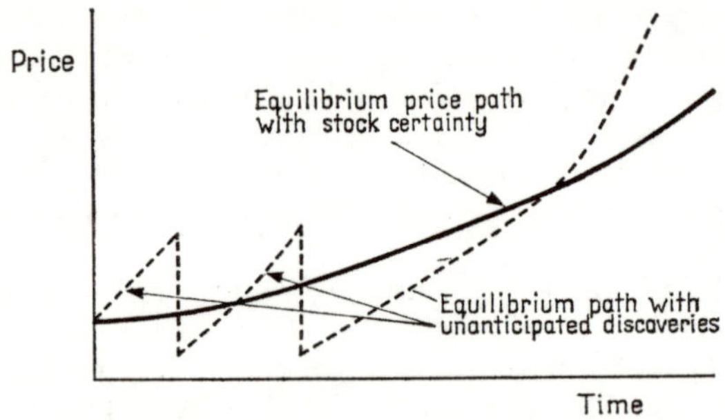

Chart 15. Equilibrium price curve in case of the discovery of new minerals

Chart 15 demonstrates the capital losses caused to the resource-owners by the discovery of new sites and the consequent temporary decrease of prices. According to Heal the owners must be compensated for bearing this risk and the only form that such compensation can take is a higher rate of price increase between discovery dates.

We can construct a competitive price curve on the basis of various suppositions. Let us take the following two assumptions:

1. The mineral resources of the Earth are fully discovered and by their extraction the increase of relative scarcity can be considered an objective trend.

2. The technology of extraction and utilization is constant and therefore the substitution of materials has already reached its limits.

Under such conditions the marginal costs and thus the prices of minerals must gradually rise, since, as a general rule, the extraction of natural resources under more favourable conditions precedes their extraction under less favourable ones.

We all know that the problem does not emerge under such conditions. More and more sources of minerals are discovered. In the case of most of the minerals relative scarcity does not increase. The methods of extraction and utilization become more and more highly developed and increasingly economical. Minerals can also be substituted by other materials. Of course, G. Heal takes these factors into consideration. However, there are some points that are debatable.

First of all, one must clarify what is meant by *the exhaustion of the resources of a certain mineral.* Different countries apply different methods in taking account of their stocks. Mineral resources are not generally taken to mean the whole, already discovered geological deposits and the possible physical maximum, but only their *extractable* part. The difference in the methods used by countries taking account of their stocks lies rather in the criteria, according to which extractability is determined. Most countries consider profitability the main criterion of extractability, or, at least, that extraction should not mean losses at prevailing prices. This also explains why, at a time of substantial price changes on the world market, countries will continue to supervise not only their development policy but will also re-evaluate their mineral stocks. A part of the stocks may be deleted from the extractable list as was the case at an ealier date with coal, when cheap oil came into large-scale use. But this process was reversed after the oil price explosion.

This could not have happened if in the development of productive forces the transition from one mineral to another, i.e. to the substitute, had taken place in the way projected in the "competitive price path" constructed by G. Heal. Quite frequently, in consequence of the discovery of new materials the extraction of traditional ones must be curbed as long as there are big stocks available, particularly when these stocks are increased by regular discoveries year after year.

G. Heal's "competitive price path" is based on conditions in which industrialization on a world scale takes place at a quicker rate than is actually the case; whereas the rate of technical development is slower. A hyperbolic price curve can more accurately characterize price movements as a result of the development of productive forces. It is a characteristic feature of this latter price curve that the individual price curve of a single mineral is a parabola: the hyperbola appears as a path, determined by the intersections of price curves where substitution takes place.

Chart 16 is based on the following two hypotheses: (1) The mass extraction of different minerals and the improvement of the appropriate technology will decrease the specific cost of extraction; the gradual inclusion into production of qualities with

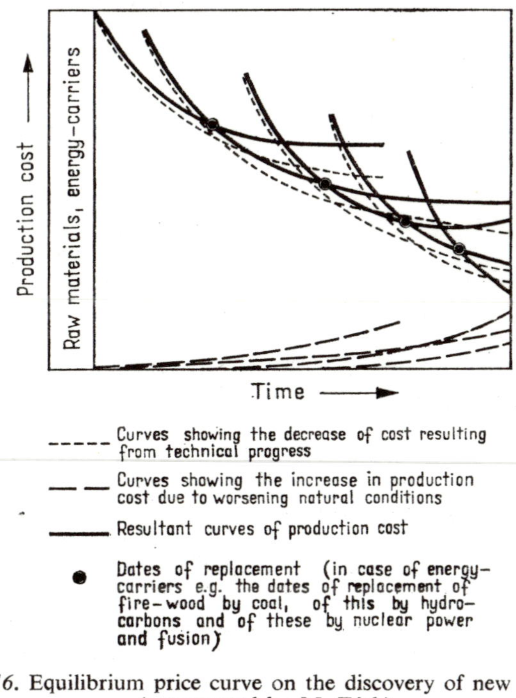

Chart 16. Equilibrium price curve on the discovery of new minerals (constructed by M. Tóth)

poorer specific values, or of stocks whose extraction takes place under more difficult natural conditions, will more and more offset the cost reducing effect of technical development and, after a certain point, specific costs will rise. (2) As a result of the development of productive forces there will be an extension of the production and utilization of new minerals or of other products suitable for replacing certain mineral raw materials, as well as of materials that can be more economically produced or used than the traditional ones.

The hydrocarbons used for replacing coal could be produced (and used) more cheaply than coal; steel and aluminium can be produced with substantially less input than a traditional metal like copper. In spite of the price increases taking place meanwhile in the raw materials of synthetics that may to some extent take the place of minerals the situation is the same. Nuclear energy is cheaper or, at least, can be cheaper, than traditional coal-based energy; and the same holds good for solar energy, supposed to provide energy in the future.

The replaceable minerals need not inevitably be more expensive than the previous ones. This follows from the fact that within the costs of the ultimate product of mineral raw materials substituting one another, namely of electric energy, metal, etc. relative costs—particularly of live labour—of primary mineral raw materials decrease, whereas relative costs of processing, utilizing in the main embodied labour, increase. This is rendered possible by the circumstance that, whilst the primary quality of identical mineral raw materials diminishes, the use-value (heating value, or metal content) of substitute mineral raw materials substantially increases. Hydrocarbons have considerably higher heating values than coal, uranium ore has a heating value several times higher than hydrocarbons; iron ore and aluminium ore have a considerably higher metal content than copper ore. Accordingly, whereas out of the costs of electrical energy produced from coal over 50% fell to the share of fuel, in a nuclear power plant they do not even amount to 20%, and the share of the uranium ore in costs is less than 5%. The situation is similar with respect to metals that can more or less substitute for one another. Whereas in the cost of copper, which can be considered the oldest of metals, the cost of copper ore amounts to 40% at least, in the case of aluminium the cost of bauxite does not amount to as much as 10%.

The future of oil prices

The price of crude oil was 4.7-times higher in 1975 than in 1970 (calculated at average prices of consumption in the USA). This change is the consequence of the 1973 oil price explosion. Since then, drastic price rises have been observed in the sphere of natural resources. But, while the majority of natural resources remain sensitive to market trends of prices, the relative price of oil has become stabilized at the level it had reached in the price explosion. However, even apart from this, oil prices deserve special attention. (1) Oil is the most important product of mining. (2) It is the main source of energy that can limit economic growth in the foreseeable future. Temporary scarcity and the production or extraction costs of substitute materials can play a determinant role in the future trend of oil prices. From this point of view the 1973 oil price explosion can be interpreted as an upgrading of the price of oil, which was previously under-priced.

Because of its suitability for heating purposes oil can be brought to a common denominator with other energy carriers, e.g. with coal. Comparability is based on *heating values*. It could in fact be assumed that the relative world market price of energy carriers is adjusted to their relative heating values. And yet, their coincidence

Table 48

relative world market price of crude oil[1] (Coal price = 100)

Year	Relative price	Year	Relative price
1928	131.5	1958	112.0
1938	125.0	1965	87.7
1948	98.0	1970	54.6
1954	101.0	1975	242.1

[1] The calculations are based on statistical data of the German Federal Republic. According to them the calorific value of a unit of coal and of crude oil was essentially identical at identical parity from GFR port or GFR mine in the period between 1953 and 1955. This period has been considered the basis of the calculations.

is only due to chance, and the possible deviations in both directions are considerable. (See Table 48.)

Let us examine the costs of *replacing oil,* which the view prevailing today considers the chief determinant of future oil prices. The following table points out the differences of opinion in this respect.

Table 49

The relative world market price of crude oil estimated for approximately 2000

	$/barrel[1]
Lowest price limit	7
Basic price (1976 price)	11.5
Highest price limit:	
Estimate I	18
Estimate II	20–30

[1] At the 1974 value of the dollar.

The 7 dollar per barrel price of oil was declared by some industrially developed countries as the minimum price after the oil price explosion. The price of 20–30 dollars per barrel is accounted for by H. Ager-Hanssen's paper.*

In order to co-ordinate their oil price policies within the framework of the so-called "West–South dialogue", the energy commission comprising the eight leading capitalist industrial countries of the world as well as 18 oil exporting developing countries, has met repeatedly. It need hardly be said that oil prices are not regulated by West–South dialogues. And yet, the significance of these must not be under-estimated, since information obtainable on such occasions is taken into consideration by the price policy of OPEC.

The only point of agreement seems to be that oil prices should not fall below the level of which projects for the reduction or substitution of oil imports in the developed capitalist countries may profitably be developed. Such considerations gave rise to the declaration by some industrially developed countries, that they would not allow the oil price to fall below 7 dollars per barrel.

* Ager-Hanssen, H.: Norwegian Oil and Alternative Energy Resources. (Manuscript.)

In the mid 1970s the prevailing assumption was that the 7 dollars per barrel price would far exceed the price of most alternative energy carriers. Calculations based on the oil price per barrel estimated the costs of North Sea oil, of American coal and of natural gas, as well as the cost of energy produced in nuclear power plants, at $ 4–4.50. The views formulated in this connexion were later modified. It turned out that the process of reducing coal production which had been started at the time of cheap oil prices, was very difficult to reverse. Despite the fact that the Earth is provided with solid energy carriers for several hundred years, and that the biggest coal stocks are in industrially developed regions, there are substantial difficulties in the way of new developments in coal production. There are, for a start, serious technical–economic obstacles and drawbacks connected with environment protection, which arise with the use of coal in industry and in households, as well as labour and other problems arising in production. That is why efforts are being made to introduce new, efficient technologies, partial or full automation; all factors that increase production costs. In the foreseeable future it is rather gasification and processes of utilization connected with it that hold out the promise of success.

It has turned out that prognoses of the building of nuclear power plants were unrealistic. One after the other the industrially developed countries narrow down, delay or cancel the building of nuclear power plants. The most important cause for curbing the construction of these plants is that the first calculations have been faulty. The projects of constructing nuclear power plants at an accelerated rate were based on the calculation that electric energy produced by them would cost half as much as that produced in oil power plants. These calculations were based on nuclear power plants put into operation in 1974 or earlier, i.e. at a time when the major part of research and development costs were covered by governments. According to the new prognoses the costs of nuclear power plants beginning operation after 1980 will be—at least in the USA—40–50% higher than that of power plants operating with fossil fuel.

Let us consider the "Offshore North Sea Oil" conference held in Stavanger, Norway in the autumn of 1976, on the basis of H. Ager-Hanssen's report. The purpose of the conference was to ascertain the cost of oil that can be extracted off the shore of the North Sea and to discuss what level the long-term world market price for this fuel can reach at which the utilization of new resources proves profitable. Attention was concentrated on the capitalist world, that is, the demand–supply situation in the Soviet Union, in East Europe and in China was not taken into consideration.

According to the basic hypothesis the oil balance will show a deficit in the capitalist world around the turn of the millenium even if the historically given annual 5.4% increase of demand decreases substantially. Ager-Hanssen outlined two alternatives for the period 1975–2000. In the first alternative a discovery rate of 20 billion barrels/year has been assumed between 1975–2000; up to 1985 the demand will increase by 4% a year and 2.5% after that time. According to the second alternative the discovery rate of 20 billion barrels/year has been assumed in the period 1975–1985 and 10 billion barrels/year after 1985, whilst the demand will increase by 3.5% till 1985, and will be 1.5% after that time. Both alternatives assume a limiting reserve to production ratio of 15:1.

Assessments indicate that oil production will fall short of demand somewhere between 1985 and 2000 on the most probable combinations of assumptions. The global oil shortage problem which the world is likely to experience some time before the year 2000, may be further enhanced if OPEC continues to put a ceiling on its production of oil. The shortage is to be covered by other sources of energy, but it must be borne in mind by the decision-makers that the full impact of the newly developed energy source on the world energy balance takes at least 15–20 years.

Having consulted energy companies and research organizations, Ager-Hanssen has drawn up the following table about the costs of alternative sources of energy. The table gives the price range for oil which is considered to be the minimum for economical exploitation of the alternative sources on a substantial scale.

Table 50

Alternative energy sources that can substitute for oil

Technology	Indicative required oil price for exploitation $/barrel	R & D status*	Max impact in year 2000 in % of total demand
Oil shale	18–23	Pilot/Study	5–7
Tar sands	17–25	Pilot/Study	? (small)
Gases and liquids from coal	15–35	Pilot/Demo	7–10
Waste heat utilization	10–20	Study/Demo	2–3
Fuels from biomass	?	Lab	0–1
Waste materials to energy	10–25	Comm	3–4
Hydrogen in energy systems**	?	Study	0
Solar heat and cooling	15–25	Pilot	3–6
Energy savings			
Transport	10–30	Study/Comm	4–6
Industry	10–30	Study/Comm	4–6
Housing and consumer products	10–30	Study/Comm	3–5

* Study = study projects; Pilot = pilot experiments; Demo = demonstration plants; Comm = commercial plants

** Impact can be expected only in the long term, i.e. the year 2000.

Chapter Six

EPILOGUE

1. Inflation theory

Inflation

We have surveyed the price trends of seven centuries and have meditated upon price conditions to be expected about the year 2000. Now we have to present a summary and draw conclusions. To achieve this we have to make a critical analysis of economics. All experience bears witness to the fact that economics does not provide an adequate basis for understanding price conditions in the present day, and it particularly fails to assist us in anticipating future price trends.

At present the price problem is primarily an inflation problem, with which, we have to admit, we are unable to cope. That is why it seems to be justified to introduce a critical analysis of economics by discussing the theory of inflation.

The notion inflation originates from the expression "inflated" and was first used in the American Civil War. It defined the state of affairs in which there was a large premium on coinage as against uncovered paper money and, parallel with it, prices generally rose, although to varying degrees.* The expression "inflation" was introduced during the period when, side by side with coinage, paper money was gaining ground. The first analysis of inflation dealt with the peculiar process of prices multiplied by two.

The classic formulation of inflation is adjusted to this: the "dilution" of money raises the price level. Its opposite is deflation: the shrinking of the quantity of money decreases the price level. As a general rule deflationary policy serves to overcome inflation. It is a monetary policy used during inflation with a view to raising the value of money. Seen in its *direct* effects, deflation is a recession and thus a painful and anti-social process. However, if used in the right time and in the right way, it is objectively necessary, because, in its indirect effects it may prevent economic shocks that bring major social tensions in their wake.

The above reference to the emergence of the concept of inflation was not meant to be an introduction to the history of theories, from which we are only picking those elements that offer useful information towards a better understanding of the inflationary problems of our time. From this point of view it may suffice to concentrate our attention on *changes which have been taking place in the concept of inflation.* On this basis we can distinguish three principal theoretical trends, according to which inflation is

- depreciation of currency,
- excess demand,
- rise in the price level.

These changed viewpoints are in chronological order. The identification of inflation with depreciation was the prevailing view up to the 1890s, and with excess

* *Közgazdasági Enciklopédia* (Encyclopedia of economics) Vol. II, Budapest, 1929.

demand up to the 'fifties of our century. In recent decades more and more economists have equated inflation with the rise in the price level, though by this the concept has become *divorced from its originally accepted meaning.*

One cannot help associating the idea with the *value concept.* The concept of value, as the quantity of labour spent on the production of commodities, became the starting-point of our understanding of the price phenomenon. If one renounces the hypothesis of labour value—as has been done by the marginal utility theory and other recent non-Marxist price theories—, then Cassel was right in proposing that value be an expression deleted from the vocabulary of economics and that science limit its attention to the study of exchange relations.* In the same way, why should we need the concept of inflation if we identify it with the rise of the price level? The very expression might not have emerged if the concept had been interpreted in the manner prevailing today.

The concept of value was introduced into economics by the classic English school, whereas that of inflation was introduced by the quantity theory of money. A connexion between value and inflation is created by money value or by its possible depreciation. Turning the pages of old textbooks one can find distinctions, sometimes only nuances, in the interpretation of inflation. By way of demonstration we should point out that Liefmann considered the influence of the multiplication of the quantity of money on price inflation,** while in Cassel's opinion inflation was the supersaturation of the market with paper money.*** One economist used the word to define a state, the other a process. But there is agreement on the view that inflation (and deflation in the same way) upsets general equilibrium, usually as a result of economic (monetary) policy.

Interpreting money value as a given price level, inflationary monetary policy is a manifestation that raises the price level and deflationary policy one that decreases it. In both cases, the change of the price level originates from the *money side.* But the price level may also change in consequence of factors appearing on the *commodity side.* This explains why old textbooks of economics separated comprehensive price analysis from the analysis of inflation and deflation and considered this latter as a peculiar manifestation of price movements induced by money regulation.

To interpret inflation as *excess demand* was a new explanation of the price level rise determined by the money side. This idea was developed by Wicksell.° According to the quantity theory, the price level will rise if the quantity of money increases, though circumstances remain otherwise unchanged. Wicksell deduced that the price effect arose from the money side, not directly from the change of the quantity of money, but from the relationship between supply and demand. The difference is significant. The increase in the quantity of money is justifiable if it is in proportion to the growth of the economy, if the share of savings increases and if, in general, the velocity of money circulation diminishes. After all, the inflationary effect exerted on the price level from the money side can only be based on the fact that people want to buy more goods and avail themselves of more services than is the supply at the given price level. For Wicksell, who thought in terms of a free market model, it seemed to be a matter of course that excess demand leads to a rise in prices.

In countries with a market economy the rise in price levels became continuous after the Second World War. The fact that excess demand has also become permanent

* Cassel, G.: *Theoretische Sozialökonomie,* Leipzig, 1918, fifth edition, 1932.

** Liefmann, R.: *Grundsätze der Volkswirtschaftslehre,* Stuttgart–Berlin, Vol. I, third ed. 1923, Vol. II, second ed. 1922.

*** Cassel, G.: *Deutschlands wirtschaftliche Widerstandskraft,* Berlin, 1916.

° Wicksell, K.: *Geldzins und Güterpreise,* Jena, 1898.

also plays a role in this. Of course, under such conditions, it became difficult to analyse separately the commodity side and the money side, that is to say to approach the problem in a way that can separate inflationary price movements from price movements determined by changes in the conditions of production. For those devising econometric models it also seemed to be simpler to identify inflation with a rise in price levels. This was done by Clark when, commissioned by the American Banker Association, he investigated price and wage trends.* In the wake of the study of Clark and others the opinion has grown general, according to which

- creeping, accelerated and galloping inflation are terms to be distinguished as functions of the annual rate of the rise in price levels; and
- cost-push and demand-pull inflation are terms to be distinguished as causes bringing about the rise of the price level.

The concept of "structural inflation" has emerged to explain the changes of relative prices, especially the rise of relative prices of certain services as a function of a differentiated increase of productivity and of proportionate wage development.

In 1958 Phillips** published a paper in which he considered three of his theses with respect to Great Britain, as statistically proved. (1) The connexion between the rate of unemployment and changes in the wage levels is not a linear one. Wage rises are larger in case of almost full employment, when there is a significant demand for labour, than are wage decreases in case of intense unemployment. (2) The extent of wage rises depends on the changes in labour demand. Labour is in a stronger position in enforcing increased wage demands if the demand for labour is increasing (if unemployment is decreasing). (3) Only in the case of a considerable rise of consumer prices does the cost of living exert an effect on wages. In the case of a rise in the cost of living by a few per cent, the rise in the consumer price level will only neutralize the difference between the improvement of productivity and the extent of wage rises. On the other hand, if the cost of living rises considerably the price–wage spiral is set into motion. The present theories of inflation are based on the Phillips curves and on their further developed variants.

There are economists who consider it merely a question of convention whether theories, the theory of inflation among them, are invested with economic content. According to this view the problem of inflation can be analysed in various frameworks of investigation; the essence is that they should reveal the causes of the price increases and find the means by which inflation can be conquered, whilst economic efficiency is also considered. However, theories, classifications, etc. shape the course of thinking. Good theories and definitions promote a fuller knowledge of the real world. Scientific research into the causes of inflation must serve the aims of economic policy. Bearing this in mind we must answer the question whether the "modern" interpretation of inflation is an advance or a distortion of the old one, and whether a switch-over from price analyses of the *commodity–money* side to analyses of the *demand* and *cost* inflation is a progressive or a retrograde step.

Let us set out from the *price relations at a given point of time,* assuming that there is no excess demand and prices are regulated by the market and operate as equilibrium prices. Regarded from the supply side these prices differ from social values. This is inevitable, since:

* Clark, J. M.: *The Wage–Price Problem.* The American Banker Association, 1960.

** Phillips, A. W.: The Relation Between Unemployment and the Rate of Change of Money Wage Rates in the United Kingdom, 1861–1957, *Economica,* November, 1959.

– The market price can maintain the equilibrium of demand and supply only in fluctuations around value.

– Various products are in a substitution relation with one another. Their relative price is influenced by the consumer, who compares it with their use-value. This is one of the reasons why value theory can only be interpreted together with rent theory.

– It is a characteristic of the production process that several products emerge simultaneously. The classification of products into main product, by-product and waste is based on this and so, where main products are linked in production, is the category of joint products. In such a manufacturing process the value per product often cannot be determined, or relative prices can be determined only as functions of substitution.

Regarded from the *demand* side it seems sufficient to assume that consumers' preferences do operate, and the adjustment of the supply structure to the demand structure is realized in an adequate manner. The question is how price movements determine the changes taking place in production and consumption conditions (the product side) (1) in the short run; (2) in the long run and (3) in the secular perspective. Likewise we will assume a general equilibrium in which the changes of the amount of money and the velocity of money circulation (the money side) do not induce price movements.

Evidently, in the *short run,* those price movements are characteristic which are naturally concomitant with the equilibrium function of prices in an economy growing under balanced conditions. Price analyses of this type investigate the price change that are connected with seasonal factors and with their movements around value. As a rule these short-run price movements do not bring about a change in price levels (and thus of the value of money). The scientific examination of price movements in the *long run* is based on the law of returns characteristic of the production factors. The decreasing returns on land and the increasing returns on capital have given rise to opinions that in the sphere of agriculture prices tend to rise, while those of industrial products are falling. Thus, in the long run, the commodity side determines changes in the price levels (value of money).

Theorists holding the quantitative theory of money studied only short-run changes, and that is how they reached the conclusion that, *regarded from the commodity side, only a change of relative prices takes place.** It should also be emphasized in general that representatives of the quantity theory of money are inclined to belittle all autonomous regularities reflecting real processes taking place in the economy and to interpret every substantial change of circumstances as a reflection of monetary processes. By this they have virtually given rise to a change in the approach to inflation, in which inflation is no longer considered as a depreciation of money but as a rise in price level.

Price stability

When characterizing the mechanism of capitalist production in the 19th century, Marx analysed the factors appearing on the commodity side, concerned with changes of value (price). He analysed a free market economy in which new forms of organiza-

* Kirmairer: *Die Quantitätstheorie,* Jena, 1922.
Neisser, H.: *Der Tauschwert des Geldes,* Jena, 1928.
Willis, P.: History of Quantity Theory, *Journal of Political Economy,* 1896.

tion and new technologies were introduced, modernization processes decided upon only if, as their result, the change in the organic composition of capital invested in production (the increase of the share of constant capital) led to a fall in the specific input per unit of product, i.e. in the value of the commodity. In the free market system of the past century this was practically enforced by the stringent competition, and was rendered possible by the oligo-centrally organized world economy, by the "industrial reserve army" and the weak position of the working class. Also, based upon this idea was Marx's hypothesis according to which the value of a commodity is in inverse ratio to the productivity of labour, which was systematically rising.

We have analysed from many aspects the general political, social and economic relations which, in the 20th century, have created new conditions for price movements. We have given voice to our opinion that in our own time the *commodity side determines the trend of rising price levels.* But, even if this is accepted, why should it be considered inflation? It would be as little justified as a theory according to which the falling price trends of the 19th century were a deflationary process.

Facts are obstinate things. They always point to the differences between reality and the way we should like things to be. Inflation is a disturbance of equilibrium, which, at first, arbitrarily re-distributies incomes, and then disrupts the economy. Of course, such a state of affairs can be maintained temporarily, but the problem must be resolved sooner or later either by a currency reform or, independently of it, by stabilization measures. Political economy, in either a socialist or a capitalist society, cannot be based on the hypothesis of a social–economic imbalance and particularly not on the prevalence of inflation which contains elements of irrationality. Nor can we consider the general process of social economic development a succession of inflation and deflation. Off and on there might appear and exist irregularities in economic life and they must be included in our analysis. But the *starting hypothesis can only be stability.* If we denied the efficiency of stabilization policy, science would offer only two alternatives to mankind: *either recurring crises and unemployment with price stability, or steady economic growth and full employment with inflation.* In fact, this is the theory of *permanent inflation.*

But what do we mean by *economic stability* and what price movements do we consider compatible with it? Opinions about price stability differ, and so do they about inflation. He who ascribes inflation to a rise of the price level, equates price stability with unchanged price levels. In interpreting price stability, one can even define it as totally unchanging (frozen) prices. Therefore it may be better to put the question in the following way: *what are the limits of price movements within basic economic stability?* The only rational interpretation of economic stability seems to be that which does not raise obstacles to the development of productive forces and is not at variance with the political, social and economic conditions necessary for economic growth. Consequently, price movements objectively determined by the changes of production and consumption conditions are to be considered justified.

The relative price of a certain product may rise or fall because relative inputs, or relative demand, rise or fall. These changes may be expressed in price movements, unless they are transitional phenomena. In the latter case it is just price stability that renders the government's temporary counterbalancing (financial) measures desirable. Price movements induced by the commodity side can be justified, since they reflect objective changes in that the relative scarcity of certain products will inevitably increase or decrease.

It was Lerner, who first expounded the theory that *rising prices without inflation* were acceptable. In his view we can imagine a state of affairs in which there is a continuous rise in demand and a continuous rise in prices, a state which is foreseeable. We can then have rising prices without any of the evils of inflation. The danger of inflation is not the rise of prices but the lack of foresight and thus of counterbalance. In the case of a foreseen price rise there is no excess demand. People expect to spend more money in the future, but they are also willing to pay the higher prices. The expected demand can be equal to the expected supply.*

While studying "modern" inflation theories we can often meet with such terms as "non-anticipated", "expected" and "actual" inflation rate. "Modern" inflation theories attach a great importance to the *expectation* motive.** One cannot help remembering the *Lerner formula*. When the excess demand – inflation formula is substituted for the price level rise – inflation formula, Lerner's distinction can be utilized within the framework of inflation. That is how an expected inflation can be differentiated from an unexpected one, and a foreseen inflation rate from an unforeseen one. If the expected price rise can be fitted into the framework of long-term equilibrium, inflation in this alternative becomes pointless.

It is often pointed out that a rising price level in harmony with the *expected rate* is meaningless in itself, since the rise of the price level leads to a change of relative prices, as a result of which various money incomes turn into real incomes in a changed ratio. This is due to the income re-distribution effect of the change of relative prices, and/or of the fact that the consumption patterns of low, medium and high income households, of childless families, or families with few or with many children show substantial differences. This, however, is not a specific feature of the price level rise.

The real wages of workers may increase from year to year, even if the price level is unchanged, rises or falls. Thus, for instance a 3% increment of real wages can be realized (1) parallel with a 6% increase of nominal wages, if the price level rises by 3%, (2) in the case of a 3% increment of nominal wages, if the price level remains unchanged and (3) with an unchanged wage level if the price level decreases by 3%. In view of this the question is what alternative is preferred by the worker. Seen from the aspect of the "average" worker, the real wage increases in the three cases by 3% exactly; thus for him it is a matter of indifference in which manner his real wages increase by 3%. But in life statistical averages are not typical. For the individual consumer the 3% average emerges in a powerful dispersion: some consumers find themselves in a better position than the average, while others are in a worse one.

What is the difference in the characteristics of the alternatives of the 3% average real wage increment? If the 3% real wage increment is realized parallel with a 3% rise of the price levels, i.e. with a 6% nominal wage, it is almost certain that there will be some marginal consumers for whom the new situation will be worse than the previous one. On the other hand, if the 3% real wage increment is realized parallel with a 3% decrease of the price level, the marginal consumer may find himself at worst in a situation in which his income does not improve. In the case of the former alternative the position becomes worse for individual consumers whose nominal wages have been raised below the average and, projected on their consumption pattern, the rise of the price level has exceeded the average. In the case of the latter alternative the position of the individual consumer does not improve where, given his consumption pattern, the price level has not decreased.

And yet, we should like to emphasize that relative prices will become transformed as a function of relative values or of demand–supply, irrespective of whether the price level remains unchanged, rises or decreases. Consequently, if somebody considers the counterbalancing of all kinds of price movements as a basic criterion of

* Lerner, A. P.: The Inflationary Process. Some Theoretical Aspects, *The Review of Economics and Statistics*, Vol. XXXI, 1949.

** Lundberg, E. (ed.): *Inflation Theory and Anti-Inflation Policy*, London, 1977.

stability, he will come up against insoluble problems in inflation, deflation or price stability alike. An uncontrolled re-distribution of incomes will arise in the three alternatives.

The presentation of the three alternatives is by no means due to chance. We see that, regarded from different aspects, priority undergoes a change.

Let us investigate the alternative in which wages do not change and real wages rise in consequence of the decrease of the price level. In this case the dispersion of the real wage increment depends on the individual consumer's consumption pattern or on the way in which he will change his consumption pattern. There is no incomes policy in this alternative, or it consists of the endeavour to change relative prices as a function of relative values, whereas real wages rise in the function of the relative consumption pattern. This will meet the requirements of economic efficiency but will certainly differ from the criteria of a just distribution of incomes.

If we interpret active incomes policy (the raising of incomes in centralized and decentralized forms) as an activity that continually corrects the distortions which the market mechanism causes in incomes distribution, obviously the alternative in which wages rise by 3% parallel with an unchanged price level is better than the one in which the price level decreases by 3%, while wages remain unchanged.

Finally, if excess demand induces a 3% rise of the price level, a 6% rise of the wage level with a 3% rise of the price level is better than when, by means of repressed inflation, wages are increased by 3% only.

Price revolution

Up to now we have emphatically argued for a wider interpretation of price stability and a narrower one of inflation. Essentially, we have attempted to interpret what is considered by opinion prevailing today as alternatives of *inflation,* as alternatives of price stability and inflation. Now we should like to study inflation from a *new aspect.* We consider it justified to regard certain cases of inflation as a price revolution and to distinguish it, as such, from all other possible cases of inflation.

Economic historians correctly differentiated the permanent inflations of the sixteenth and early seventeenth centuries from the short-run inflations following them. To convey this they have introduced the term "price revolution", but failed to describe satisfactorily the criteria of price revolutions. What can be the specific features of a price revolution?

1. Inflation is a particular state, whereas a price revolution is a departure from economic laws. If, on account of war or of any other reasons, a country, or a group of countries, finds itself in an emergency, governments feel authorized to "suspend" the economic laws that control economic life under normal circumstances. Of course, economic laws cannot be quashed, but their scope of action can be restricted, the conditions of their operation can be changed and, what is more, they can be put to the service of an emergency situation. This is realized in a *restrictive war economy.*

On the other hand, we can speak about a price revolution if, owing to the changes of external factors, the operation of the free market mechanism is shattered, nevertheless price movements are still automatically controlled. Thus a price revolution is a peculiar manifestation of a market economy, which operates under peaceful conditions, moreover under market forces. In relation to economics this state can be qualified as "unlawful" because, under the impact of external factors, economic laws give rise to irrational behaviour, prices cannot provide an orientation for rational economic decisions and thus the economy *runs into a blind alley.*

In the case of excess demand, the value of money decreases, and, under such conditions the only modification in the connexion of commodity value and price is that the changes of relative prices occur within a rising price level. The levelling of profit rates and the flow of capital promoting it are characteristic of the whole process —with all the usual exceptions, including those due to monopoly. But the essential point is that, in the case of simple inflation, no commodity can acquire and maintain for a long time a privileged position, even if the demand structure on which excess demand is based is concentrated upon definite commodities. As a result of inter-sector capital flows, prices of commodities approach their value: monopoly profits and rents diminish to their normal level in the price structure.

What differentiates a price revolution from simple inflation is the circumstance that the role of the law of value in regulating relative prices terminates or, at least, considerably weakens. Under such conditions the law of value merely expresses the simple truth that the output at the given prices is equal to the amount of total value.

2. Inflation may be on a world scale, it might be regional or limited to the economy of some countries or of only one. *A price revolution is a phenomenon on a world scale.* Not even socialist countries can avoid its effect. On the one hand, socialist countries can purchase goods only on the world market at prices prevailing there, and they have to adjust their sales prices to the price relations of the world market. On the other hand, in CMEA trade, integrating the socialist economies, the world market price is considered the main criterion for foreign trade pricing.

Any country can create an inflation and will actually do so if a situation arises which can be overcome only by means of inflation. In such cases it is the society of that nation itself that bears the costs of inflation. The income re-distribution brought about by inflation mostly takes place within the country. A price revolution is also created by countries, but it definitely relates to *world economy as a whole.* A price explosion is a peculiar profit inflation, with a view to the international re-distribution of national incomes.

Profit inflation characterized the price revolution of the sixteenth century, and tendencies towards profit inflation are also visible at present. The sixteenth century profit inflation was connected with the emergence of a world economy, whereas the present tendencies of profit inflation are rooted in the secular changes in the world economy. Primitive (previous) accumulation laid the foundations of capitalist production in the sixteenth century. In our time it is the developing world that is trying to find ways and means by which it can ensure the capital required for an equitable economic growth.

3. Inflation is a way out of problems. A price revolution is a *challenge,* in the background of which there is an endeavour to re-arrange the power structures as well as political and social values.

The recognition of the self-regulating capacity of economic life created economics. Regarded from a historical aspect it seems that, relying on a philosophy which professed the natural freedom of man, the physiocratic and the English classic schools developed economics into an independent science in their fight against the constraints of mercantilist economic policy. They put forward a theory that, as it were, brought economic knowledge into line with economic policy, in a theory in which what is natural seems to be right. This was the extolling of the price mechanism and of the regulating role of the market. That is why, in pure theory, the "right price", the "natural price" and the "free market price" blend into a unity.

All this may suggest that the order of values that emerged came into being purely through the search for economic rationality, as a result of social evolution, and that the new challenge endangers this natural process. In fact, philosophy professing the natural freedom of man and the economic policy embracing it had been preceded by the emergence of the power structure whose survival and consolidation could be best ensured by this very philosophy. The challenge of the developing world is levelled against this economic mechanism.

2. Price theory

Market price

The history of political economy under capitalism is, it may be said, the history of the price theory. The very close link between the two is observable in the theory which treats the state as an exogenous factor of the economy. In their abstraction from practice the representatives of pure theory reached a different conclusion and considered different phases in the spontaneous movements of the market to be determinant. The different explanations of processes taking place in economic life that can be inserted into the framework of pure theory, as well as the different views regarding them also give rise to possible variants in price theory.

It is not possible for us to introduce the different variants and we need not do so. It is enough if we concentrate our attention on the following:

– the *basic hypotheses,* which, according to the representatives of pure theory, prevail under the conditions of perfect competition;
– the *modifications* that occur under monopoly conditions. In what follows we will start from the assumption that the *Pareto optimum** offers sufficient explanation for the basic hypotheses; and
– the modifications are well characterized by the theories of imperfect competition and monopolistic competition.**

The price theory created by the political economy of capitalism is integrated within the framework of the *general equilibrium theory.* This is a natural concomitant of the scientific approach prevailing in a free market system based on capitalist private ownership. If economics is pursued as a pure theory, in effect without any politics, the analysis can characterize only the state that emerges under the conditions of *self-regulation.* On the other hand, the price mechanism and the self-regulation of the market based on it, can only be accepted if we assume that by their nature factors exerting an effect on economic life are striving for an equilibrium in which there is no reason for change. This concept has been expounded by representatives of the marginal utility school. Indeed, it was they who provided the equilibrium theory with the objective foundation of price theory. According to this, the optimal state is one in which no one can gain without causing a loss to others, because

– all costs are minimized and
– all prices—seen from the demand side—conform to the marginal utility and, seen from the supply side, conform to the marginal cost.

According to the representatives of pure theory, rationality under capitalism must be limited, since in practice *the conditions of perfect competition cannot be ensured.* That is why attention is focussed on a manysided analysis of market relations. Price

* Pareto, V.: *Cours d'économie politique,* Lausanne, 1897.
** Robinson, J.: *Economics of Imperfect Competition,* London, 1954. Chamberlin, E. H.: *The Theory of Monopolistic Competition,* Cambridge, Mass., USA, 1947.

theory takes into account differences in the numbers of the participants in the market and in the character of commodities sold on the market. Depending on the number of participants, there exists a competitive market, a monopoly market and an oligopoly market. In this connexion there appear differences between the prices ruling under competition and under monopoly. The equilibrium price is independent of the intentions of the participants in the market, while the monopoly price is the result of enterprise policy (concerning supply or demand and/or price). Depending on the character of the product there exist markets of standardized and of differentiated products. Price stratification and harmonization are dealt with in close connexion with their possible market effects.

Price policy relates to two linked processes: One is that of *capital concentration* and centralization; the other is *product substitution* which is increasingly gaining ground as a result of technical progress. Capital concentration and centralization create the system of big firms and parallel with this oligopoly markets become predominant. With the growth of productive forces the market price is more and more controlled by big firms, which can influence prices; indeed, they pursue an active price policy. At the same time the spread of substitutability of products changes the competition between enterprises into a competition between products.

All these connexions are interpreted by a price theory closely linked with the *elasticity of demand.* Investigations of the elasticity of demand are based on the generally prevailing axiom that price changes transform demand in opposite directions, whereas income changes transform it in the same direction. Price rises and/or the decrease in incomes constrain demand, whilst the decrease in prices and/or the rise of incomes increase demand. When the co-efficient of elasticity of demand is one, we are confronted with proportionate changes. In the case of elastic demand, demand changes progressively; in the case of inelastic demand it changes regressively.

Society and economy

But are relative prices and their changes satisfactorily explained by the hypotheses on which price theory is based? The 1973 oil price explosion makes this question timely. Investigating the world market price trends for natural resources in the period 1973–1976, we can make two remarks. (1) Since the 1973 oil price explosion there have been hectic price rises in raw materials and fuels. (2) In case of most natural resources prices continued to be more or less sensitive to market conditions, whereas the relative price of oil, which soared after the oil price explosion, became more or less stabilized.

We would be faced with an insoluble task if, basing ourselves on price theory, we had to explain the 1973 oil price explosion *ex post* or forecast price trends *ex ante.* Yet, economics endeavours to give an explanation to processes taking place in economic life, and some kind of answer can be offered even within the framework of the traditional price theory. It is also possible to interpret in mathematical formulae factors that determine prices. In this connexion the debate the author of this work had with G. Heal at the fifth World Congress of Economists held in Tokyo in 1977 may deserve attention.* The debate which has recurred since the advance of econometrics was pursued once more on the question: what is in fact the task of our science? Is it to reveal in general the logical system of the interactions of economic life, or is it

* Heal, G.: *The Long-Run Movement of Prices of Exhaustable Resources,* and Csikós-Nagy, B.: *Past and Prospective Price Trends of Natural Resources.* Proceedings of the World Congress of the I. E. A., Tokyo, 29 August–3 September 1977.

more than that? May it transcend the boundaries of pure theory? If we practise economics as a normative science, how should the scientific foundations of economic policy be interpreted? The author of the present work belongs to the camp that emphasizes the role of economics in the service of practice. He who approaches the problem in this way imposes more rigorous requirements on our science.

Let us make the situation created by the 1973 oil price explosion clearer. The world market price of crude oil rose fivefold overnight. Demand, in accordance with the course prescribed by the demand curve, ought to have decreased. But the oil price explosion had hardly any influence on the demand for oil. The only thing that happened was that development projects previously rejected as causing losses were put on the agenda again and greater stress was laid upon energy saving. All this had a perceivable and important effect, and yet deviated in its character from the assumptions of conventional price theory. And what is more, the most important decisions on oil saving did not emerge in accord with the market mechanism, but unfolded in consequence of government decisions on new trends to be encouraged by economic policy. Thus it seems that economy

– *in the short run* made a weak response to the oil price change and that only the positions of international creditors and debtors altered; on the other hand,

– *in the long run,* new trends of development policy based on the possibility of oil substitution came to the fore.

How could the essence of the problem under examination be indicated? Under commodity production, consumption adopts the form of demand and production that of supply, both of them being determined by a given price. On the market, supply and demand mean the quantity the producer is willing to put on the market and the consumer is willing to buy. All this is regulated, among other means, by the price. This connexion is expressed by the supply and demand schedules. For different commodities, the supply curve and the demand curve differ; regularities are controlled by price elasticity.

When all is said and done, the question is what the content of the demand–supply equilibrium is; how the market clearing function of price can be interpreted, and what stand we should take in the matter of demand and supply curves. One can start from the view that economics provides only a logical framework for economic analysis, and price theory can be interpreted in the same way. In this interpretation, price theory is the explanation of possible alternatives that may occur in the relationship between demand–supply and price. The starting hypothesis of "other things being equal" is well known. To formulate the demand schedule of a product we vary the price of the product and observe what would happen to its quantity bought at any one period of time in which no other factors alter to confuse our experiment. Thus, like any scientist who wants to isolate the effects of one causal factor, we must try to vary only one thing at a time.

However, in economics we are unable to perform a controlled laboratory experiment, and if we observe economic magnitudes statistically we can but seldom consider other things to be equal. Our capacity to experiment empirically in economics is limited and this emphasizes the importance of the clarity of our logical thinking, which may enable us to hope to recognize the essential tendencies even under conditions when—at the same time—other tendencies also influence the situation.*

* Samuelson, P. A.: *Economics,* 9th ed., New York, 1973.

Anyhow, price theory endeavours to convey the close connexion between price and demand.

Price theory characterizes the relation between society and economy by stating that society will adjust itself to the changing circumstances of the economy. This is the concept of a free market system, which, in practice, may have been most characteristic in the 19th century, in the classic stage of capitalism. At that time economic laws were seen almost as laws of nature, in the face of which man is helpless. In the traditional market price theory the state is to be considered an exogenous factor, and recurring economic crises as self-clearing processes of the economy were taken for granted.

If the rules of the game of classic capitalism had been valid in the 1970s OPEC would have had no chance at all to perform the 1973 oil price explosion, or, if it had, this would have appeared in price history only as a short-term episode. But in the 'seventies of our century the relationship between society and economy is significantly different from what it was at the time when the theses of the *Pareto optimum* were formulated and even from what was characteristic when the modified theses of imperfect competition and monopolistic competition were elaborated. An *increase in society's expectations and requirements* is characteristic of the changes gradually taking place in the relationship of society and the economy.

Parallel with the development of productive forces and with the rise of living standards, the ideas about prime necessities are undergoing a change. This change is best demonstrated by the debates about living costs. When there is wage indexation, the way in which consumption structure and changes in price levels are calculated becomes of basic importance. The traditional commodity structure representing the consumption of a sample worker's family used to differ qualitatively from the average consumption pattern of society. Owing to the development of productive forces this consumption pattern becomes continually changed and enriched. In industrially developed countries workers' consumption patterns approach the average. Indeed, the differentiation used in household statistics still continues. But this rather serves to give information for decisions of economic policy about the differentiating effect on the price index of the different consumption patterns of different social classes, or of different magnitudes of incomes. If we consider the demand for products belonging to the sphere of prime necessities as inelastic, this in itself points to the fact that, with the development of productive forces and the modification of the notion of what constitutes necessities, the sphere in which demand is inelastic is expanding, simply because incomes are becoming adjusted to new price relations.

Alternatives of the social equilibrium

The classical economists considered our science as economics of production and considered labour expended on producing commodities to be the substance of value. Smith and Ricardo revealed the laws of the exchange of equal quantities of labour, which regulate social production and by which requirements affect production on the one hand and requirements adapt themselves to production on the other.* Further developing the theory of labour value Marx put forward the theory of surplus value and showed that the exchange of commodities at their labour value is a natural law of their equilibrium.**

* Smith, A.: *Inquiry into the Nature and Causes of the Wealth of Nations,* Edinburgh, 1776. Ricardo, D.: *Principles of Political Economy and Taxation,* London, 1817.

** Marx, K.: *Das Kapital,* Vol. I, Hamburg, 1867; Vol. II, 1885; Vol. III, 1913.

The theory of surplus value directed attention to capitalist exploitation. Therefore the defenders of the capitalist system considered it important to lay the theoretical system of capitalist production on new foundations. This was done by the school of marginal utility, which changed the economics of production into economics of consumption. The rules set forth by Gossen on the satisfaction of needs provided a foundation for this.* Marginal utility calculated in consumption took the place of labour value calculated in production. Efforts in the field of theory were directed to explain economic phenomena on the basis of consumer sovereignty. Praxeology was created and so was the theory of rational economic behaviour.** Pareto founded praxeological economics,*** Mises transformed price theory into a theory of decision alternatives.° All this is closely connected with the assumption according to which

– *optimum* equilibrium (the so-called Pareto optimum) can come into being only under conditions of perfect competition and consequently,

– every other equilibrium, including the one in monopolistic (oligopolistic) markets may be *sub-optimal.*

The two alternatives can also be formulated in the following way: monopoly price is higher than the competitive price; the monopoly supply is smaller than supply would be in perfect competition. That is to say, in the case of a monopoly enterprise the maximization of profit is based on a constraint of production. In perfect competition price coincides with marginal cost. A monopoly enterprise will optimize production where marginal returns equal marginal costs; but here marginal returns are lower than the price. According to the assumptions of price theory, a monopoly enterprise calculates in the following way: The raising of supply by any single unit depending on the elasticity of demand decreases the price. Consequently, the increment in costs is not compared with the price but only with the profit that appears when the price decrease (the marginal returns curve) is taken into consideration.

When creating the economics of praxeology, Pareto assumed that efficiency (the Pareto optimum) could also assert itself under socialism. And yet, when the revolution overthrew capitalism in Russia, Mises delivered a scientific challenge to the socialization of the means of production. He wanted to prove that capitalist private ownership and the free market were indispensable conditions of rational behaviour. In his opinion there is no price mechanism where there is no free market and, without the former, there is no economic calculation. He also emphasized that exchange conditions of commodities could only be established where the means of production were in private ownership, consequently, every step that removed the private ownership of the means of production, was, at the same time, a move away from rational calculation.°°

In the period between the two world wars the theory of marginal utility, and the explanation of economic phenomena by the principle of consumer sovereignty, prevailed in general in non-Marxist economic thinking. This explains why, at that time, some Marxist economists also tried to prove that the social ownership of the means of production and a planned economy were not contradictory to rational behaviour as

* Gossen, H. M.: *Entwicklung des Gesetzes des menschlichen Verkehrs,* Braunschweig, 1854.

** The notion of praxeology originates from Espinas. On the theory of praxeology see: Slutsky, B.: Beitrag zur formalpraxeologischen Grundlegung der Ökonomik. *Wirtschaftswissenschaftliche Informationen,* No. 46, 1966, Berlin.

*** Pareto, V.: *Cours d'économie politique,* Lausanne, 1897.

° Mises, L.: *Nationalökonomie. Theorie des Handels und Wirtschaftens,* Geneva, 1940.

°° Mises, L.: Die Wirtschaftsrechnung im sozialistischen Gemeinwesen, *Archiv für Sozialwissenschaften,* April 1920.

interpreted by the school of marginal utility, or that the Pareto optimum could be realized in socialism too. The answer to Mises's challenge is known in economics as the Lange–Lerner solution.*

It was only later when *welfare economics* was pursued, that the recognition gained ground that the market model of general equilibrium left out of consideration the sociological context, along with essential elements that played a role in social–economic development. The integration of sociological factors into the equilibrium model, as well as the endeavours to achieve this created welfare economics.** The "social welfare function" introduced by Bergson indicated that an optimum state could be determined only as a function of *social utility*.*** Seen from this aspect, one can approach problems that have been created by the co-existence of different socio-economic systems and by the endeavours of the developing world to catch up with the developed countries.

If we consider economics not as "pure theory" but as a normative science and if, in close connexion with this, we consider the state an endogenous factor of the economy and not an exogenous one, it becomes clear at once that different optimal states are conceivable and that they can come into existence only by the *state*'s organizing and controlling actions. Seen from this aspect *equilibrium and efficiency appear as questions separated from each other*. Quantitative and qualitative elements are expressed in the economy's general state of equilibrium. The general equilibrium of the purchasing power and of the commodity fund and, on individual markets, the partial equilibrium of supply and demand represent the quantitative element. The maximization of social utility, the optimum of efficiency represent the qualitative element.

As soon as government control becomes the chief regulator of economic processes, the economy may develop either in an equilibrium or in a disequilibrium, and it can achieve in either case varying degrees of efficiency. *Socialist price theory* has defined the system of conditions under which a state is optimal in the normative system of social utility.° This is realized in efficiency-oriented planning (shadow price planning), a system based on a tripartite structure of the aims of economic policy: (1) objective function, (2) system of constraints, (3) program. The *objective function* is the growth rates, which can be of different magnitudes according to plan variants; the optimum plan being the variant that yields the highest growth rate. The *system of constraints* comprises, in the function of social utility, the timely requirements of policy determined in an identical way for all plan variants. The program is the possible hierarchic structure of aims, its internal connexions being determined by the consistency of the plan. Program variants are obtained by mathematical programming.

Our exposition of price theory has led us to the conclusion that the market mechanism—even if we disregard inflation—can represent a kind of rationality only to the extent to which the objective processes occurring in social–economic development can be brought into harmony with the operation of the market mechanism

* Lange, O.: On the Economic Theory of Socialism, *Review of Economic Studies,* October 1936; February 1937.

Lerner, A. P.: Economic Theory and Socialist Economy, *Review of Economic Studies,* October 1936.

** Pigou, A. C.: *Economics of Welfare,* London, 1920.

*** Bergson, A.: *Essays in Normative Economics,* Cambridge, Mass., 1966.

° (Fedorenko, N. P.) Федоренко, Н. П.: Цена и оптимальное планирование (Price and optimal planning), *Коммунист,* 1970.

Kornai, J.: A gazdasági szerkezet matematikai tervezése (Mathematical planning of the economic structure), Budapest, 1965.

Csikós-Nagy, B.: *Socialist Price Theory and Price Policy,* Budapest, 1975.

This is becoming less and less possible because the socialization of economy is taking place:

– The relationship of society and economy changes, society's willingness to adjust itself to fluctuations in the economy diminishes.

– The relationship of state and economy changes: from being an exogenous factor the state becomes an endogenous one, endeavouring—in harmony with society's expectations—to prevent economic crises, to achieve full employment, etc.

What remains of the market price theory if we abstract it from the theory of general equilibrium? This theory may still provide a number of useful sidelights on prices, but these cannot furnish a solution to general social–economic development.

3. Price policy

Power structure and price structure

Every market mechanism serves a given power structure. A free market could not exist if it did not ensure the greatest advantage for those who keep it operating. That is why one must reject the assumption that the free market is a rational system of economic processes unrelated to political considerations. In a market economy the price exists as an equilibrium price, but in its background there is always a definite economic policy and thus a price policy.

It is only through market forms that price theory has included in the sphere of its examination the problems of power. But on this basis the peculiarities of the price structure that express a given power structure cannot be revealed. Let us take, for instance, the oil price policy of the 'fifties (and partly of the 'sixties). At that time the oil resources of the developing world were exploited by the multi-national monopolies of the Western world. By means of foreign capital investments these enterprises could lay the foundation of market conditions favourable for their own—industrially developed—countries. Their own business interests also dictated that a part of the land and monopoly rent should not be realized in the oil price, and, moreover, that as large a part of the rent as possible should be realized in higher stages of the production process—that is to say in the home country. This rendered it possible that oil price policy should appropriately contribute to the industrial development of the developed countries.

Multi-national enterprises, as a general rule, kept the world market price of oil below its use-value. This *price structure brought into being a definite production structure,* which was favourable for the industrially developed capitalist countries, since it contributed to the financing of industrial investment. This price policy was supported by a peculiar budget policy. (1) A *customs duty system,* which ensured tax-free import for natural resources and levied increasing duties in the function of the degree of industrial processing. (2) A *taxation system,* in which a part of the ground rent of natural resources is drawn off at the stage of consumption goods (petrol, sugar, etc.); i.e. not in the area of exploitation of natural resources, but at the place of the consumption of end-products.

If we do not integrate into the price theory these characteristics of price structure originating in the power structure, we simply cannot understand the secondary redistribution of net incomes created by labour. Through the price policy of multi-national enterprises and the budget policy of governments supporting it, this, as we have seen, takes place:

– first, in favour of all non-extractive branches, due to the fact that the extractive branches only realize a small part of the land (monopoly) rent;
– secondly, in favour of the monopolized non-extractive branches, by realizing a part of the rent in the processing stages.

Vertically operating monopolies will, of course, re-distribute incomes also within a country. This takes place since the monopolies have to adjust themselves to the price structure created by the price policy of multi-national enterprises and by the budget policy of governments.

What, in the mechanism of oil prices, differentiates the present from the past is the circumstance that the *oil price policy more and more evades the control of multi-national enterprises, and that the role of oil exporting countries is growing.* The historical price structure must, as a matter of course, change when the power structure changes. The *historical price structure* could only be concomitant with the power structure which was characteristic of the oligo-centric world economy and of which the colonial system was an organic part. It follows from the nature of things that, by the colonial territories becoming independent, the criteria of economic decisions change, and so does the system of pricing.

Both within and without the framework of the UN the developing world is pursuing a price policy aimed at upgrading natural resources. Outside the framework of the UN, the OPEC's price policy is the most spectacular challenge, its essence being to change the chemical centred oil price policy of the multi-national oil enterprises into a raw material centred oil price policy. Such a switch-over is the point that first and foremost deserves attention when we want to judge the future price of natural resources. The *oil price policy of OPEC* has raised the world market price of oil above its relative use-value. This price policy has laid the foundations for a new production structure policy, and therefore the hypothesis is justified according to which the secular change of world economy has created a structural crisis.

The oil embargo ordered by OPEC in 1973 and the explosion of the prices of energy carriers and of certain raw materials following it—or rather the success of these actions—exposed the relative vulnerability of the developed capitalist countries, the problems of their unity and the relative limits of their possibilities of retaliation. Evidently, OPEC also reckoned with the inelasticity of demand, brought about by the basic interests of economic growth and of employment in the industrially developed capitalist countries. To summarize: by traditional methods within the system of market automatism there is no rational solution to the challenge of the developing world. The hypothesis exists: *the free market mechanism was workable only in the period when power-political discipline and, as a last resort, war could be used to enforce it.*

Under such circumstances the hypothesis of pure theory is absolutely untenable. What superficially appears to be politically neutral is, in reality, in the interest of a determined policy. But how could *the new power structure* be defined in which the oil price explosion could be realized, a power structure which, in general, is favourable to endeavours aimed at revaluing natural resources? *Prima facie* one might assume that the change in power relations can be characterized as the "South" having made headway against the "North". This is the conclusion we reach if we think of the following: (1) The upward revaluation of natural resources is one of the central questions put on the agenda by the developing world. (2) The program of solving problems was laid down by the UN in the resolution on the new international economic order in harmony with the Manila Declaration of the developing countries.

However, if we examine the fundamentals, our judgement must be modified. Three factors are to be taken into consideration at least.

1. In themselves the demands of the developing countries evidently cannot determine the processes of the world economy. For individual countries the UN resolution does not mean any, or hardly any, concrete obligation. That is why it could be adopted as a UN resolution. It indicates, at the same time, the basic differences of opinion in the concrete interpretation of certain elements of the new international economic order. On the development of power relations will depend how consistently the new international economic order—and particularly its institutional framework—will develop.

2. *On a world scale* the relative price problem of the extractive and non-extractive sectors is, in *foreign trade* (in inter-state economic relations) a problem of the terms of trade. By dint of a *change of the terms of trade* one group of countries will obtain additional financial sources, which can be used, in a determined ratio, for accelerating economic growth or for raising living standards. Another group of countries will get into an unfavourable position.

The rise in the relative prices of natural resources cannot be unambigously interpreted as being unequivocally advantageous for the developing world. From time to time differentiated price movements are advantageous for different groups of countries, while, at the same time, they create grave economic difficulties in other developing countries. Thus, what at first sight appears to be the North–South problem arises, in fact, not in connexion with "rich" and "poor" countries, but rather countries "rich in raw materials" and "poor in raw materials". Moreover, a general reference to natural resources is not accurate, since even within the extractive sectors relative prices may also undergo substantial changes in both directions.

3. It seems to be only natural that one group of countries endeavours to improve its position in the world economy. However, it is equally natural that others try to avoid changes to their disadvantage. This conflict can hardly be resolved on an ethical basis since it is not connected with the international distribution or re-distribution of value created by labour but of monopoly rent. The country exploiting a natural resource may claim that the whole rent income is its rightful due, whereas the country utilizing a natural resource may claim that the formation of the rent income is not independent of the general state of productive forces and of the results achieved by processing technologies. Indeed, the country utilizing a natural resource also plays a part in raising the social utility of the resource in question. The essence of the conflict is that, by means of the price, an income which has been created in the process of social–economic development, thanks to various factors, has to be distributed internationally.

We have reached a point in our analysis in which the whole intricacy of the problem is revealed for anyone who has followed as a "neutral" observer the often heated debate. We cannot fail to notice the formidable difficulties which confront the harmonization of the interests involved. Societies living under relatively favourable economic conditions expect their governments to pursue an economic policy that can ensure systematic economic growth and, based on it, a raising of living standards. On the other hand, societies under relatively poor economic conditions demand that their governments pursue an economic policy aimed at abolishing backwardness and at catching up with developed countries. It seems to be natural for all of us that the *per capita* economic growth should be more valid in the developing world than in the economically developed world; that the gap between degrees of development should not grow but be reduced. However, there is an excessive emphasis upon the price category in this attempt at levelling.

One alternative: co-ordinated price policy

Many kinds of international economic co-operation involve co-ordination of price policy, since in a market economy all manifestations of economic policy affect either demand or supply, or else the price directly. However, when this co-operation is based on the principle of the free market, the main form of co-ordinated price policy is monetary co-operation, or rather the expectation that the countries participating in the co-operation should completely liberalize their foreign trade. Therefore, it is not due to chance that GATT, particularly in the 'sixties, kept on the agenda the investigation of objectionable measures taken by some member countries with a view to keeping export prices lower than prices at which the product was sold within the country. Member countries of GATT undertook the obligation not to permit any direct or indirect export subsidy that would reduce export price below the comparable price of the domestic market. The following were considered to be methods used for this purpose:

- the granting of currency bonuses for exports and re-exports;
- a direct subsidy for exporters;
- the refunding of direct taxes or of social charges in the case of export;
- an exemption from general taxation, except the indirect taxes levied at different production phases of export goods;
- the transfer for export purposes of raw materials imported by government organizations at prices different from the domestic ones and lower than world market prices;
- disproportionate premiums for export credits;
- the granting of government credits at artificially low interest rates;
- the paying of credit costs by the government.

The GATT rules are, of course, not an appropriate basis for solving the problem. The UN resolution on the new international economic order might serve as a basis for transforming the price structure of the world market in the desired way.

The *significance of government policies* in world price trends has increased. These policies exert a major influence, in a direct or indirect way, upon the economic processes taking place on a world level, and upon the conditions of the division of labour among different countries. If we want to avoid, or put an end to trade wars, there is no way other than the application of an internationally harmonized price policy, which takes into account economic stability. *An agreement on the interpretation and practical application of the new international economic order is needed* and so is an *operative price policy in this spirit, a policy which always aims at mutual advantage.*

So far it has been mostly the socialist countries that have gained experiences in the international co-ordination of price policies. That is why it is well worthwhile to pay attention to the ideas which arose in the debates of the CMEA about contractual prices in foreign trade. In this respect the CMEA is a good model, because its members significantly differ from one another with respect to their economic potential, the level of the development of productive forces, their production structure and their foreign trade sensitivity. At the same time the economic control systems of these countries are of the same type. From the standpoint of the question under investigation this is a definite advantage, for in the model in which the application of an internationally co-ordinated price policy seems to be possible, a harmony of economic policy on a governmental level must also be assumed.

Criteria expressing comparative advantage play, necessarily, a significant role in the debate about economic co-operation to be realized in the CMEA. The problem is the co-ordination of the development of productive forces, which facilitates the optimum utilization of the productive forces of the single countries. It is not the optimum of integrated unity that takes the place of the several countries' optimum; the desirable state of affairs comes into being through a co-ordination of national interests. But what is recognized as a criterion of mutual advantage by the individual countries within the CMEA? The possible alternatives that point to divergent views in this respect are

- comparative costs,
- labour time input as an equivalent,
- capital requirements as an equivalent.

As we can see, there are different approaches brought to a common denominator by the concept of input. This enables one to appreciate the effort made over two decades to find a substitute for world market prices in the contractual pricing of the CMEA, which should be based on the value relations of the socialist world market. This price system would leave out of consideration the problem of rent, and would place the products of extractive and non-extractive branches on an identical basis of evaluation. However, this has been one of the reasons why relative inputs of the socialist world market have not gained ground. In other words: the question whether rents are justified or not has given rise to the view according to which *the prices of natural resources should be controlled by world market prices and the prices of industrial products by the relative inputs of the socialist world market.*

But in cases where the question of a "dual" price basis arises (prices of industrial products = value; prices of natural resources = value + rent), this must be fitted into the framework of a consistent price system. We consider a price system consistent if it considers the interdependencies of prices and costs. Evidently, a foreign trade price system is unacceptable if it raises the relative price of natural resources to a level at which processing, taking into consideration the circumstances of industrial mass production, is unprofitable even with up-to-day technologies. Evidently, the prices of semi-finished and of finished goods must be in harmony with the prices of the natural resources which are utilized in their manufacture. Thus the duality of the price basis can only mean that the returns gained by the extraction of natural resources are higher than the average profit that can be realized in the processing industries.

The author of this book does not wish to give the impression that he interprets his reference to the contractual price of the CMEA as a solution of the world market price problem. We do not refer to the CMEA as a mechanism of economic co-operation which could be applied on a world scale. In the CMEA, commodity and price relations play only a very limited role. Within the economic co-operation of the CMEA, the economic integration is based, first of all, on the following features: a harmonization of national economic policies, the co-ordination of national plans, the organized ensuring of energy and material supply, industrial specialization and production co-operation, a unification of standards, a harmonized solution of transport tasks as well as a harmonization of technical–scientific research. In such a co-operation system *price cannot play a decisive role in shaping structural problems.* However, even under such conditions relative prices play a role in the re-distribution of national incomes.

In the CMEA, foreign trade takes place on the terms and at prices set by price policy guidelines laid down in inter-state agreements. At present the basis of CMEA contractual prices is the world market price cleared of elements of "irregularities". In this way the fluctuations of prices of natural resources are smoothed, since the world market prices of natural resources are interpreted as prices averaged over several years. Thus the pricing in CMEA contracts pre-supposes the existence of world market prices outside the CMEA.

Independent of all this, in the case of a world-scale co-ordination of price policy a number of questions arise which spring from the differences in socio-economic systems. Such a price policy cannot set out from the assumption that a world organization endowed with appropriate authority would be able to co-ordinate supply and demand by methods outside the sphere of prices. World price policy cannot disregard the market value of products to be sold, or rather it can operate only by influencing market relations. This happens for instance in the case of stock-piling policy. Consequently the main form of manifestation of a co-ordinated price policy on a world scale cannot be fixed prices but guideline prices, combined with adequate market control. In addition, in relation to strategic economic factors, a more precise policy for energy carriers, for staple foodstuffs and minerals may seem to be justified. This mechanism may correspond to the one introduced by the banks of issue through open market operations in the field of currencies.

The other possible outcome: price revolution

The problem is complex, in fact it is even contradictory. If we take everything into consideration, we *cannot exclude a possibility of trade war,* or of its running rampant. This itself is a price revolution, concomitant with a structural crisis or with structural change, and is inevitable unless government action is consciously taken to keep it in check. Let us add that at present, forces operating for stabilization are very weak.

As long as price policy remains concealed and the world market appears from the outside as a competitive market, countries will accept world market prices as objective facts. When world market (foreign trade) prices are a magnitude independent of the single countries, every one of them will evidently endeavour to safeguard its international competitiveness, to ensure the stability of its national currency. When this is threatened by the rules of the game of the market mechanism, governments spend a part of national reserves on the support of foreign trade and payments.

However, when *world market prices (foreign trade prices) appear in an open form as depending on political decisions,* radical changes of behaviour may occur. In such a case the question arises what power enables its holder to interfere in price policy, and to what extent the change of the relative price by coercion can be justified in terms of international economic co-operation based on mutual advantage. If a country, or a group of countries, is in a position to control the world market price of a single commodity, or of several, on grounds of their dominance over supply, another country, or a group of other countries, will, at a time favourable for it, evidently do the same with respect to another commodity or a group of other commodities. All this also exerts an effect on the export price policy of industrially developed capitalist countries. The change of the co-efficient of export deflation also refers to a changing export price policy. (See Table 51.)

The tendency indicated in Table 52 shows differences in individual countries.

The challenge of the developing world may also have played a part in the *industrially developed capitalist countries' having changed their export price policy.* Up to the 1970s there was a relative price stability on the world market in spite of the fact that inflation was continually increasing in the industrially developed capital-

Table 51

The inflation rate of industrially developed capitalist countries and the inflation rate of the world market

Year	Average national inflation rate*	World market inflation rate**	Export deflation co-efficient 2:1
	1	2	3
1960	2.0	1.0	0.50
1961	2.3	1.0	0.43
1962	2.4	0.01	0.004
1963	2.6	0.01	0.004
1964	2.7	3.0	1.11
1965	3.0	1.0	0.33
1966	3.4	2.0	0.59
1967	3.2	0.1	0.03
1968	3.7	−1.0	−0.29
1969	4.8	3.2	0.66
1970	5.9	6.3	1.06
1971	5.4	5.0	0.93
1972	4.8	8.6	1.79
1973	7.0	21.0	3.0
1974	11.7	24.6	2.10
1975***	11.3	11.6	1.07
1976***	7.7	0.01	0.001

* See Table 28: GNP deflator.

** Export price indices of industrially developed capitalist countries, *Monthly Bulletin of Statistics*, June 1969; April 1977.

*** GDP deflator, *Source: World Economic Outlook 1977–78*, Report by UNCTAD Secretariat.

Table 52

The rise of export prices as a percentage of the annual rate of increase of wholesale prices in some capitalist countries

Country	1956–1960	1960–1965	1965–1970	1970–1975
USA	30	250	120	129
Japan	+	+	74	92
GFR	+	130	314	94
Great Britain	+	107	42	75
France	+	39	30	120
Italy	+	7	60	109
Holland	+	83	28	120
Sweden	+	35	52	110
Switzerland	+	172	180	92
Austria	+	11	24	204
Spain	+	61	16	114
Greece	+	100	36	95

+ indicates decrease of export prices.

Source: Calculated on grounds of International Financial Statistics.

ist countries. As we have seen, in the 1970s this inflation extended over the world market too. It is worth-while to examine how this price change is connected with the inflation of the world market price of raw materials.

Table 53

The average rate of inflation within single countries and on the world market

Period	Annual average inflation rate			
	World market*			Within single countries**
	extractive branches	non-extractive branches	total	
1950–1959	−0.5	2.4	1.0	3.1
1960–1969	0.6	1.3	0.8	3.0
1970–1975	25.4	12.9	17.9	9.0

* The respective numbers of the *Monthly Bulletin of Statistics* and the *Yearbook of International Trade Statistics.*

** Calculated by averaging the annual rate based on data of 14 industrially developed capitalist countries of the International Monetary Fund's Research Department, International Financial Statistics (wholesale price index).

From the end of the Second World War up to the 1970s the industrially developed capitalist countries endeavoured to avoid, as much as possible, the spill-over effect of domestic inflation onto the world market. The business policy of enterprises considered this important with a view to preserving *international competitiveness,* supported by governmental economic policy in the interest of preserving *the stability of the currency.* Thus, as it were, the domestic inflation rate financed the policy of relatively stable export prices. But in the 1970s the situation changed. In that period —at least in some industrially developed capitalist countries—the endeavour could be observed to make *world market inflation serve the ends of anti-inflationary policy within the country.* The course of the export deflation co-efficient in the period 1970–1972 bears witness to this. In subsequent years the raising of export prices of industrially developed capitalist countries was set going, first of all, with a view to shifting back the rise of import prices. Assumably the price rise of crude oil, which began already in 1972 and was quite considerable in 1973, played a significant role within import prices. (See Table 54.)

For the time being we cannot draw far-reaching conclusions from the changes of export price policy. Namely, 1976 prices (Table 51) show that the changes begun

Table 54

Foreign trade price index of industrially developed capitalist countries (1970 = 100)

	1971	1972	1973	1974	1975	1976
Imports	106	114	140	197	217	216
Out of this:						
Petroleum	125	133	175	582	602	717
Exports	105	114	138	172	192	192

Source: Monthly Bulletin of Statistics, April 1977.

in 1970 returned to the previous trend; domestic inflation was again significantly higher than what had been realized in the countries' export prices.

The chances of an internationally harmonized price policy are impaired by the fact that the problem of relative prices of natural resources has arisen in a period of *inflation* and is thus connected with the problem of *indexation.* All things considered, indexation raises the inflation rate, because it removes a certain circle of products from the trend of averages, since it considers the average a minimum measure of price increases.

The 1973 oil price explosion introduced elements of a new price revolution, by *introducing profit inflation in the scope of a trade war.* Only its political–social framework differs basically from that of the price revolution of the 16th – early 17th centuries. Then the price revolution was in the service of primitive (previous) accumulation, laying the material foundations for the elimination of the constraints of feudalism and for the unfolding of capitalist commodity production. Now it strives chiefly for a re-distribution of national incomes in favour of the developing world. The risk in the oil price explosion brought about by OPEC in 1973 lies in the debatable proposition that price conditions of the world market can be controlled in the long run, in the interests of the "price policy of one commodity".

*

We assume that the normative principles of the "New International Economic Order" declared in the UN resolution will, first of all, determine in the next decade the processes of economic life. As we have experienced, the transition from the traditional order of world economy into a new one does not take place smoothly. We may witness a secular change, which may create the new equilibrium adjusted to the changes in world economy, but accompanied by several smaller or greater shocks. Our hypothesis that a new price revolution now threatens—or that perhaps we are already experiencing it—is connected with this.

With a certain simplification we may interpret the secular change taking place in the world economy as a *transition into a new equilibrium, which can take place only with a basic transformation of the economic structure.* The question is whether one can hope for co-operation between governments to ensure the transition by mutually safeguarding national interests, that is to say, by minimizing tensions. This is a realistic alternative, since the agreement on the basic principles of a new international economic order at the level of the UN has clearly indicated that there has been a general recognition that the system of international economic co-operation is to be laid on new foundations. But the principles agreed upon are too general and can thus be interpreted in different ways. The clashing of national interests is basic, and that is why debates about the interpretation of principles may come to the fore. This may lead to a situation favourable to a price revolution. Nevertheless it is to be hoped that understanding and common interests will in the end decide the course of economic development.